From Corsets to Communism

Jenny Robertson

From Corsets
to Communism

JENNY ROBERTSON

First Published in the UK in 2019 by
Scotland Street Press
100 Willowbrae Avenue
Edinburgh EH8 7HU

A CIP record for this book is available from the British Library.

ISBN 978-1-910895-32-0

Note on permissions: while all efforts have been made to contact
the copyright holders for certain text quotations and illustrations,
they have not all been found. The publishers would welcome
any contact from or recognition of these copyright holders.

Typeset by Hewer Text UK Ltd, Edinburgh
Printed in Scotland by Bell & Bain Limited, Glasgow

Cover designed by Anne Sophie Fraser

To Stuart
Our shared commitment to Poland has underscored our lives
from our first meeting when those six words you uttered,
'Would you like to learn Polish?' turned out to be an invitation
to far more than the intricacies of Polish grammar.

Contents

	List of Illustrations	ix
	A word about Polish	xii
	Introduction	1
1	Youth absorbed in the third person	3
2	Icy fields – the challenge of a woman writer	11
3	Life in its entirety	19
4	Laying out life in patterns	30
5	Encircled by fire	39
6	Independent employment	50
7	Living on the edge	57
8	Unkind love	72
9	House of women	86
10	My highest level	101
11	Literature rejuvenates	114
12	Boundary and beyond	124
13	Storm clouds near and far	132
14	Taken to the gates of hell	142
15	Bombardment	149
16	A rosary of deaths	163
17	That smoking wound	176
18	Cameos of crime	188
19	Restored to life	202
20	Knots of life	214
	In Memoriam	223
	Notes	225
	Bibliography	239
	Acknowledgements	243

A Timeline for Zofia Nalkowska   245
A Timeline of Polish History   251
Index   255

List of illustrations

Front cover: Zofia Nałkowska, from her Diary 1909, volume 2, courtesy of Jan Kujawski.

1. Family: Zofia and her sister Hanna with their parents and grandmother. Taken by Maurycy Pusch, courtesy of Hanna Kirchner.

2. Wacław Nałkowski, portrait located in the *Meadow House* Museum in Wołomin, courtesy of photographer Katarzyna Humińska.

3. Works on geography by Wacław Nałkowski, *Meadow House*, Katarzyna Humińska.

4. Page from the collection of poems *Pierwocin* with a drawing by Zofia, courtesy of Irene Korsak and Joanna Kujawska (from Hanna Kirchner's biography of Zofia Nałkowska).

5. Page from *Pierwocin* with later comments, courtesy of Irene Korsak and Joanna Kujawska (from Hanna Kirchner).

6. Zofia Nałkowska in 1903, from the archive of Hanna Kirchner.

7. Leon Rygier, 1922, Hanna Kirchner.

8. Zofia with some major writers of the time, Nałęczów 1907, Hanna Kirchner.

9. Ludwik Liciński, 1904, Hanna Kirchner.

10. Edmund Szalit, Hanna Kirchner.

11. Zofia Villaume, c. 1903, Hanna Kirchner.

12. Zofia Nałkowska, picture first published in her novel *Narcyza* (1910), https://www.revolvy.com/page/Zofia-Nałkowska.

13. Family piano in *Meadow House*, Katarzyna Humińska.

14. Disarming Germans on the streets of Warsaw 1916, Hanna Kirchner (from the Polish News Agency archive, author unknown).

15. Jan Gorzechowski in 1914, Hanna Kirchner (from Małgorzata Olbrycht's collection).

16. Janusz Korczak's memorial stone in Treblinka extermination camp, photograph taken by the author.

17. Zofia and Gorzechowski's house in Grodno, Hanna Kirchner.

18. Zofia and Gorzechowski with their pets, including the greyhound Diana and the deer Basia, Grodno 1924, from the Reproduction Section of the National Library in Warsaw.

19. Jan Gorzechowski in his office, Hanna Kirchner.

20. PEN Club party in honour of Russian poet Konstantin Balmont, 1927, Hanna Kirchner (from the Archive of Mechanical Documentation in Warsaw).

21. Pastel portrait of Zofia by Stanisław Witkiewicz (Witkacy), 1930, Hanna Kirchner.

22. Zofia with Karol Szymanowski and his sister Stanisława in Zakopane, 1931, Hanna Kirchner (reproduction made by photographer Andrzej Zborski).

23. Michał Choromański, late 1930s, Hanna Kirchner (from the Archive of Mechanical Documentation in Warsaw).

24. Portrait of Bruno Schultz, https://www.revolvy.com/page/ Bruno-Schulz.

25. First cover of Schultz's *Sklepy cynamonowe* ("Cinnamon Shops"), 1934, https://www.revolvy.com/page/The-Street-of-Crocodiles.

26. Bogusław Kuczyński, late 1930s, Hanna Kirchner.

27. Truskavets, spa in Ukraine where Zofia and Schultz met for the last time in 1939, https://www.revolvy.com/page/Truskavets.

28. Three Crosses Square, Warsaw, 1940, photograph by W. Szczeciński, from the Historical Museum of the City of Warsaw.

29. Ruins of the Warsaw Ghetto, photograph by Wacław Żdżarski, property of Poland's National Digital Archives.

30. First cover of *Medallions*, 1946, https://www.revolvy.com/page/Medallions.

31. Tablet commemorating the "corpse factory" in which soap was produced from human bodies, Stutthof concentration camp, https://www.revolvy.com/page/Zofia-Nałkowska.

32. Holy Cross Church and Staszic Palace, with figure of Christ among the ruins, 1946, property of Poland's National Digital Archives.

33. Bust that marks Zofia's grave, made by her sister Hanna, photograph by Katarzyna Humińska.

34. Zofia's grave in the Powązki Cemetery in Warsaw, Hanna Kirchner.

35. Front view of the *Meadow House*, Katarzyna Humińska.

A word about Polish

Polish looks formidable with its clusters of consonants but once we understand the structure it is simpler to pronounce than English. For example, *szcz* looks awful but when we know that sz sounds like sh and cz like ch all is straightforward. After all no-one has any difficulty saying "Scottish Cheese."

Ch in Polish sounds like Scottish Loch

W in Polish sounds like V while l with a stroke through it, ł, as in Zofia Nałkowska sounds like English w. So Zofia's surname sounds rather like Now-kov-ska and her father Wacław's name sounds like Vats –wav.

The city of Łódź where Zofia lived after the Second World War sounds rather like English woodge and the most difficult name in the book, the surname of Zofia's second husband Jan Gorzechowski, looks simply dreadful but breaks down like this Gor –zh (or *je* as in French) e as in egg, ch as in loch, ov ski: Gor –zhe –chov –ski.

Pan and Pani literally mean lord and lady, also Sir and Madam, or simply Mr and Mrs.

Introduction

Born in 1884, Zofia Nałkowska's life spans seventy explosive years of Polish history, from Tsarist government in Warsaw to the iron fist of Communism. From her teens she chafed at the repressive conventions society dictated to women. Her early literary work elevates hitherto barely voiced issues of femininity to the highest level of literature. Her writing was always contemporary and offers some of the bravest and most perceptive analysis of the complex world of twentieth century Poland, yet, tyrannised by her second husband this award-wining author wrote of their relationship, 'I had to make myself simple to be understood.'

Largely self-educated, a woman in a man's world, Zofia Nałkowska looked unflinchingly at life and prised it open with her pen.

I knew nothing about this a lifetime ago when I first discovered the writing of this woman whose life and work have absorbed twenty years of my later, more recent life.

My path to Poland began in my teenage years in Glasgow when I started to correspond with a thirty-three year old Polish woman who lived in a displaced person's camp in Northern Germany. The connection came through a small charity and, at the end of my first undergraduate year at Glasgow University, I worked in Hamburg as a volunteer with this charity. I returned to Glasgow determined to study Polish.

A new world opened up for me, a lifetime of learning, On my first visit to Warsaw I came across a slender book, *Medaliony, Medallions.* This slim-mest of slim books is a literary masterpiece, totally simple, totally profound and absolutely unforgettable. Ten short stories make the unsay-able real and present, for all time and for everyone. They charted my course through life and finally mapped my way to the diaries and literary works of the author of that little book, Zofia Nałkowska.

CHAPTER I

Youth absorbed in the third person

She was a unique phenomenon, not only in Polish literature but in Polish
cultural life. No other famous Polish woman possessed so many of the
highest gifts of talent and charm or triumphs or top literary positions . . .[1]

Zofia Nałkowska – a woman, a writer. Tall and striking, of large proportions, 'a ship in full sail,' Zofia was famous for her wit, her charm and her
piercingly blue eyes. 'Forget-me-not blue,' said her admirers. 'Rapacious,'[2]
her critics said. They were eyes before which even an armed enemy
quailed. Those eyes looked unflinchingly at human nature in all its foibles
and turned their gaze on herself too as she confided her inner thoughts to
the diaries she kept lifelong. Published years after her death, from 1970
onwards, painstakingly annotated by Professor Hanna Kirchner, the nine
volumes of hitherto unknown memoir became an outstanding literary
success, surprising readers with their intimate portrait of a major writer
who constantly pushed the boundaries of the novel while battling a crippling sense of personal inadequacy, her need to be adored, constant ill-
health along with early deafness and tinnitus.

Her public knew such a different picture! Zofia presented herself as the
grand lady of Polish letters and crafted her outer persona as carefully as
her award-winning prose. The only woman in the Polish Academy of
Literature, Zofia became an institution in her own right. Young people
attending her secret gatherings in Occupied Warsaw during the Second
World War referred to her as though she were a university course. 'I'm on
my second year of Nałkowska . . . I've just finished Nałkowska.'[3]

She had her rivals and critics, notably another leading author, Maria
Dąbrowska, who wrote sarcastically of the self-assurance and imposing
manner of sixty-three year old Zofia in 1947:

Nałkowska was radiant. She holds herself better all the time. She must have splendid masseurs and beauticians because even her mouth and neck look smooth, but what self-assurance, not just of an excellent writer, but also a major political figure. Oh, those patronising little wags of her finger at men who jump up trembling to offer her a cigarette or bend their ears to receive some whispered commission from their queen. I was astounded. I've never seen her in such form, triumphant and dictatorial. She must have a new lover, because it's not likely that her career successes alone would give her such arrogance.[4]

Zofia Nałkowska was a European on a grand scale. She read French, English and Russian in the original language and took part in literary events all over Europe, from Norway to the Balkans, including a visit to London and Edinburgh in 1935.

Intimately involved with the 'movers and shakers' of Polish political and literary life, Zofia portrayed people at the top of society as well as bringing to life those at the bottom whose hopes and dreams went unnoticed. The thing that mattered most to her was people. 'The most interesting thing that a person can get to know is another person,' she always said and made it her life's work to understand others. Her appointment to the Committee for the Investigation of Nazi war crimes in Poland in 1945 gave rise to *Medallions*, short stories, immediately acknowledged as a masterpiece. One colleague concluded, 'If you wrote in French, English or even Norwegian you would be the most famous writer in the world.'[5]

Zofia was born into a political situation that denied Poles the right to be Polish. The child of an impoverished radical, Zofia opened those startlingly blue eyes on the 10th November 1884 in the Polish capital which was firmly under the control of Alexander III, Emperor of All the Russias. Warsaw had become little more than a provincial outpost of a mighty foreign Empire. Street signs were in Cyrillic. Roman Catholic Baroque Churches had been clumsily topped by the golden domes of the Eastern Orthodox, the press was tightly controlled and all schooling was conducted in Russian.

Poland had not existed as a political entity since 1795 when it had been divided between three all-controlling Empires: Prussia, Russia and Austro-Hungary. Poland's ancient capital, Kraków, home of Zofia's maternal grandmother, belonged to the Austro-Hungarian Empire; the family needed visas to make that journey within their own country.

This situation for freedom-loving Poles was deeply hurtful and universally resented. Zofia later wrote that this near annihilation of Polish-ness was like a constant wound and such an acute emotional disadvantage that it felt like living with a disability.[6]

Because of the political and cultural pressures of Tsarist censorship Zofia and her sister Hanna, two years younger than she, were educated at home. There had been an older sister, Celina, who had died in infancy before Zofia was born.

As they grew older both girls were painfully aware that lack of political and cultural freedom also meant deprivation in terms of lifestyle and career choice. Their father Wacław Nałkowski (1851 – 1911), a radical intellectual, was a member of a group of writers, artists and thinkers, prophets of a new revolutionary age who were constantly under the survey of the Tsar's secret police.

The son of an impoverished landowner, young Wacław Nałkowski, even as a teenager, had been forced to support his parents with his meagre earnings from tutoring while his feckless father lost land and property. Wacław was forced to work late into the night, doing his schoolwork at the cost of his eyesight. He loved logic, mathematics, geography and the world of natural sciences. Because all his schoolwork was in Russian, Wacław immersed himself in forbidden Polish literature at home, reading alone in his room where he would gaze out at the night sky and view the stars, 'those millions of worlds like an open page of a mathematical thesis.'[7]

Wacław gained a place at the prestigious Jagiellonian University in Kraków and often went hungry, even to the point of starvation; he shivered in an unheated room where the ink froze in the bottle. Here Wacław embraced radical political ideas and here too he met his future wife Anna, the second of three attractive sisters, all of Czech parentage.

The couple moved to Warsaw where Wacław continued his work in geography without any hope of an academic post. He gave lessons for minimal or no pay in the Polish 'flying university', so called because it met in various locations for fear of intervention by the heavy-handed Tsarist police and their many spies.

His bride Anna, who was only nineteen, immersed herself in her husband's academic passion and devoted her own considerable intellectual abilities to his work.

Into her husband's office she would pull her little desk and entered when the children were already asleep in order to write her own books, silently and engrossed, at his side.[8]

Before long Zofia and Hanna were helping too – their father dictated his work to them and trained them to be his copy editors.

The family moved from one poor set of rooms to another. Zofia recalled that they were always filled with the scent of hyacinths, which her mother cultivated, and with music. Anna had a beautiful alto voice and sang light classical music, accompanying herself on the piano.[9]

Teenage Zofia became a close intellectual companion for her intensely academic father whom she described as 'the most intelligent man I know.' They read and discussed Nietzsche, Voltaire and other free-thinking philosophers and writers – Zofia grasped some of Nietzsche's concepts more quickly than her father. Around the table of their small apartment sat many of the best minds of so-called progressive Warsaw - the teenage girl fancied herself in love with several of them. Her father's close friendship with these literary luminaries helped Zofia find outlets when she began to publish her poetry, at the age of fifteen. Her sister Hanna became a distinguished sculptor.

Growing up among intellectual adults, lost in a world of serious books, in debate and discussions of science, philosophy and literature, Zofia thought that this was a normal way of life and only later realised that few girls lived on these rarefied academic heights. Although Zofia admired her father and adored her mother, she chafed at the privations of her life, the lack of attractive clothes and of social life with other young people. The fifteen year old girl complained to her diary:

> Poverty is robbing me of the most beautiful years of my life. I try to be away from home as much as I can. I feel fine at class, and outside on the street I'm just like everyone else, but when I come back here, up the dark, dirty stairs to two rooms, one leading through to the other, where there is nowhere to escape to, where the ugly furniture is only what is the most essential – my wings fall away from me. I, loving beauty above all else, live surrounded by ugliness. I feel victimised as a person, as a woman and as a spiritual being. I'm often amazed that this fate has happened to me, exactly to me. I shall never accept it and I torture myself and those closest to me[10].

Still wearing a schoolgirl's brown dress and black apron, Zofia knew that she would soon be bound within the confining stays of womanhood, and her parents, remarkable though she knew them to be, were no help in her quest for personal freedom.

Her father was a man – and therefore free; besides, complained Zofia, 'he wants to change the world, and I'm just concerned about myself.'[11]

Her mother, quiet and self-sacrificing, modelled the sort of wifely dedication that Zofia found too restricting. She carried the burdens of domestic life and child-care to set her husband free.

Thinking through the imbalance between the possibilities for women and men, fifteen year old Zofia complained to her diary:

> A man gets married only when he's tired of real love, when he desires – in the worst case – home-cooked food and nicely darned linen, or at most commonly shared convictions, a companion for his thought and friendship.
>
> I don't want to be anyone's ideal or the 'angel of the hearth'. I just want to be a woman. I want true love, not marriage, only love. [. . .] I'm crying as I write. I know I want impossible things [. . .] I feel that I've already passed through all the stages of a virgin's development and I'm ready to receive a man.[12]

The young schoolgirl recalls a scene she had seen through her window as she studied, trying to catch the last of the evening light. The room opposite was lit and she watched an army officer and his woman 'friend' jump about, lifting their legs as high as they could. Zofia guessed this must be the famous can-can. The soldier then uncorked a bottle. They sat down, drank, ate something, the woman flung her arms round his neck and they both went into the unlit room next door.

> It was all too banal for me to feel threatened and revolted – so I don't feel anything, but it's frightful just the same [. . .] Although they are both 'sinning' in the identical way, the consequences are not identical. She is an outcast, despised [. . .] while he's a nice young man who, a few years hence, will marry an innocent girl as a respite after a too-merrily spent youth.

I know a drama in which an anxious father asks a doctor for advice about his son who is ill as a result of an excessive life. 'Let him get married, that's the best medicine.'

That's enough to make me stop wanting to live, to stop wanting anything.[13]

In her diary, the teenager documents her everyday struggles, bent over her desk from Sundays to Thursdays, working on translations from French and Russian, writing her own poetry as well as taking down dictation from her father who, although charming to his friends could also be dictatorial to his daughters – and perhaps also to his wife. Zofia recalled a scene when a young man visited the family. He sat chatting to Zofia in one of the only two rooms when Wacław burst in from the adjoining room and scolded his daughter for disturbing his work, thereby definitely cramping her style.[14]

Yet although Zofia chafed at the restrictions her father laid upon her, she respected his dedication to his work and to the end of her days Wacław Nałkowski remained his daughter's closest mentor.

However, the teenage girl wanted a life beyond the home and was often forced to turn down invitations because she had no money to buy new clothes. Once when she had been invited to a party, seventeen year old Zofia made excuses not to go until a friend realised that the real reason was that the teenager had nothing to wear. She immediately offered to lend her something. Zofia accepted, though with shame.

And so, Cinderella went to the ball and waltzed the night away. She would not have been Zofia if she had not been only too aware of her reflection in long mirrors and noted her slim figure, flushed face and happy eyes (although in her diary she wrote that this happiness was really a pretence). And she would not have been Zofia if she had failed to notice that the two hired musicians, a violinist and a pianist, both blind, were exhausted by hours of playing at a hectic pace.

Zofia's partners whirled her around in lively Polish folk dances – and then disaster struck:

While we were spinning around in some kind of mad waltz we bumped against another couple and one of buttons on the other boy's sleeve scratched my arm high above my elbow. I felt a sharp pain. My partner apologised and said, 'Oh, you've torn your blouse.'

'It doesn't matter, only my arm hurts a bit. You see how vicious this eagle is, even just on a button.'[15]

It did matter, though, for now Zofia had to buy a new blouse to replace the torn one she had borrowed, and where was the money to come from? This jokey little interchange was typical. The young man blamed her for the rip in her blouse while Zofia concealed her pain with a witticism – the 'vicious' eagle was a reference to the two-headed Tsarist eagle on the student's uniform.

A diary entry for May 1902 notes that at a concert one of Zofia's friends whispered, shocked, 'Zofia, you've forgotten your corset!'

And Zofia commented, 'If only *he'd* been there! He would have fallen in love with me at once.'[16]

Still unsure of herself and her future, Zofia realised that diary writing had now become essential to her, although she wasn't sure why. Was it something to do with a desire to live on after her death, even if only in words in a notebook? Brought up as a materialist, Zofia remained convinced to the end of her life, and often emphasised in her writing, that this life is our one and only life. But was there not a deeper reason:

> I analyse everything in my life in a *literary* way; I have a particular style in receiving impressions, dreams and recollections – an epic style, I call it. I always introduce myself in the third person, my actions in the past tense, my feelings in the form of facial expressions, poses, gestures, dreams – all in the style of something that has already happened and has been told [. . .] My brain is constantly at work [. . .] And yet I never write novellas or novels [. . .] I have stories in my mind, worked out in the most minute details [. . .] yet when I pick up my pen and see in front of me a cold, white, empty piece of paper – suddenly everything escapes my mind, every dialogue, comma, description – and I can't write.[17]

Zofia's confidential musings in her diary also highlight moments of tension between her teenage self who wanted fun and her father who stuck to firm socialist principles.

The family was invited to a reception at the house of a nouveau-riche millionaire. Wacław flatly refused to go, arguing 'logically and correctly,' as Zofia wrote, that rich people not only make him work for them, they even expect him to waste the time he should be using to do that work. Zofia however argued back 'equally logically', that if we want to enjoy ourselves we have to waive these principles sometimes – or else become an anarchist or commit suicide.[18]

Zofia was never an anarchist and didn't intend to commit suicide, so she went to the reception, chaperoned by family friends who were also ready to forego their principles for a moment's pleasure at the rich table of a millionaire. That reception, at a table drowned in flowers, among capitalist millionaires 'theoretically our enemies' would soon be woven into a novel, *Women* (1906).

Zofia Nałkowska's major books are now being translated in English. But what did the early years of the twentieth century in unfree Poland offer this young girl who later said of herself, that adults write for children, but that she had been a child writing for adults?[19]

Her talents were many but her career options were few. She could become an actress with the dubiety of that profession for women in those restricted years or, in a worst-case scenario, become a rich man's 'kept woman' and enjoy the foreign travel, art and music, beautiful clothes her parents' lifestyle denied her. Or else, a virgin and desirable, she could get married.

Which she disastrously did . . .

CHAPTER 2

Icy fields – the challenge of a woman writer

'So let my one and only man be primeval, strong, despotic . . . I want to be a woman, only a woman'[1]

In 1903 eighteen year old Zofia lamented to her diary that she had spent the three previous years of her life pining for the love of an older man. 'I only saw him seven times and he has spoilt three years of my life,' she complained. 'But he it is whom I must thank for the loveliest poems that I have ever written – they were all for him!'[2]

Torn between the 'icy fields' of celibacy – her metaphor – and the erotic longing for physical love, Zofia was already earning her living from her pen. The books she translated were published with her name on the cover – a proud moment for the teenage author. Her poetry appeared in quality journals, heavily deformed by Tsarist censorship. One such poem had a challenging feminist title, *The White She-Eagle*. Called to an editorial meeting, Zofia saw to her horror that her poem 'was covered in red.' Forced to re-work the whole text she found the new version 'dreadfully bland.'[3]

Nevertheless she started work on her first lengthy prose piece, a novella, *Icy Fields*, which became the opening of a trilogy entitled, defiantly, *Women*.

In *Icy Fields* the main protagonist is a young woman, poor and self-educated like the author herself. Zofia puts into her heroine's mouth her own thoughts on love, life and being:

> I am [. . .] young and attractive – and so I want to live. Nietzsche recommends the use of a whip on women [. . .] (Others say) that we should go everywhere with a chaperone so that our future husband will have no reason to be suspicious. Just the same, in spite of that, I want to

be a woman [. . .] So let my one and only man be primeval, strong, despotic. I shall pleasure his siesta and cigar with my wise conversation, I shall unbind my hair and dance before him, keeping time with my tambourine. I shall reveal only my eyes to others, covering my face with a veil . . . I want to be a woman, only a woman.[4]

With this highly-charged agenda, the eighteen year old met Leon Rygier, nine years her senior, a valued teacher of Polish and an up and coming poet, a dandy, beautifully dressed, a man (ominously) 'with a way with women.'

Zofia liked 'his kind, dreamy looks, his pleasant voice, his handsome, elegant figure. He is gentle and soft with so much subtlety, so much charm.'[5] She loved his musical voice and decided that he was definitely the man for her, although he had said – his voice smooth as velvet, 'It would be wonderful if I could say that you, madam, are my beloved.'

'So why doesn't he say it?' eighteen year old Zofia asked her diary.[6]

And then, it happened. 'Yesterday the electric doorbell sounded in the hall, just the same as always. It was Sunday afternoon, the maid had gone out. I opened the door myself. And in came – Rygier. And [. . .] into my house came the sun.'[7]

Passionate about this handsome man whose exquisite manners were reflected in his stylish dress, Zofia responded to his declarations of love; soon she Leon were writing poems to each other, singing together, she wrote, like nightingales.

We're terribly like one another, almost identical. We don't have any money but we love artistic comfort. We have fair hair, blue eyes and we write poetry. We look at one another with our mournful blue eyes and smile in silence.[8]

With astonishing insight, however, Zofia saw the danger signals. For a start, she noted, Rygier's poems could have been written for any eighteen year old girl not just for her, and she quoted as an example: 'Across your tears love's rainbow unfurls. You are the first for me, the one and only girl.'

And, even more importantly:

He needs an iron, but caring hand, just as I do. Neither of us can be a support for the other and we both require that as a basic necessity

[. . .][9] I love him through and through . . . but I imagine marriage differently. It's not about money, it's about support, which I need. [. . .] I want
(my husband) to take on the burden of steering my life. I am not weak,
only too complicated and unbalanced, too sensitive and dreamy. I've
always been inclined to throw myself into the grace and disgrace of a
hurricane.'[10]

In her diary Zofia agonises, reflects and analyses. The personal strengths
and weaknesses she explores on its pages will bedevil every relationship
throughout her life, as she continually sought that longed-for male support
– and found a hurricane instead.

In May, the season she always loved, came that dazzling, irrecoverable
moment: her first kiss on the mouth, making this May the most wonderful of all, 'my first May of love, full of flowers, kisses and sunshine,
wonderful, extravagant May, the first May in my life [. . .]'[11]

And soon she notes, 'I am engaged to *Ryś*,' and adds, 'I saw how the
uncertainty was torturing him.' Later she said of herself that she stayed in
difficult, indeed dangerous relationships because she was so aware of the
effect that her leaving would have on her partner. For all her subsequent
reputation as a woman surrounded by adoring men, a kind of literary
femme fatale, Zofia responded to the compliments and flattery of her male
admirers – only to be tossed around in that inevitable hurricane.

All too soon a cloud darkened the engaged couple's happy scene. Zofia's
mother, the rock and mainstay of her family, became ill with gall bladder
problems and suddenly became childish and demanding. Household cares
fell on Zofia's unaccustomed shoulders. Leon listened patiently to Zofia's
worries – and became ever more passionate. Zofia was torn between her
intense desire and her invalid mother's needs, certain that, 'Mother too is
full of suppressed tears and rebellion [. . .] after such a sad, closed, profoundly
empty life, after this single chain of injuries and disappointments.'[12]

Zofia doesn't specify what these 'injuries and disappointments' were.
Could there have been marital infidelity? When Zofia was only ten a
talented young woman, Maria (also known as Marynia) Komornicka had
burst into the 'sad, closed' intensely intellectual world of the Nałkowski
household.

At first Maria, then aged eighteen, charmed Zofia as they shared ideas,
particularly about the fate of women. Like Zofia, Maria believed that

women were obliged to partake in life only as partial people since 'man' described all humankind – how could a 'woman' be 'man'? Teenage Zofia's diaries and her first novels are full of these tensions.

Maria Komornicka had grown up on a country estate with a tyrannical, violent father. Sent to an eminent literary scholar to be tutored in Warsaw, the young girl was deeply unhappy, fell in love with her cousin and tried to drown herself in the River Vistula. A passing police patrol saved her life – but the officers decided she must be a prostitute. She was taken to a police station, forced to endure a humiliating internal examination which she perceived as rape, and, given the way in which prostitutes were treated at the time, she may indeed have been sexually violated.

Maria's troubled personality produced thought-provoking, highly original writing and Wacław Nałkowski, always attracted to bright young minds, adored her as an outstanding person whose sensitivity and intellect would outlast the narrow-minded times in which she was forced to live. His close friend, Cezary Jellenta (1861 – 1935) was equally fascinated by young Maria Kormonicka; the three of them edited a radical, modernist journal, *Vanguard*. Too inflammatory for the Tsarist censorship, this journal was published in the more liberal, Austrian-controlled city of Lwów, now L'viv.

Maria's father was furious at his daughter's involvement with the avant-garde – and even more with her entanglement with 'a Socialist (Wacław) and a Jew (Cezary)'. He sent Maria to Cambridge University where, however, she was only allowed to take part in preparatory courses. Deeply disillusioned by this experience and by the English suffragette movement, Maria returned to Warsaw, to her two intellectual admirers, Wacław and Cezary, and to Zofia's increasing jealously.

Teenage Zofia was fascinated by Cezary and imagined herself in love with him, despite the age difference and the fact that he was married, so Maria's intrusion into her family life distressed young Zofia terribly. She was jealous too of Maria's friendship with her dearest friend and name-sake, Zofia Villaume; she also saw that her mother was upset by the relationship of the young 'meteor' Maria with Wacław as they worked closely together, one to one.

Maria must have sensed the tensions. When her father died, although the family disinherited her and blamed her for his early death, Maria returned home to the estate. She wrote to Cezary, explaining that she had noticed that Wacław had been distancing himself from her because he didn't want an affair that would poison his life and tear himself in two, nor did he want to torment his wife.

Later on, Maria Komornicka removed herself even further from possible love affairs, and from Poland. She moved to Paris and in 1907 burnt her dresses, put on men's clothing, pulled out all her teeth, smoked a pipe and changed her name to Piotr Włast, a medieval dignitary who had been a family forbear. Maria continued to write under this name for the next forty years during which s/he was either plunged into actual mental illness or was felt to be so by his/her family. Piotr Włast endured many years in metal institutions and only at the end of his life, having been placed in an institution in the care of nuns, did she return to female dress and to her name, Maria. She died in obscurity in 1947.

It is not clear whether Maria's 'nervous disorders' were caused by the way in which society as a whole and her family in particular regarded a transgender woman, or whether this change of sexual identity was driven by increasing psychosis or by her protest against the power of the stronger sex against women, linked to her sufferings at the hands of the police. It is however significant that while Zofia Villaume kept in touch with the brilliant person who had fascinated her in her late teens, Zofia N never visited her erstwhile mentor – and perhaps tormentor. Perhaps this rather callous attitude towards a destitute old woman was Zofia's last act of loyalty to her adored mother who had suffered 'injury and disappointment' all those years ago.[13]

In 1903, however, with Maria's influence removed from the Nałkowski household, Anna recovered from her illness and Zofia had an unpleasant surprise – she was brought face to face with Leon's former fiancée, a woman with whom he had shared three years of life.

> She's back in Warsaw, she comes often and meets up with him, she weeps over the past and writes many letters, kissing 'his hands and feet.' Ryś is terribly weak [. . .]. He doesn't know how to finish with her . . .[14]

Zofia took this quite calmly at first, saying that she was so sure of Leon's love that she could accept his past – he talked to her quite openly about his previous love affairs, so she could never accuse him of hiding anything from her.

'I've accepted all his colourful past – though not without difficulty,' she wrote and turned a chance sighting of the jilted woman into a joke. As the lady approached, Zofia hid Leon in a gateway while she had a good look at the woman who had known him so intimately. 'We ran home giggling like children,' she wrote afterwards.[15]

Friends of the family warned Zofia that she was making a serious mistake. Young and proud, she was confident she could trust her own judgment. Rygier had successfully persuaded her that although there had indeed been other women, Zofia was his first and only real love.

She transmuted her doubts into literature. Writing *Icy Fields*, the young author makes one of her characters explain why she had broken off her relationship with the man she loved.

> 'You see – I simply couldn't bear the thought that I wasn't the first . . . One marvellous winter evening, silver-bright, I dreamt that a long row of female figures was walking across the snow-covered fields, they were beautiful like spring flowers, because he's one of those men who 'have a way with women'. A whole garden of red flowers grew on the white wilderness and shone from afar like puddles of blood . . . the thing that might have become happiness for me had become for others an injury, shame, the torment of humiliation, the trampling of the rights to life, pushed to the depth of poverty and abandonment, closing the gates to all happiness – that very thing that might have been happiness for me.'[16]

Well aware of these other rejected women and sharp-eyed as ever, Zofia probes Leon Rygier with her pen as pitilessly as she analyses herself.

> He has known too many women too well and so he doesn't consider me beautiful. [. . .] He thinks I'm the wisest woman he's ever known, exceptional and original but he only says that occasionally, without enthusiasm. He loves me with his thoughts and his heart, but not in the depths of his soul. Actually he's in love with himself, exactly as I am – and, like me, he too must feel himself the object of admiration. He doesn't know how to admire others.[17]

And yet he brought her sunshine and fun. He took her out to cafes and theatres. With no money for smart clothes, Zofia added a lace collar here, a frill or two to old dresses, to a new hat – and knew that she looked good.

Then – another blow and a deep wound to her carefully cultivated egoism. During a visit to a little outdoor theatre Rygier pointed out an actress with whom he had had a brief affair. Zofia smiled and stuck to her theory – it didn't matter – but, 'I felt a searing pain in my breasts and somewhere around my throat and everything went dark.'[18]

She wanted to escape somewhere far away – even to die. Why did he torment her so frightfully? She couldn't take revenge because he was so kind to her – and he seemed to be suffering terribly – he even had tears in his eyes at the sight of her pain and she saw this as a sign of his enduring love for her. Yet her thoughts tormented her still. She didn't doubt her love for him but now knew that terrible times lay ahead for her within that love. She wrote: 'My real homeland is in fields of ice.'[19] This phrase would become the title of her first short novel, already quoted above. Naïve and yet profound, this novella, published for the first time in 1904, is like the opening chords of a vast musical symphony that would become the literary output of Poland's leading modernist writer, Zofia Nałkowska.

The sun soon shone between them once more. Rygier liked to have a good time and didn't mind if Zofia had a mild flirt – he liked her to look good and to know that people admired her. They went out to avant-garde cafes where she enjoyed the compliments of literary giants: men who had been part of the family circle when she was a schoolgirl now bowed to her as a woman. She felt that she had become a modern 'progressive woman.'

'It's very pleasant to be engaged, in fact to be Zofia Nałkowska. People are angry, but I am content,' she wrote in almost the last entry of the diary she had kept since the age of twelve.[20]

Zofia felt that diary writing had lost its point because she could now confide in her dear Ryś. Besides, she wanted to write fiction and felt that diary-writing would become a parody of the real thing.

So, how could she wind up this important document of her youth without sounding pathetic or banal?

'Usually a novel ends with a wedding – and in a few months I am getting married,' she wrote and tidied her dairy away.[21]

The marriage between nineteen year old Zofia Nałkowska and Leon Rygier took place on the 11th February 1904 beneath the neo-classical rotunda of the Reformed Church of the Holy Trinity on Królewska Street in Warsaw. The church was famous for its acoustics and for its music, Chopin had played here once in front of the Russian Tsar. Zofia, a materialist and non-religious, had chosen a Protestant wedding because it was possible to get divorced; she had already decided that although she would love Ryś and be faithful to him, she didn't want, as she wrote in a letter to her friend Zofia V, to close off the possibility of escape.

The marriage was a sensation, attended by many people from the Warsaw literary and social scene. The bride had teased her long hair with her fingers, and parted it into two layers, twisted in a heavy knot at the nape of her neck. She coiled two gleaming knots over each ear to hide a scar from an operation she had endured aged sixteen when she had been troubled with inflammation in her inner ear. [22]

The newly-weds had hoped to go abroad for their honeymoon, to Italy or Paris, where Leon Rygier's uncle Tadeusz lived; he was a well-known sculptor whose statue to the poet Adam Mickiewicz still stands in Kraków's Old Market Square, but, as usual, there was no money and so they spent their honeymoon in the place Zofia liked most on earth – her family summer home outside Warsaw, a small wooden house that she would later immortalise as *The House above the Meadows* in one of her most popular books.

And, at first, they were happy . . .

CHAPTER 3

Life in its entirety[1]

We look at the world through the prism of our slavery, through the tiny window in our cages. From statistics and brochures we know about prostitutes, we know that our friend's husband isn't faithful, while ours is the great exception, we know our own sins and in deepest secrecy we know the sins of our friend. But life in its entirety is a secret for us.[2]

Zofia's married life began in her little earthly Paradise, the wooden house the family called *Górki*, later renamed as 'The House above the Meadows', after the title of Zofia's popular book. Situated among pinewoods and low-lying marshland close to the small town of Wołomin, about twenty kilometres east of the capital, this modest *Meadow House* offered the family a summer retreat from city streets. Financial pressures meant that sometimes they took up more permanent residence there, living simply among the tall pine trees.

The family always travelled out of Warsaw by train, then trekked two kilometres along sandy paths through the forests. Once there, the growing girls shed their shoes – though the pine needles prickled their bare feet[3]. They immersed themselves in all that the countryside could offer, including a range of likely and unlikely pets, both sisters were lifelong animal lovers. Their neighbours were simple people whom Zofia would later immortalise in her much acclaimed book, *The House above the Meadows* (1925). Life here brought the two sisters into contact with women and men who were mostly illiterate – a world away from the intense intellectual society of Warsaw, though social norms were still strictly obeyed. Friends from the city, writers, poets, artists and social activists often visited, making the little wooden house a hothouse of left-wing intellectual endeavour.

All this would be woven into Zofia's literary work. The family's retreat in the flat, marshy countryside became part of Zofia's own identity, an affirmation of herself amidst the simple things of nature that she loved.

It's wonderful here. Everywhere else you have to go somewhere far away in order to see the world of nature. Here it's enough to stand on the porch or the balcony. The night sky is dark blue, a brassy moon will emerge from behind the forest, closer and closer until, right under the little hill the meadow swims in shadow and the alders stand scattered on its surface. Sometimes the summer nights are black, full of stars. But this night is entirely in the new impressionistic style – very elegant. It is divine, full of a strange kind of rapture[4].

No light pollution there! In 1904 the first electric street lights illuminated parts of Warsaw – but did not contaminate the sandy roads or the meadows and marshlands, bright with kingcups and marsh-marigolds, Zofia's favourite flowers.

So when Mr and Mrs Leon Rygier moved in after their wedding, the house was full of Zofia's happiest memories.

Her father Wacław's room was painted white 'like a cell' and faced east. Maps hung on the walls; the table and shelves were full of books. The family's dogs – there were always pets in the Nałkowski household – were allowed to come into the sparsely furnished room where they lay in the strip of sunlight across the floor while Wacław worked on his enormous treatise, unfinished at his death, *The territory of historical Poland as a geographical entity*. Wacław hoped to show that the scientific facts of Polish geography made the most convincing case for its independence.

When he was tired after long hours of academic work, he would go outside and water his prized peach trees, which, because the soil was poor and the pine forests absorbed the rain, he had planted on a terrace, Italian style, at the side of the house.[5] Young Zofia and Hanna were given the task of watering these sandy terraces.[6]

At his desk Wacław always worked in complete isolation, often till three or four in the morning and many of his major works were written in his quiet room. He wrote in pencil on long strips of paper which he laid in meticulous order on the top of an ancient, out of tune piano. Zofia recalled a disaster when a storm suddenly blew the window open and the precious papers flew outside. Luckily no rain fell and the family searched the garden and the forest beyond, until all was safely gathered in.[7]

At first Leon and Zofia enjoyed a period of wedded bliss in the quiet countryside. Zofia wrote to her friend Zofia Villaume that – to her great surprise – she loved married life and appreciated the fact that Leon now fully shared the Nałkowski family's political views. However, beyond the happy love nest, Poland was in turmoil.

Cracks began to appear in the political heart of the maimed non-entity of Partitioned Poland. Political factions in all three Partitions actively worked towards Independence without any clear idea of how an independent Polish state might be governed. In 1904 Russia's war with Japan brought armed demonstrators to the streets of Warsaw in protest at enforced mobilisation. The 'icy fields' of Polish captivity began to thaw as the absolutist Tsarist regime made a few concessions. A few Polish-language schools and teacher training colleges were opened, public libraries came into being and educational clubs were organised for workers' children. Polish presses and publishers made use of the new freedom. Previously, authors had to seek publication in the Austrian controlled part of Poland. Now, thanks to the slight thaw, Władysław Reymont (1867 – 1925) was able to publish the first instalments of his Nobel prizewinning novel *Chłopi, Peasants* in a Warsaw journal. Women also enjoyed a little more freedom. Skirts were raised, ankles were visible and ladies could ride unaccompanied in trams and horse-drawn taxis.

Unrest in St Petersburg in 1905 made such deep cracks in the Tsar's repressive system that Polish independence looked more and more likely, though as perceptive people saw, it could only come about if Germany and Russia went to war. Factory workers went on strike – which made political leaders on the Polish Right, notably Roman Dmowski (1864 – 1939), favour Polish nationalism over social reform, while the charismatic leader of the socialist party, Józef Piłsudski (1867 – 1935), began preparations for military action.

Through this turbulence, happy in her new married life, Zofia Rygier-Nałkowska worked intensively on poetry, collections of short stories, the beginning of her trilogy, *Women* (dedicated to her mother) and a novel with the fairy-tale title *Prince* which dealt with broken dreams, revolution and tyranny.

1904 saw the publication of her stand-alone novella, *Icy fields*, written before her marriage, in which the main character, Janka, is certainly Zofia: self-educated, too poor to buy attractive clothes, longing to be noticed and envied. Janka flirts outrageously with a young landowner's son, but declares unrequited love to an older man and retreats to the 'icy fields' of academic work.

Various critics have read in this very obviously autobiographical work a sub-text of Zofia's personality: too much in love with herself, she too fails to leave her own 'icy fields' in order to fulfil the obligations and responsibilities of a true relationship. However, Zofia's marriage to Leon Rygier shows that she was able to take that risk in an era when women were, as teenage Zofia saw so clearly, denied sexual equality even within marriage. The restrictions on women, those corsets of conventionality, shaped Zofia's icily intellectual heroines. She later rejected these early novels, written in the flowery style of the period, although younger women at the time saw them as ground-breaking. Perceptive critics who recognised the art beyond the polemic, concluded that Mrs Rygier-Nałkowska had created a new thing in Polish literature: she wrote as a woman about women, penetrating deep into the female psyche and sexuality. An important writer and artist, Stanislaw Witkiewicz, also known as Witkacy (1885–1939), described Nałkowska's early novels as works of genius which were sadly undervalued.[8] They influenced emerging Polish writers, both men and women.

In *Prince*, a young woman who had been married for convenience falls deeply in love with a revolutionary hero. Another such figure, a friend of the Nałkowski family, Ludwik Liciński (1874 – 1908) would soon engage Zofia deeply in real life. In her novel her young heroine joins the revolutionaries, begins a sexual liaison with their leader, Jerzy and, pregnant with his child, keeps a lonely vigil the night before his execution:

> Today – at the hour of five thirty . . .
> I look at my watch – I know every moment what time it is and I don't understand why I long for this night to last longer and longer – because after all each second of this night which you too are experiencing, comes closer to everything that only the most monstrous imagination might dream up in madness.
> O do you hear the hour strike? Do you hear footsteps? I know, I already know. They are coming in for you. They have come to take you

away. And the priest. You don't confess. You despise all that – it is your last small pleasure – and how frightfully small it is in the face of what is to come . . .

Jerzy, you're crying out, you're afraid – Oh God, why have they frightened you like this, Why all these monstrous accessories of death which only make it even more frightful . . . Don't go! Free yourself, shout, Jerzy! Sing that wonderful, triumphant song once again . . . Why don't you shout, why don't you writhe across the earth? Why in this moment you are still enduring that inhuman comedy?

And now they are moving forward so slowly – to this place where you will die[9]. (1907)

Not only is this powerful, it is also prophetic. This young woman's experience foreshadows that of millions of others whose loved ones were murdered by the barbaric terror unleashed throughout the twentieth century by tyrants East and West. The Russian poet Anna Akhmatova later joined the endless queue of grieving women outside the barred windows of a Leningrad prison in the 1930s when her son was a victim of the Stalinist purges. 'Can you write about this?' someone asked her – and Akhmatova produced a poem, *Requiem*, (1940) that went to the heart of every wife or mother's pain. Zofia's early prose, however, was both requiem and a call to arms.

By 1907 Zofia Rygier-Nałkowska was already a significant published author and poet. A photograph of the time shows her seated in company of some of the major writers of the day. She is wearing white with lace about her throat. Her shining hair is sleek at the sides and piled high on the top of her head. Her face is half in shadow and has a slightly sulky look; no one else in the picture is smiling either– this was in the days before anyone said 'cheese.' In that same year Zofia moved with her husband to the city of Kielce where they shared a literary life, working together on a radical newspaper. Zofia also taught illiterate adults and life seemed happy.

All too soon, though, deep rifts appeared within their marriage. Zofia's work was winning significant admirers while Leon was a poor shadow, a poetaster, who soon showed his preference for hanging out in cafes, piling up debts – and meeting other women. 1907, the year in which *The Prince* was published, was a year in which twenty-three year old Zofia had many illusions shattered.

Leon had seduced and made pregnant a young chambermaid whose mother had sent from the country to work for Zofia, entrusting her to the young wife's care. Right at the very end of her life Zofia wrote about the little girl to her friend and namesake Zofia V:

> She was delicate and charming. Her mother, a country housewife put her under my protection but for her he was a prince from a fairy tale. She came to me for help. How could he have dared! I wasn't jealous of her, I just felt such human, sisterly compassion. Such sorrow for the injury he had done her. How did he dare?[10]

Affairs of the heart however painful, became part of the tapestry she wove into her creative work. Far into the future, the seduced country girl would become one of the greatest characters in pre-war Polish literature, Justyna in Zofia's much-acclaimed novel, *Boundary*.

Later that year Zofia was invited to speak at the first ever Women's Conference in Poland, during which she gave a message so explosive that an older, well-established woman writer walked out – though she later claimed she had left because she had an engagement and not because she was offended. In that lecture Zofia called for sexual equality for women and confronted the dilemma that had engaged her during her teenage years: since humankind is referred to as 'man', can a woman be fully 'man' (human), being a woman? She challenged her audience: where are the prostitutes? Why are none invited to our conference?

'Men need prostitutes,' twenty-one year old Zofia declared. 'We honest women create them, yet we despise 'fallen women':

> We look at the world through the prism of our slavery, through the tiny window in our cages. From statistics and brochures we know about prostitutes, we know that our friend's husband isn't faithful, while ours is the great exception, we know our own sins and in deepest secrecy we know the sins of our friend. But life in its totality is a secret for us.

Zofia ended her lengthy speech with a challenge: we want life in its entirety![11]

Her speech created an outcry and a backlash, but Zofia had no need to shout. Bad manners were never for her. These feminist ideas were woven into the personages and dilemmas of the sophisticated women of her early novels.

Even so, confronted with increasing evidence of her husband's infidelity, Zofia knew herself betrayed as a wife, and this may have been a reason why she had a romance with the publisher of the literary paper both she and Rygier worked for. The affair was brief, but gave her happiness. The couple went out into the countryside and picked Zofia's favourite marigolds and wild white anemones. Her marriage had been rocked to its foundations and her emotions were shattered by the death of a close friend, Ludwik Liciński (1874 – 1908), a political activist, writer and revolutionary. Ludwik's self-sacrificing life made Leon Rygier's seem even more shallow and worthless. Liciński's attacks on the Tsarist regime had forced him to become a homeless wanderer, crossing borders, dodging the police. He decided to escape beyond the Urals to Siberia to study the life of imprisoned Polish deportees, but his poverty and rough living had ruined his health and he was too ill to travel. Wacław Nałkowski set up a fund to raise money to send Ludwik to a warmer climate for treatment. Friends responded generously, but it was too late. Instead, the monies raised paid for his care in a sanatorium in Otwock, near Warsaw where thirty-four year old Ludwik was soon to die. Zofia spent hours at his bedside and when they were apart they wrote long letters to each other. The physical facts of severe illness cast an enormous shadow on her, but even more wounding was the emotional content of this bedside vigil, for Liciński loved her and she, knowing that he was dying, felt obliged to pretend to love him in return. She hated this deception but felt forced into it. After his death she followed his coffin to the grave. She kept all his letters until they went up in flames when Hitler's army burnt Warsaw to the ground in 1944. Only one letter from him remained:

'There have been terrible things in my life [. . .] but you should remember above all that you are the only person whom I love perhaps more than life, even my own.'[12]

Zofia would paint a faithful portrait of Ludwik Liciński in her next novel with its feminine title, *Narcyza*. After Ludwik's death and fleeing from her shattered marriage, Zofia took refuge with Zofia Villaume – they had been friends since Zofia was fifteen. Zofia V. was a landowner's daughter, half-French. Her abundant dark hair reached her ankles. She lived a sheltered life and enjoyed many of the privileges denied to her younger namesake; their friendship lasted life-long. Zofia N often spent her holidays at the Villaume family estate and the two girls sat in the garden in the shadow of the trees, one of them reclining in a hammock, as they read serious literature aloud.

Zofia V was always a major support to Zofia N, so now the two friends discussed Zofia's plans for divorce. Zofia felt so sorry for Leon in his empty life that she found it hard to make a final decision – a feature of her personality which would repeat itself more destructively later on, yet the treachery had been so cruel that she did not hurry back to Kielce after Ludwik's Liciński's death.

Meantime Zofia was busy on a collection of short stories which were not considered appropriate reading for young ladies because they so radically challenged stereotypes about women. One young reader later confessed to having read them in secret and acknowledged the input of Zofia's work on her own writing life.[13]

The title story, called, innocently, *Little kitten or white tulips* (1909) is painted as delicately as the subtlest water colour, yet is explosive in its understatement – a technique that would mark Zofia's later work. This story also makes a bitterly ironic comment on Zofia's own marriage to a man nine years' older – Koteczka (little kitten) is engaged to an older man who confesses that he has had many love affairs. The distressed girl bursts into tears and then admits that she had once gone to an artist to have her portrait painted. She wasn't in love with him, oh no, because he was too young and handsome to be married. The kind of men who looked for marriage were grey about the temples, like her fiancé, and not handsome, because handsome men betray their wives; while women like little Koteczka, are destined to be wives but not lovers, just wives.[14]

In 1909, too, Zofia returned to her diary writing and continued in this to the end of her life while in the outer world political events were about to engage her time and attention. The Nałkowski family were involved with the trial and imprisonment of a philosopher, writer and controversial literary critic, Stanisław Brzozowski (1878 – 1911).

Brzozowski's Marxist, and particularly his literary views influenced many younger Polish thinkers and writers, not least the Nobel Laureate Czesław Miłosz (1911 – 2004) who later, having defected from Communist Poland in 1955 wrote a biography of Brzozowski in which he compared his own situation with the harsh and demeaning treatment that critics meted out to Stanisław – both had been persecuted by authoritarian conformist regimes and both had branded as traitors.[15]

Brzozowski's trial took place in Krakow. Zofia, formally separated though not yet divorced, travelled there with her father, both of them boldly standing out in support of the accused, along with several other left wing literary giants of the day, 'the flower of the socialist world,' wrote Zofia.[16] She might more accurately have written 'underground.' Although she hated public speaking, Zofia gave lectures in Stanisław's defence and actively campaigned on behalf of the accused.

The painful destruction of Zofia's illusions about herself as a woman and a wife had flung her into the cauldron of political protest.

The background to the trial of the controversial young man was also complex. Stanisław Brzozowski had been involved in a student secret society. As treasurer, he had helped himself to funds – his father was dying and he wanted to help him. He promised to pay the money back, nevertheless his fellow students put him on trial. This brought the group to the attention of the Tsarist police who arrested the leaders. In grim prison conditions, Stanisław contracted the first stages of TB. He fled to Florence where the long arm of the secret police reached him. Dragged back to Kraków in desperately poor health Brzozowski was accused of collaborating with Tsarist police. His trial proved nothing, yet did not clear his name – nor did it improve his health. Suffering from advanced tuberculosis, he returned to enforced exile in Florence with his wife and little girl. He was already a dying man.

Zofia too plunged into ill-health and depression. Still not formally divorced from Leon Rygier, she was tormented by his explicit descriptions of his talents as a lover of other women. Her obvious distress massaged his male ego. Zofia later confided to Zofia V. that Leon would 'return at dawn, full of emotion and tell me that I smell of lily of the valley and of spring – whereas that other one a few hours ago . . . Oh there were so many of these comparisons, so cruel and unnecessary.'[17]

Leon Rygier then began an affair with one of Zofia's close friends and Zofia, knowing that her marriage had reached the point of no return, took refuge with her parents, with reading and writing – and with her diary which she began again in 1909 and continued for the rest of her life.

She found consolation too in a new, and entirely unconsummated love affair with a handsome young lawyer, Edmund Joachim Szalit, brother-in-law of the accused man, Brzozowski. Zofia's bruised heart now found true love with a man who could have been her ideal husband, the only man, she confided to her diary, whose child she wished she could bear, a love that had to be kept secret and could never become reality because Edmund was married with a little girl. Knowing too well the wretchedness of betrayal, Zofia refused to let Edmund take their love to its physical conclusion, nor would she let him tell his wife about the affair that brought them both such happiness. Nevertheless, in spite of the torment of leading a secret life, the affair restored Zofia's self-belief during a year of sweetness and passionate kisses, of walks and talks, and a blissful time together in *Meadow House*. It was paid for at a huge emotional cost but she was always glad that she had not been the cause of break-up within her beloved Edmund's family, glad that they had both behaved honoura-bly, making their love even more true.

When the affair ended Zofia found a partial escape from her troubles in travel in Poland and abroad – as a paid companion to a wealthy woman. She was still reading widely, in French and Russian as well as in Polish but ill-health dogged her. She felt demeaned in her role and very definitely out of her comfort zone in the world of rich business men and financiers, a world she had met only at that reception in Warsaw which her father had refused to attend. In spite of her illnesses, some of which may have been caused by her longing for Edmund and perhaps even more acutely, Leon's continual pressure, Zofia used this time for self-education, immersing herself in works of art in Florence, Venice and Rome. And of course in her writing.

1910 saw the publication of short stories, including *Heavenly Night*, a marvellously evocative novella with a chilling ending worthy of a Hitchcock film. Here Zofia brings on stage betrayed love, the silent cry of an aborted child and an act of irreversible revenge. The drama is set against a mountain landscape, where a frozen lake reflects the stars, so that fish might swallow them, while the colour on the surface is some-times hyacinth and sometimes blood . . .

These motifs will echo throughout many of Zofia's novels; fish and deep water will always be used as a hint of death.

Modern readers in Poland find Nałkowska's early prose flowery and pretentious – but many marvel at her ability to use words like a painter. She is able to sketch a complete portrait or a description of a landscape in impressionistic detail so that we see how feathers that adorn a woman's hat shimmer and float around her face (*The Palatine Rose*). In her novel *Narcysa* (1910) as we drive with one of her characters in an open carriage through the Mazovian dusk, we almost smell the fresh scents of spring, and watch the landscape darken as the moon rises and perspectives change.

These early books are of their time but a hundred years on they are still powerfully drawn pictures of a world long gone, brought to light by a young writer's careful pen who claimed 'life in its entirety' for women in an almost pathologically patriarchal world.

CHAPTER 4

Laying out life in patterns

> Pani Zofia, already adorned with the nimbus of a famous writer, charmed me with the light of her improbably blue eyes and with something which awoke deep trust from the very first moment. She was one of those rare people who simply radiate interest in other people, never mind whether old or young [. . .][1]

On her return from her Italian sojourn, still bedevilled by ill-health and depression, Zofia found refuge in *Meadow House* where she gradually recovered from the assault on her inner life, which her husband had torn apart. Leon Rygier continued to dance on the ruins. Zofia even paid his debts, and to her increasing revulsion, was sufficiently seduced by him to sleep with him. Leon was obviously a talented lover and it's not clear when Zofia finally achieved a divorce. At the end of his life, three marriages later, Rygier boasted of his connection with the famous writer who 'had so cruelly cast him off.' He told one student. 'Never tell your secrets to the woman you love.'

This student recalled in his memoir of Nałkowska:

> He told us about his break up with Nałkowska. According to Rygier, it happened because he'd been away somewhere and had an affair which he confessed to her on his return home. The very next day Nałkowska packed her bags and went back to her mother.
>
> 'You just couldn't talk to her, she got into such a temper [. . .]
>
> As he spoke he looked somewhere in the distance with such sorrow as if it had just happened yesterday [. . .] Rygier was already an old man, yet he had never stopped feeling sad about it (the separation). Her charm was undimmed, its strength so powerful that he remembered it

still and referred to it on his death bed a quarter of a century after our conversation.[2]

The little vignette casts light on the dynamics of the mismatch that Zofia had guessed at even before the marriage.

Anti-Jewish action broke out in Warsaw in May 1913. The immediate catalyst was an influx of immigrants from the Russian Empire, so-called *Litvaks*, who supported socialism, This flood of immigrants with a suspect ideology gave the National Democratic Party a pretext to boycott Jewish traders. Jewish students were expelled from college, while writers, artists and musicians were threatened with expulsion from the Polish cultural scene. Zofia attended a concert at which the conductor Zdzisław Birnbaum (1878-1921) was the victim of an attempted boycott. Thus the scandal reached the hallowed temple of music itself, the Warsaw Philharmonic. Zofia deplored every manifestation of nationalistic fervour and was branded as a 'non-anti-Semite' by some social groups.[3]

She also witnessed hardship among the countrywomen who lived around *Meadow House*.

A hard-working woman 'so small you can hardly see her . . . who is in her forties but looks like a hundred' fled to the protective hospitality of *Meadow House* from her abusive husband. 'If he just took a whip I wouldn't mind but he grabs whatever he can and kicks me around the head,' she said in dialect, a phrase that Zofia used in later work. This woman's tyrannical husband stormed round to *Meadow House* to force her to come back home because he needed her earnings. Zofia recorded the terror in her eyes 'so red, that when they wept, it was like tears of blood.'[4]

In highlighting the plight of simple people, Zofia gave their lives value and worth. She would use this story in her other work, but she was never repetitive and her writing came at great personal cost. She was always full of misgivings, certain of failure and often felt unable to write. 'My only support is my family . . . I love them with all reserves of my feelings,' she wrote.[5]

The family rejoiced when the other daughter Hanna's first major piece of sculpture was included in an exhibition in the prestigious Zachęta Gallery in Warsaw. Hanna was tall like Zofia and prettier, with finer, more delicate features. 'My beautiful sister, slender and pale like a Rossetti virgin . . .' wrote Zofia.[6]

When autumn weather set in, the family returned from *Meadow House* to their flat in Warsaw. Zofia's room looked on to a windowless wall, which 'causes me physical torture.'[7] She reorganised this little room to her own tastes, spinning around, she wrote, like a bee in a honey cell. Here she completed *Narcysa*, a novel sometimes called the Polish *Madame Bovary*, which laid her open to the charge of having a narcissistic personality. Her analogy of herself as a bee within the honeycomb or a spider spinning a web points to aspects of femininity both nourishing and predatory. Critics who hold the view of Zofia's vulnerable egoistic personality point to her two destructive marriages and other equally harmful relationships; it must however be remembered that the young woman was forging her career in a country that was virulently patriarchal. Although there had been several major women writers in nineteenth century Polish literature, women's writing and art were considered second-rate. A contemporary and namesake Zofia Stryjeńska (1891 – 1976) had to dress as a man to be admitted to an art college in Munich in 1911, was twice forcibly admitted to psychiatric hospital by her husband and was finally affected so badly with syphilis from another liaison that she could no longer see to paint.[8]

Roman Catholic Polish women were offered the Virgin Mary as a role model and whilst this was also true in other Roman Catholic countries, the Holy Virgin has a deeply patriotic dimension in Poland. In 1656 when Poland was overrun by Swedish Protestant forces, the King, trying to whip up national unity, crowned the Virgin Mary Queen of Poland; she is acknowledged as such to this day. Thus the Heavenly, yet uniquely Polish Queen held a political as well as religious place in the nation's hearts, and particularly in the hearts of patriotic women. In 1830, the year of a major Polish Uprising, the national poet Adam Mickiewicz (1798 – 1855), issued a poetic call to mothers to:

> Kneel before our Mother of Sorrows,
> See the sword which made her bleed:
> The foe will pierce you too with painful blows.
> No matter if the world blossoms with peace,
> Your son's destiny is crucifixion;
> Though allied nations declare that war will cease,
> His call his death and martyrdom, not resurrection.[9]

Women were required to express their patriotism through their devotion to the Virgin, while socially they were corseted in conventionality and bore the brunt of male infidelity, including venereal disease. Out-of-wedlock pregnancy was a scandal. Within the matrimonial bonds a wife was required to accept unwanted pregnancies and turn a blind eye to her husband's love affairs. Zofia Nałkowska exposed all these scenarios in her writing and in that sense she can certainly be considered a feminist writer. Her cry as a young woman had been 'we want life in its entirety'. She never flinched from analysis of this entirety. Her work is not just women-focussed. People were her meat and drink and a wide-ranging portrait gallery is presented in her books. Her characters, women and men, leap from the page and remain with the reader long after the book is closed.

Zofia loved to dance the night away. She could ride and skate, she enjoyed foreign travel, loved to flirt and to joke, always within the conventions of decency. She was also a life-long learner. She read widely and thoughtfully, always with a pencil in hand and she allowed her work to change as she came into contact with other younger writers. Later, well-established herself, when she generously encouraged emerging writers, she was never too precious or proud not to let them influence her writing style. She drew from life and her diaries are her sketchbook.

> I don't make anything up, I don't imagine things, just lay out in patterns details which only and always come from my own psychological experiences. My deepest characteristic is a fundamental inability to cope with facts of reality that happen outside myself.[10]

This self-confessed characteristic, coupled with her penetrating, even fearless intellect allowed Zofia to write novels that still have relevance today. However, one example of this completely truthful use of detail from her experience (this time her father's) which Zofia employs in *Narcysa* has disturbing undertones.

Wacław must have shared with his family an incident from his boyhood on the family estate near Lublin which left him deeply ashamed, and forged his later political and social convictions. He, the landowner's son, had come upon a little barefoot girl who was carrying two buckets of water across a hilly meadow from the river. The heavy buckets and the steep incline were too much for her. Wacław cruelly knocked the buckets out of her hand. Water soaked the grass and splashed the child's muddy feet and torn dress. She didn't cry or make a sound, simply turned round and went back to the river to fill the buckets all over again.

This cruel action and the child's unspoken acceptance were seared upon Wacław's conscience for the rest of his life and only much later Zofia discovered that the incident had been preceded by a severe beating and kicking by Wacław's own father.[11]

By contrast Zofia uses the incident in her novel *Narcysa* to define the awakening sexual responses of one of her characters, Maurycy. About to betray his pregnant wife, Maurycy decides that he is not guilty of any wrong:

> To the best of his knowledge his feeling of tenderness for a woman always contained within it a certain moment of affectionate, totally non-malicious cruelty [. . .] which dated back to the distant days of his childhood, to that memorable event when the child's water had poured out [. . .] because, as he had looked down at the little girl and watched her go away without a word, without tears, saddened but humble, he had experienced for the first time a deep, undefined sweetness which foretold from the depths of his boyish body all his future love affairs. He must have sensed then that, just as she had accepted that injury, she would also respond to the cruellest, brutal caresses without tears, just with the same humble, sweet sadness [. . .]
>
> He saw the little girl once or twice afterwards but he felt a kind of shame, supposedly because of those buckets and he didn't accost her again.[12]

The chapter ends when Maurycy has already experienced the 'madness' and 'sunny happiness' of sexual pleasure which leaves him deeply saddened and always reminds him of the child who had first aroused his sexual instincts:

> It happened that in the fragrant darkness of a stable he then met the child, the same small girl whom he had hurt long ago. And there – already acquainted with the art of love, he inflicted a new injury on her.
>
> She was his second lover. Humbly, without complaint and without a smile, she gave him happiness. But he didn't have long to enjoy her because she died soon afterwards.[13]

Modern readers rightly find this offensive, but Zofia Nałkowska was always concerned with the truth. She never tried to gloss over unpleasant, even criminal actions until in the end she forged the facts of unimaginable crime into the masterpiece for which she is still remembered, *Medallions*.

Still plagued with ill-health, Zofia resumed her ill-starred marriage, partly because she didn't want to bring disharmony into the family life – Wacław was unwell; until in January 1911 tragedy hit, an event so shattering that this woman of words could only sum it up in just two words: *father's death*.

Wacław had collapsed in the street with a cerebral haemorrhage and was taken to hospital. His wife and two daughters hurried, shocked, to his bedside where they kept watch beside him but he never regained consciousness.

Anna Nałkowska, faithful to Wacław's philosophy, refused to admit a priest to his bedside. His funeral on 31st of January 1911 was a huge occasion, a political manifestation. Crowds gathered to honour this academic who had devoted his life to the geography of a country that didn't officially exist on any map. Friends, students, colleagues and admirers followed the coffin whose only decoration was a crown of thorns. Someone attached a red ribbon to the crown of thorns, an act of protest which produced an immediate reaction from the Tsarist police. The offending ribbon however, was not removed completely, tucked beneath the thorns it was still visible to the mourners. Political prisoners in the grim Pawiak prison watched through barred windows the final journey of a man whose early death was brought on by childhood poverty, overwork, increasing ill-health and his steadfast refusal to consult a doctor which cost money he could never afford.

Wacław was buried in the Powązki cemetery in Warsaw. Fifteen years later, in 1926, at the instigation of the Polish Geographical Society which he had founded, Hanna Nałkowska, now a much admired sculptor, cast a bronze figure of a knight in armour entitled *The Warrior*, in recognition of Nałkowski's long fight for Marxist principles and this was placed on Wacław's grave.[14]

That was already in another era when Poland was an independent country; the immediate impact of Wacław's death on his family was desperate poverty and illness. The three grieving women could no longer afford to live in Warsaw and moved to *Meadow House*. Anna, loyally pursuing her husband's professional work, wrote geography text books, greatly appreciated by future generations of school children. Hanna taught village children geography while Zofia set aside her own literary pursuits and devoted herself to preparing Wacław's manuscripts for publication. The year 1911 also saw the publication of a novella, *Heavenly Night* and two years later came *Mirrors*, a collection of short stories which won widespread critical acclaim.

Their deep mourning lasted two years. In January 1913, Zofia and Hanna attended a New Year ball. The two tall sisters attracted much admiration, particularly Hanna who wore a classically inspired gown with violets on her shoulder and in her hair. The two lovely sisters soon attracted new admirers who made the train journey out of town to the wooden house in the forests. Here Anna and her daughters delighted guests with their beauty, elegance, charm and by their genuine interest in the people, old and young who visited.

A friend of the family, Karolina Beylin (1899 – 1977) gives a child's insight into *Meadow House* and the three tall ladies who lived there:

> The house seemed truly magical.
>
> Three beautiful tall ladies whose low melodious voices were all alike . . . the mother and her two daughter, each one different and each filled with her own kind of unusual charm. The mother, Pani Anna, whose geography text books were used in schools was dark-haired and although she seemed stern, she was in fact full of warmth and greeted us with such a genuine smile that all my shyness about entering an unknown house disappeared.
>
> Standing beside her, Pani Zofia, already wearing the nimbus of a famous writer, charmed me with the light of her improbably blue eyes and with something which awoke deep trust from the very first moment. She was one of those rare people who simply radiate interest in other people, never mind whether old or young, or even a small girl as I was then. With every question, even every glance she seemed to open up the person she was talking to right from the very inside.
>
> Next to her was her younger sister Hanna, already a well-known sculptor, slender with ash-blond hair and subtle features as if she had been cut out from a painting by Burne-Jones, who was popular at that time.

The interior of the house was just as unusual as its three mistresses. In the spacious, but low-ceilinged dining room, right opposite the door, an owl sat on a perch, totally without a cage and looked at the people coming in with its round, spooky eyes.

'That's Wunia,' Pani Zofia said. 'She's a big surprise to all our visitors and she shows her anger in such a funny way.'

She wagged her finger at the bird and without making a single sound, Wunia shook her neck feathers out like a sort of boa.

'That feathery necklace is a sign that she's upset,' Pani Zofia explained.

Thus Wunia was my first introduction to the house of the Nałkowska ladies and so she has always stayed in my memory.[15]

This owl and other unusual pets, including a jackdaw with a wing missing, a hare and a hedgehog would later feature in a collection of short stories called *My Animals* (1934).

Tall and statuesque, with brilliant forget-me-not blue eyes (cold as crystal, some critics said) which contrasted with her darker brows and with her abundant curly brown hair carefully arranged to conceal her rather high forehead, Zofia was sought after as an adornment at balls or concerts or theatres. So she flirted and charmed and did not let anyone except her mother and her close friend Zofia V see her inner pain. Only with Zofia V, she confessed, could she cast aside the art and artifice of her social life and drop the mask with she wore, as she put it, for the sake of whichever man she was with. She did not reveal to outsiders the poverty that made her reuse worn clothing, nor did she reveal ill health or any complaint that made that dazzling smile an effort, or her sparkling wit a weariness. Zofia maintained a high intellectual life with deep reading in many languages. And all the time too, she kept on writing and fought to stay in the market as a powerful new voice for women.

So now, in 1913 on the eve of a war which would destroy three crumbling empires and restore Poland to full statehood, twenty-seven year old Zofia began to claim that 'full erotic life' she had longed for. There were secret affairs, kisses in the back of horse-drawn taxi-cabs. Unfortunately most eligible men were already married and wanted a wife to be a background figure, domesticated and trivial. Zofia was never trivial or domesticated – and nor was she a woman of easy virtue. Her attempt at free love was hollow, empty of emotional satisfaction. 'This is all so against my nature,' she lamented. 'Because, after all, I am, par excellence, a home bird, constant and faithful, dreaming of the one love which will bring me happiness.'[16]

Thus, on the eve of world war, Zofia longed for stability, for a man whom she could rely on, with whom she could share her formidable intellect, who would love her for herself and not for what he could get out of her. She would chase that elusive dream for the rest of her life. The First World War, which saw fighting on the streets of Warsaw in ever-changing battle zones between the warring powers, brought her a love both passionate and cruel. This love would degrade and demean her, attempt to rob her of everything she had fought so hard to achieve, yet enrich her writing and provide her with some of the most challenging and dangerous male characters in Polish and European literature.

CHAPTER 5

Encircled by fire[1]

I am defenceless in the face emotional despotism. I don't know how to
be either abrasive or straightforward, I don't know how to break off
relationships with people, even when I absolutely can't stand them . . .
when someone else is annoyed or upset in my presence I feel their
unpleasantness as if it were my own. But my so-called 'goodness' has a
basis that is completely false and ignoble.[2]

These words written when Zofia was almost twenty-nine sum up the
dilemma which would haunt her whole life. Soon, however, external
events impinged on the three Nałkowska women. The First World War
began, Zofia commented, like the opening of a bad novel. A burglar
climbed into the upper storey of *Meadow House* and stole a watch, a
gold brooch, a bag with documents and an eiderdown, while their dog
killed a neighbour's chicken. Nothing is wasted in a literary life and this
latter episode later wove its way into a humorous story (*My Animals*
1915).

The war soon made its presence felt. Friends were called up, banks and
post offices were closed. The three women were totally dependent on
these services and even had to borrow money to pay the milk bill. In the
midst of this chaos and confusion Zofia recorded that a squirrel had just
taken a nut from her hand.[3]

Trains were full of Russian soldiers moving westwards to fight the
invading Germans. People cheered these troops because Polish soldiers
were among them but these men were about to fight their compatriots in
the enemy German and Austrian armies. Zofia commented sadly that few
people were aware of that irony. Soon, she noted, the trains were returning with the wounded and no-one cheered then.[4]

Meadow House was no longer safe for three vulnerable women now that the countryside was full of invading soldiers and other marauders. They moved back to Warsaw and crowded into an unheated room in a friend's flat along with other refugees. Zofia longed even more desperately for a home of her own, a husband and child; feelings that she had stifled because of Leon's infidelity and because of her own ambition to succeed as a writer.

Warsaw was under continued attack, thousands of deaths were reported.[5] Cezary Jellenta, the close friend of Wacław Nałkowski whom teenage Zofia had imagined herself in love with, wrote a memoir of the year 1914 showing how people supported one another and maintained high morale by continuing to meet at concerts and in cafes. As the German armies drew closer and outlying cities were bombed, Jellenta commented:

> Warsaw is nervous and impatient. She feels the approaching blow and the old city can only guess what it will be like. Will we be able to bear it? Will it come to street fighting? Will there be mob theft, will the police maintain order? Uncertainty and fear grip our necks like a noose.[6]

On a more optimistic note, however, he noted:

> The Russians have only just grasped something unfathomable, unde-finable in the soul of Warsaw. She is like a queen in lethargy, bewitched in a golden coffin. She was born to wear a crown, all she needs to do is wake up . . .
>
> We've already shown who we really are, stewards of mercy, organis-ing help and self-help, we've impressed everyone with our up-to date medical provision, with the hospitality and charm of our women, with the fire of our sympathy, the way our young people are so wildly passionate to engage in every kind of noble action.[7]

However, as Jellenta tried to imagine the future for Poland he predicted gloomily that the country would slide down a precipice and, like a river, would flow into the vast oceans of Russia and be lost once again.[8]

Zofia too feared for the future even as she used the experiences of war to craft new stories. In 1915, along with her sister and mother, she made the difficult journey out of town only to discover that their beloved

Meadow House had been plundered. Russian soldiers had set up camp in the forests; guards conducted the three Polish ladies politely along the forest paths and promised to keep watch while they sorted through their remaining possessions.

Zofia was moved by their 'naïve words' as they told her of the loss of their comrades: 'These simple men, exhausted after a whole year of bloody warfare yearned for their far-off Siberia as if for a Promised Land,' she wrote[9], little knowing that two years later the Tsarist armies would disintegrate and a new theatre of war would be played out across lands that Poland would reclaim as its eastern territories.

On that August day of 'gloomy idyll' a Russian officer, a book lover, spent hours helping Zofia pack her scattered books – the men had gazed in awe at the sight of all these books and had told Zofia with laughter, 'Why would we steal your books – we can't read them!' The officer asked Zofia to play for him – their ancient piano had been left in *Meadow House*.[10]

Zofia crafted these encounters into a short story called *P.P.C pour prendre congé* (in order to take a break). It was published in a Warsaw literary journal, in a children's anthology (incredibly!) and included in her collection of war-time short stories, *Secrets of Blood*. This collection shows Zofia's new voice. As a detached, calm observer she explores the impact of war on characters depicted from life, including a simple woman on a crowded platform when families saw their menfolk off to fight. 'He forgot his gloves,' the woman complained in dialect – as if that were the biggest loss he would sustain in that war. This became the subject of a story called *Gloves*.

As Warsaw was shaken by gunfire and bombs, Zofia began to tease out a theory of war. Her view was that war exposes the reality of evil which already exists in everyday life, in harsh labour in mines and factories, in the drudgery of peasant labour and in punitive conditions in hospitals for the mentally ill.[11]

However, during the unrelenting bombardment she was honest enough to confess in her diary that she was afraid to go down to the cellar because her nightdress was shabby and she would have to sit huddled up too closely with repulsive neighbours.[12]

In August 1915 the Russian army was driven back eastwards across the River Vistula. Warsaw was torn in two, with civilians caught in the crossfire, before the German army took the city. The officers installed themselves in the best cafes and hotels.

'Nothing changes,' Zofia commented wryly, 'except the colours of the uniforms and the flags.'[13]

In the midst of smoke and the clamour of war, a new hope began to shine for the beleaguered people of Warsaw. Improbable as it seemed, people began to feel that their vision of a free and independent Poland might become a reality, although the bravest and best would shed their blood in the battle. Zofia did not agree with nationalistic slogans and feared that if it came into being, the new Poland would be nationalistic, right-wing and anti-Semitic.

As starving people queued outside empty bakeries and Zofia shivered in an unheated room with only a candle to read and write by, she kept on working. Her mother's geography text books brought in a little income. Both sisters were ill and their mother ventured through the war-torn streets to take Zofia's latest work to the publisher – and returned with a silk bed cover.[14] Wrapped in the silk coverlet Zofia received visitors, believing herself loved 'as never before' by a major literary critic who brought her flowers but never voiced the marriage proposal which Zofia longed to hear and which she was too proud – and perhaps too bound by convention, to request.

So, she concluded, 'I only see that no one is happy. It's bad to be a wife and it's bad to be a mistress.' She gave herself a wise piece of advice: 'No need to eat yourself up with regrets, you just have to go back to books.'[15]

Which she did. 1915 saw the publication of a novel, *Snakes and Roses*. It was greatly praised in its day and still remains a powerful critique of the world of high finance that Zofia had met with (and had been repulsed by) in her travels as a lady companion. Although she portrays some Jewish characters in a rather stereotypical way, the book also demonstrates a sympathetic knowledge of Judaism. When she was a teenager Zofia had chanced upon a deserted Jewish cemetery. She was always fascinated by gravestones, because they bore silent witness to the lost biographies of vanished people and thus were a sign that life is more lasting than death. In her first published novel, (*Icy Fields*) Zofia describes this abandoned Jewish cemetery:

> The carved stone grave slabs stand in long straight rows; some strange Kabbalistic signs are carved on them, lions, broken candles, bookshelves, some kind of secret decoration. Moss, heather and thyme

cover the almost invisible hillock of graves; the wooden fence we have to crawl through is lost among the trunks of the pine trees. Thus, symmetrical rows of grave stones rise in the midst of a forest seemingly untouched by human hands. I feel as if I've gone back into some sort of remote past.

I like graveyards, I like to look at the triumph of life over death . . .'[16]

Words in Polish on one of these abandoned gravestones had captured her attention, *węzeł życia*, the knot of life. She repeated the phrase in many of her books and used it as the title of her last published novel, *Knots of Life* (1953). A lover of life, and utterly absorbed in its knotty complications, Zofia understood this phrase literally, so in *Snakes and Roses* a young woman, Raissa, uses the phrase as she explains the place of the Hebrew Scriptures in the life of 'the masses':

'They study this book for years on end, that's the way it's always been. And still its wisdom has not been exhausted.' Raissa's small mouth twisted in an imperceptible smile [. . .] 'Just think, that's after all the only thing by which the eternal spiritual hunger of the masses is fed; it's the only thing that keeps them alive, it's their fatherland and faith, their only heart, their soul [. . .] The knot of life,' she said [. . .] She took out another book and began to read, 'I took this from the headstone of Joseph son of Elias, dead from the creation of the world 4130, 'May his soul be woven into the knot of life.'[. . .] Inscriptions on gravestones from some old Jewish cemetery,' she explained.[17]

Later critics pointed out that the Polish word *węzeł*, knot or tie which Zofia saw on the gravestone, does not exactly translate the Hebrew צרור *tseror* as used in the Scriptures: 'The soul of my lord shall be bound in the bundle of life with the Lord thy God.' (1 Samuel 25:29 KJV).[18] However another twist in the 'knots of life' in *Snakes and Roses* is the murder of a brain-damaged child by her mother, unloved in her marriage and stigmatised in her social life by the awful fact of her crippled child.

'I shall kill her,' she thought. There was no horror in her heart, only the hard, stony feeling of necessity [. . .] Her fingers stiffened and

became crooked like a bird's claws [. . .] Marusia's hard fingers twisted
around the little one's throat. It was warm, choking a little from the
pressure, alive [. . .]. Oh, quicker, quicker, she whispered between her
teeth, squeezing the slender neck more strongly, with all her strength,
with all her strength . . .[19]

Thereafter Marusia is led inexorably to suicide in the forbiddingly dark
water of a canal.

The themes of child murder and of suicide are two dark threads in the
tapestry of Zofia's complete work. Taken as a whole her work is like a musical symphony with themes repeated, re-worked and developed in different
ways. A friend and fellow-writer wrote that to appreciate Nałkowska you
have to 'read her whole'. Forty years later, right at the end of her life, Zofia
wrote a short story In the dark in which Jewish women in hiding with 'no
other way out' are forced to suffocate a crying child. Marusia's 'crooked'
fingers from 1915 become the 'curved' fingers in this piece:

> They clearly heard slow footsteps in the room next door. The little
> girl screamed again [. . .] There was no other way out. Already several
> curved fingers pressed on the small throat. The child snorted, but she
> still held out, defending herself with her little hands. They held her hard
> but she kept moving, struggling. There was no other way out. The
> child weakened, she fell on to someone's lap. Silence fell. Nothing more
> was heard behind the door. They were saved.[20]

When the story In the dark appeared in the journal New Culture (1952
number 22), Zofia prefaced it with a short introduction:

> I offer this little note, found among my papers, written long ago
> during the fearful time of the Occupation, as a small contribution to
> knowledge about the fate which war prepares for children.[21]

This last phrase, a deliberate echo of Medallions, shows that war is
responsible for crime, not the women in the story who are its victims. The
problem of evil, or suffering and pain is very present in all Zofia
Nałkowska's work, and in this story she presents it by painting on a dark
canvas a scene which the reader cannot see.

It is a crime too monstrous and vast for one small canvas – and yet the very smallness of the portrait, its precision and its darkness reveal the enormity of that crime.

It takes great perseverance, enormous intelligence and a remarkable memory to weave this complex tapestry in which words echo and reflect one another over many years, not least when we consider that Zofia's life was lived always in flux as she moved from one address to another, especially in the Second World War when so many of her papers shared the fate of her beloved Warsaw and went up in flames.

However, in 1915, Zofia's personal world was widening. She met army officers upon whose valour hopes of freedom for Poland depended. 'The clank of swords when they greet you,' she reported, 'and the ring of spurs accompany their respectful bows.' She then adds a more sinister comment. A young field gendarme, an artist in peace time, told her in an offhand way how he had hanged several Jewish men, some supposedly for spying, the others as an example. This young man had immediately pulled out his sketch book and had drawn the murdered men hanging on the gibbet. 'No one voiced any concern,' Zofia recorded, 'so deep in human kind is this racial hatred.'

Zofia also heard stories of tragic deaths on the field – including one that shook her utterly. She asked if these military men knew Edmund Szalit, a Doctor of Law from Kraków. 'Yes,' she was told. 'He's dead too.'[22]

In her silent sorrow for the young man she had loved so dearly, Zofia longed even more intensely for that one special person whom she could take seriously and with whom she could share happiness in her own quiet home.

However, in summer 1916, despite the hardships of war – the three women had to wash their own clothes in cheap soap and exist on a restricted diet, with no meat for weeks (they started to keep rabbits), thirty-one year old Zofia nevertheless decided that she felt 'healthier, prettier and even younger.'[23] She chiselled her reflections on war into the collection of short stories called appropriately, *Secrets of Blood* (published 1917) And now she was caterpulted into the cruellest love affair of her life.

He was a renowned hero, a legendary figure who fought for Polish independence, and, disguised as a Tsarist officer in 1906, had breached tight security in the notorious Russian prison in Warsaw and rescued ten Polish freedom fighters who had been condemned to death. Zofia's new lover, Jan Gorzechowski, known as 'Jur' by his comrades in arms, was ten years older than she, a close friend of the charismatic leader Marshal Piłsudski. He was a married man with three children, totally unsuited to this charming intellectual, the darling of the literary salons who had already forged her place in Polish literature. Jan had absolutely no interest in literature.

In his travelogue *Journey to Poland*, written in 1924, the German novelist Alfred Doblin, anxious to find his Jewish roots and also to learn the story of Poland, is told about the above-mentioned heroic rescue of ten Polish revolutionaries by a 'Baron von Bindberg. The baron,' Doblin writes, 'was Grozechowski (sic); he is still alive today, a colonel in the Polish army.' [24]

Doblin also asked about outstanding Polish writers and was told about Zofia Nałkowska 'a woman,' he added, little knowing the volatile connection between these two people.[25]

Zofia was only too aware of the huge discrepancies between them; nevertheless that unlikely suitor filled her wartime summer with happiness.

She knew all the danger signs, oh yes, she knew:

> I thought to myself, woman is the prize of a warrior. I thought, a hero is allowed to be wild and cruel. I tenderly caressed those small, aristocratic hands, bloodstained, after all, and hardened from the sword and the reins. His deeds are legendary and his soul is simple, active and strict, thirsting for tenderness and goodness with a mad longing that is hard to resist. I would like the affair to finish with this and not go beyond a July romance, a platonic pastoral idyll and only in deepest secret do I contemplate marriage.[26]

And a month later:

> Oh God, what happiness [. . .] This man is a complete psychological revelation [. . .] a man of action, free from any ambition. This action is chemically pure, elemental like a phenomenon of nature, made out of the same necessity with which a tree grows or a bird sings. Huge things, performed with the simplicity of a child.[27]

By October, she could write:

I live encircled by fire, loved as never before [. . .] I am no longer free, I am not my own person, denied everything – thought, desire, friendship, memories. And that is good. In exchange for this loss I have the ceaseless gift of viewing and discovering a spirit that is monochrome and fearless, rock hard, violent and yet immeasurably tender. Almost from the beginning the whole initiative of emotion was on his side. And that is good too.[28]

Thanks to Jan, Zofia was drawn into new spheres of life beyond her highly intellectual world of debate and reason. She began to understand the legendary Polish Legionaries and their fight for freedom under Józef Piłsudski, whom she had earlier viewed as little better than a terrorist.

At this time too her sister Hanna's piece of sculpture, *The Warrior*, won first prize in a competition. It would later adorn their father Wacław's grave, a tribute to a warrior in a very different sense from Jan, but one who perhaps shared some of the same severity and hardness.

On 5th November 1916 an act proclaiming Poland's independence in the German controlled areas was read out in Warsaw; a gesture designed to win Poles to the German war effort. Zofia greeted the announcement with joy and bitterness – and a return to ill-health. For the third time in her life she was troubled by inflammation of the inner ear, and was tenderly cared for by her mother and by Jan. This infection would bring on deafness and tinnitus by the time she was forty.

On the home front a girl who worked as a domestic help for the three Nałkowska women suffered a psychotic breakdown.[29] Zofia wove this tragedy into *Marcjia's Family* which was included in a collection of stories, *The Walls of the World*, published in 1931.

For now, though, completely enveloped in Jan's 'boundless love', which she began to understand as 'sweet despotism', Zofia felt obliged take up a new pursuit. Field sports were Jan's great passion and the couple rode out to hunt in the Mazovian countryside.

The 'sweet despotism' soon turned out to be, in Zofia's own words, 'an unbearable, continually rattling chain.'[30] Still believing in Jan's love, but understanding that should their affair become marriage she would be completely controlled by her war hero, Zofia faced a psychological chasm. She wasn't allowed to meet friends (especially men friends) or to have any private life. Jan read her letters, even her diary and she records bitterly:

No affair has ever been so hostile to my creativity as this [. . .] I have
to be completely transparent, pure to the depth of my soul. I have to be
simple in order to be understood.'[31]

Although she felt the sweetness of being totally loved, she was so terrorized by this man that she did not know how to end the affair, and perhaps
was afraid to. Luckily, in September 1917 Jan left her on his own affairs. He
was away for three months. Zofia did not question his absence. Instead, she
picked up her pen again. Her new work was completely different from
anything she had done before: a series of character sketches which portrayed
real people under cleverly thought out pseudonyms. Written with wit, brev-
ity and clarity, this was a new discipline in Zofia's writing craft as she focussed
on other people, trying to understand their motives and actions. She
described herself as a receptacle to process the world around her with all the
precision she could muster. Without Jan's 'sweet' tyranny, she returned
happily to her own world, reading and writing, working in the garden of
Meadow House, enjoying her friendship with her dear Zofia V, now married
and still her closest friend. She began a new novel, *Count Emil*, a neglected
masterpiece, which contains one of the greatest hunting scenes in European
literature. And although her longing for the continually absent Jan was so
great that she felt she would die, she assessed their love coolly and soberly:

His priceless worth in my life, his love, unlike anything before, his
wild jealousy, sensitivity, ceaseless loving, loving without pause for
breath. His wicked, uncontrolled spirit, violent as nature, his mad heart.
What have I done, o God! The thought that he might even yet come
into the room, push in, angry, hot, always, each moment, greedy for me
like air. I can't believe that his departure was possible – his departure
that I demanded [. . .] Nothing united us except love – and no one can
be so far from me and hostile to me as him.' [32]

Weeping by day, dosing herself on tranquillizers, reading and writing
no matter how anguished she felt, Zofia agonised and grieved until Jan
returned at the beginning of December. He seized her diary and wrote in
it, 'I came back and I love you terribly, Jan.'[33]

It was the end of her freedom – and it coincided with great changes in
Poland. Zofia entered fully into the life of her newly independent nation.

She was about to create her greatest novels written in a concise, detached form. At the end of her life she summed up the changes in her writing:

'The world had altered and had to be written in a different way. The form which the critics call simplicity was my response to this view of the world, in which small things and small people are precisely the things worthy of attention.'[34]

CHAPTER 6

Independent employment

I don't want what is good, only what is necessary.[1]

The signing of the Armistice and the defeat of Germany and Austria in 1918 brought freedom to a newly independent Poland. Warsaw went mad with joy, but Zofia was full of foreboding: this newly emerged state was so dangerously situated between ruined Germany and revolutionary Russia. She thought back to her father's socialist ideals and reflected on her place in the new Poland as a writer.

The capital began to buzz with life. Warsaw became the smart place to be. Zofia took part in the new literary milieu; still struggling for money, she was a person of acknowledged significance, beauty and charm. She saw the publication of her new novel *Count Emil*. It was not well received; it showed the unheroic side of war, and has almost been forgotten now. The novel sheds light on Zofia's own inner life, as described through her main character, a young man called Emil:

> Emil was always defenceless in the face of someone else's feelings, embarrassed and moved to the depths . . . Each new event was a pretext for work of an enormous magnitude . . . He couldn't bear it if there was still something he hadn't thought through right to the end [. . .]

> And this stubborn and exclusive intellectual work was like a battle. He experienced each thing and each person as something alien which had forcibly burst into his field of knowledge from the world outside, a hostile thing, fixed on his memory for ever. He had to process it somehow, reshape it in himself, so that it would stay there, not wounding everything around him, not giving pain.[2]

Zofia too understood the world by thinking about it deeply and reflecting it back to herself exactly as she describes here. When we read this we begin to understand the 'stubborn and exclusive intellectual work' which complicated Zofia's love life and enabled her to create fully achieved characters in her fiction. We also understand that when Jan, her warrior lover 'forcibly burst into her field of knowledge from the world outside,' and declared his passionate love, she, longing for love and anxious not to give pain, 'thought' it all out 'to the end' and responded – to her great cost.

Jan Gorzechowski saw none of this enormous endeavour in his mistress. All he could say of this brilliant woman was that he wished she didn't get so upset when he killed animals whilst out hunting! In a hunting scene in *Count Emil*, Zofia writes a subversive elegy for wilfully killed creatures. Three pheasants with 'wing feathers like Byzantine jewels' shot up out of the birches:

Emil's heart beat as he took aim . . . two heavy birds fell close by, their little red faces and wonderful dappled wings scoured the white snow [. . .] Then with fateful charm, lightness and wildness a timid, furry, beautiful forest creature emerged from bushes close by. Its slender little snout, immeasurably subtle and seeming a little sad, its reddish-gold fur, its shape lengthened by a wonderful plume, its silken movements, wise, attentive and supple [. . .]

(*Emil shot it* . . .) The fox's beautiful little head buried itself between its small paws in the soft downy snow – with a childish sorrowful gesture of despair.[3]

A writer's revenge on her lover's passion in a book about war? Zofia deconstructs war, patriotism and nationalism in ways that were not part of the wave of enthusiasm that greeted the newly independent Poland.

Count Emil was written just before Polish independence. Zofia accurately describes her country's lack of freedom as:

a fact that affects every sphere of life, like an injury or an amputation. In a captive land philosophy and art cannot extend beyond the problems of the homeland. Language and tradition become the secret of existence, work and religion are the only a category of patriotism.

It must be thus, that from the iron of the manacles that shackle one's wrists, one forges thorny ornaments to wreath one's head. The master-pieces of our major writers were destined to incite us to fight the parti-tioning power, our crowning philosophical epic is closed within the charmed circle of the nation's martyrdom.[4]

These words sum up the complex Polish story which has given rise to a view of literature, culture and even of religion that still sets Poland apart from the rest of the Europe. Zofia well knew – as every Polish person knows – the beautiful, tragic opening of the Polish national epic, *Pan Tadeusz*:

O, Litwo, Ojczyzno moja! ty jesteś jak zdrowie;
Ile cię trzeba cenić, ten tylko się dowie,
Kto cię stracił. Dziś piękność twą w całej ozdobie
Widzę i opisuję, bo tęsknię po tobie [. . .]

O Lithuania, my native land, you are like health; only the person who has lost you knows how much to appreciate you. I see and describe today your beauty in all its splendour, because I yearn for you.

The Polish National Bard, Adam Mickiewicz (1798-1855) who wrote these poignant words in exile in Paris developed the image of Poland as 'the Christ of the nations', crucified on the map of Europe. In his poem *To a Polish Mother* quoted in chapter 4 Mickiewicz writes:

In Nazareth our young Redeemer played
With tiny crosses, toyed with future pain:
Polish mother, make your son unafraid,
Give him his future toys, an iron chain
To wreathe his infant wrists [. . .][5]

Hence Zofia's words about 'iron shackles and thorny wreathes'. She might well have recalled the wreath of thorns on her father's coffin.

Even after 1918 the newly independent Poland still had to fight for survival. Its eastern borders were insecure. Revolution had torn Russia apart and the conflict spilt over into countries which had been under the

Tsarist yoke. The White army waged war against the Bolsheviks, ethnic groups tried to forge their own nationalisms, with the large Jewish populations in those eastern provincial towns always at risk from cruel pogroms. Polish landowners were murdered, their properties were devastated, while in towns and cities factory workers rose against their bosses. There was political unrest in the former Congress Poland as nationalist factions tried to wrest power from the socialists. Members of the National Committee under the right wing leader Roman Dmowski planned a coup which aimed at calling a new Cabinet headed by the composer, Ignacy Paderewski (1860 – 1941), a life-long supporter of the Polish cause. In January 1919, political unrest became violent. Jan Gorzechowski, now superintendent of the Warsaw City Police, was threatened at pistol point. True to style, war hero Jan kept his cool and overcame his attacker but was beaten up, dragged out unconscious to a waiting car and put under arrest.

The impact on Zofia must have been huge although she made only a passing mention of it in her diary – indeed between 1918 – 1922 the diary entries are sparse – very likely as a result of the strict censorship imposed on her by Jan.

Perhaps political events were too overwhelming. Zofia was torn between her lover's devoted loyalty to Marshall Piłsudski, who fascinated her as a personality of immense strength and intelligence, while she personally supported Bolshevik ideals, if not their extremism. This inner tension was heightened in 1919 when armed conflict broke out between the Polish armies and the Bolsheviks who aimed to spread world Communism 'over the corpse of white Poland'.[6] Jan was now right at the heart of the conflict. Jan, whom she now described as both secretive and wild, both bad and good.

> I don't need to watch over this love, it's stronger than anything I can think of. It is certain because it is not built on any kind of misunderstanding or illusion, only on necessity.[7]

Zofia believed in necessity. 'I don't want what is good, only what is necessary,' she declared.[8]

In these uncertain years, with Jan still not divorced and their relationship therefore highly compromising for them both, Zofia tried to keep their affair a secret, but Jan paid no attention to her wishes, and to her intense embarrassment would seize her by the arm in public and march along with his captive in tow – a captive who was already one of the literary greats.

In August 1920 Warsaw was encircled by Soviet armies. Against all the odds, thanks to Polish intelligence and to Marshal Pilsudski's military strategy, the outnumbered Poles drove back the Soviet armies, and by 1922 the eastern border was secured – for barely two decades. Historians now acknowledge that this war with its successful outcome for Poland was one of the most significant victories in the twentieth century. The Polish armies stemmed the onslaught of Soviet communism, saved Western Europe from Soviet terror and gave the fragile states in Eastern Europe a brief taste of political freedom.

In 1920 Zofia organised a literary conference in Warsaw and in autumn of that year she started work as head of the literary department in the Office of Foreign Propaganda which aimed to showcase Poland through literature. This work and her secret life with Jan gave her a view into the intensive, but often fraught life of the new Polish Republic – she would write about it with authority in her next novels.

Zofia's office was situated in in central Warsaw in a building which is now the much-photographed President's Palace. Built in the mid seventeenth century it served as a residence for leading princely families until the Russian Occupation.

Zofia's job in the Office of Foreign Propaganda only lasted until the following March (1921), when the department closed down because of lack of money. Poland, recovering from six years of war, had to collate three different tax systems and cope with hyper-inflation.

According to Wanda Melcer (1896 – 1972), Zofia was a strict supervisor.[9] Wanda had known the Nałkowski family from her earliest childhood. Her father Henryk was a composer and Zofia and her family often attended his concerts. Wanda's uncle by marriage, Jan Dawid (1859 – 1914) was a close friend of Wacław Nałkowski and a leading figure in the Flying University movement at which Wacław taught and Zofia studied. He edited the radical journal *Voice* and was often under pressure from the Tsarist police. Zofia herself was present during a police search and recorded Dawid's deep shock and fear and the heroism of his wife, Jadwiga. Such were the pressures from the authorities that Jadwiga finally took her own life. Wanda, however, recalled happier times when Zofia and Hanna, both wearing identical floral print dresses with ribbons in their hair, perched on low armchairs in Auntie Jadwiga's big drawing room and played at sailing on long sea journeys along with Dr Janusz Korczak, a family friend.[10]

Dr Janusz Korczak, born Henryk or Hersz Goldszmit (1878 – 1942), a writer and medical doctor, dedicated his life to the care of children, aiming to give them an independent voice and a strong sense of personal responsibility. He wrote popular children's fiction, edited children's newspapers to which children contributed their views, broadcast on radio, founded and directed orphanages at which children were allowed to assess their adult mentors. Korczak totally opposed corporal punishment and every kind of aggression from adults against children. In the end, although Polish friends wanted to save him, Korczak went into the Warsaw ghetto with his children and with them was murdered in Treblinka in August 1942. Wacław Nałkowski counted Korczak as his closest friend and mentor. As an esteemed educator he had drawn Leon Rygier, a teacher into his circle. The good doctor' features in Zofia's youthful memoirs.

With typical kindness Zofia got Wanda the job in the typing room when the younger woman needed work. However, said Wanda, Zofia arrived at work at 11 am while Wanda had been working at her desk since eight, proof reading manuscripts, collating translations. Wanda realised that Zofia had probably been working at home, writing as usual in bed, propped up on cushions using long strips of paper. This was the way she had served her apprenticeship, writing for *The Voice*. These strips of paper had made it easier for the typesetters and Zofia stuck to that method all her writing life. She wrote in pencil – or in green ink, often sketching out the ending first and in this way, wrote Wanda, Zofia Nałkowska 'pushed the Polish novel forward and widened its boundaries,'[11] being the first writer to explore as a woman the motivation and inner life of women. Wanda compared this 'lazy workaholic' to a potter constantly re-shaping the clay, rewriting each sentence many times.[12] Only when she was satisfied with this arduous work would she then spread those strips of handwritten paper on the floor and literally pin them together. Late in her career friends noted how this grand lady of letters knelt on the floor with pins in her mouth like a dressmaker, pinning her next novel together in her own version of 'cut and paste', or, as one amused observer noted, pecking among the scraps of paper like a hen.[13]

Caught up with work and with other pressures, Zofia abandoned her diary writing for almost two years. Her next diary entry comes not from Warsaw but from a small village five kilometres from Vilnius, the capital of present-day Lithuania:

27th July 1922. A month ago on 25th June, I married Jan Gorzechowski, Lieutenant-Colonel and Chief of the Military Police in Vilnius. I am thirty-seven years old.[14]

An entirely new life had begun.

CHAPTER 7

Living on the edge

Sometimes I tell myself with astonishment that in the autumn of my life I've found myself here, so far from the whole of my past life, that I came here with a man whose love for me is like some sort of frightful misunderstanding.[1]

Zofia Nałkowska, literary star, Varsovian to the core, had moved far beyond her comfort zone to live in Poland's newly regained eastern territories with a passionate, violent man, in whose shadow she was supposed to conform to the rigid standards of the Polish Army's officer class.

The newly-married couple found lodgings outside Vilnius. Their living quarters bore the traces of occupying armies:

Our first shelter in this land was a small lodge house, half in ruins which nestled beside an ugly rural palace, no longer inhabited by the wealthy. Our doors had no locks or keys, just a latch on either side. They actually looked like a much-written parchment. One of them bore the message, written in black, *Gott mit uns* which had been crossed through with crooked letters in chalk: *Magazyn prowiantowy i broni 1 kompanii* (1st Company's provisions and weapons store). On the other door were the words: *Kwatera plutonu łączności 1 brygady kawalerii* (quarters for the First Cavalry Brigade liaisons platoon).[2]

Rooms that had been used as army stores cannot have been cosy or homely. Zofia was left on her own, Jan travelled to Vilnius each day. His goings and comings marked Zofia's day as she struggled to come to terms with her new environment and new status, no longer as a famous writer, but 'only' as an officer's wife in a hierarchical military society.

Jan and Zofia shared a passion for nature (though from different view-points, his was a hunter's eye). She explored the countryside alone or with Jan, and always with her beloved greyhound Diana, a present from her husband. Always ready to listen and learn, Zofia absorbed the landscape about which she had read from her earliest childhood. This territory had once belonged to the great Polish-Lithuanian Commonwealth. Marshal Piłsudski and his loyal band of war heroes now wanted to resettle these formerly Polish lands and create a federal buffer state against the newly formed Union of Soviet Socialist Republics.

Zofia loved the views of beautiful, historic Vilnius, the capital city of Lithuania, which she glimpsed from her horse-drawn carriage, 'a city of mixed-up, overlapping regions' as Czesław Miłosz, a Lithuanian Pole later called the city he viewed as home.[3]

Jews called the city *Vilna*, and when Zofia enjoyed the view of the city she was looking at 'the Jerusalem of the North' with over a hundred syna-gogues and major teaching and cultural institutions; almost half the popu-lation was Jewish. Vilnius became a major centre for Zionism, while the Bund, an international socialist party was also founded there.[4]

Vilnius had been home to Elijah ben Solomon Zalman (1720 – 1797), the saintly teacher known as the Vilna Gaon who had reputedly given his first lecture in the Great Synagogue when he was seven and when he was nine knew by heart the whole Hebrew Bible.[5] There is now a monument to this widely revered scholar in the Lithuanian capital. It stands on the site of the Great Synagogue which had been destroyed by the Nazis along with almost every Jewish woman, man and child in Vilnius.

Christian devotion in Vilnius finds a focus in the icon of the Blessed Virgin of the Dawn Gates. In Lithuanian she is *Aušros Vartų Dievo Motina*, in Polish *Matka Boska Ostrobramska*, and in Belarussian Маці Божая Вастрабрамская, a linguistic mix which transcends nationality. The icon is revered by all three cultures. Adorned in costly silver garments, the icon, placed above the Dawn Gates, is said to have protected Vilnius when marauding Swedish armies attacked. The Protestant soldiers mocked the Virgin – and even put a bullet through one of her sleeves. Next day, however, the massive iron gates beneath the icon collapsed, crushing the impious Swedes. Thus the place of the Protective Mother was assured for all time in the affection of the faithful, and Vilnius is still an important centre for Polish pilgrims and visitors.

Polish culture had long flourished in Vilnius. Leading writers, thinkers, artists, politicians all regarded the city as their spiritual home. The great Marshal of Poland, Józef Piłsudski chose Vilnius for his heart's resting place. His body lies in state in the Wawel Castle in Kraków, he donated his brain to medical research, but his heart was interred in his mother's tomb in the historic Rasu cemetery in Vilnius, along with a quotation from a great Romantic poet, Juliusz Słowacki (1809 – 1849), Piłsudski's favourite poet. The words that are his only epitaph sum up the man and his mission.

> *Kto mogąc wybrać, wybrał zamiast domu*
> *Gniazdo na skałach orła, niechaj umie*
> *Spać, gdy źrenice czerwone od gromu*
> *I słychać jęk szatanów w sosen szumie.*
> *Tak żyłem [. . .]*[6]

If, having the choice, you chose an eagle's nest on the clifftops instead of a home, you must learn to sleep when your pupils are reddened by thunder, and to listen to the moan of devils in the rustle of the pines. So have I lived.

Piłsudski chose the 'eagle's nest' and perhaps preferred this image of Poland as a fearless eagle rather than that of the crucified Christ. His great desire was to win Vilnius back for Poland. He received the keys of the city in 1919 and fought for it against the Bolsheviks, and against Lithuanians who did not welcome the Polish colonisers.

Zofia and Jan had hoped to settle in Vilnius where Zofia would certainly have felt at home, but opposition from Lithuanian nationalists made the capital too dangerous for the Polish government to set up a strong military presence there. Polish military men and their families, including. Lt-Colonel and Mrs Jan Gorzechowski, therefore, made their base in the historic town of Grodno, now in Belarus. Grodno was rapidly turning into a large garrison town, which brought about an upturn in the local economy. The Gorzechowskis lived in army quarters on Kirk Street – so named because there had once been a Protestant Church on this street, its abandoned graveyard was visible from the house, where crows clustered and crowed.

Crows seemed to have been a feature of Grodno. Zofia wrote that sometimes the western sky was darkened by flocks of these birds.[7] Some nested in two birch trees nearby and added to the general sense of gloom she felt about the city almost three hundred kilometres from Warsaw and the life she knew best.

She explored her new place of residence, but could never bring herself to like this far-flung outpost on the edge of Polish civilisation.

Situated on the banks of the River Niemen and several trade routes, Grodno had a long and sometimes prosperous history. Churches, monasteries and palaces, a wooden Orthodox church and an equally historic synagogue bore witness to past glory. The last Polish Parliament, the *Sejm*, had met in Grodno and the last King of Poland, Stanisław Poniatowski had abdicated there. Ruled by the Romanovs since 1795, Grodno had become a Russian provincial town with a large Jewish population, while local Belarussians mostly lived on the land, often employed as labourers on the Polish gentry's estates. During the First World War Grodno had passed from Russia to Germany, briefly to the short-lived Belarussian Republic and finally to Poland. For Zofia its main significance was that it had been home to an important nineteenth century writer, Eliza Orzeszkowa (1841 – 1910). Zofia re-read her novels, but could not understand what Eliza had seen in this town (beyond the fact that it had been her birthplace) that had made this distinguished writer want to settle there. 'This wooden house with its long flat frontage stands directly on the street, it is painted grey and is simply ugly,' she wrote.[8]

To understand the problems faced by Polish rule in its eastern territories after the First World War, we have to think (as Zofia explains in a later novel, *Unkind Love*, 1928) of the English in Ireland, or of landowners in the Highlands and Islands of Scotland. The occupiers at first ruled by force with guns and armies and later developed a strong, even romantic attachment to the land and their 'native' retainers, which was never reciprocated. Poland had a long connection with these eastern territories with roots going back to the sixteenth century and earlier; but now the new Union of Soviet Socialist Republics was putting pressure on the Polish eastern border while local nationalistic movements also engaged Jan's attention. As chief of the Border Police he was required to suppress such movements. Zofia transposed these realities into literature. Her much-acclaimed novel, *The Romance of Teresa Hennert* (1924)[9] encapsulates the difficulties faced by the Polish state that had emerged from oppression to become in its turn an oppressor of ethnic terrorists (or freedom fighters). It is a brave as well as penetrating analysis of the complexities of the new state which she knew at first hand from her work in the Cultural Propaganda Bureau in Warsaw and, intimately, in her marriage to a former war hero now head of police. Her novel brings on stage the elite of the newly emerged Second Republic of Poland, the nouveau riche, bureaucrats and military top brass, who felt rootless and uncertain now that the independence they had dreamt of and fought for had finally been won. Her relationship with Jan had opened her eyes to the dilemmas faced by men who had given their all to free their Poland, but now were at a loss as to how their hard-won nation should be governed, not least in the parts of Poland (exactly like Grodno) with large populations of ethnic groups who longed for their own freedom. Zofia would analyse their suppressed voices in this book, in her novel *Unkind Love* and a short story collection, *Walls of the World* (1931) as well as in *Teresa Hennert*. Other viewpoints in this powerful book are expressed by an ardent young Communist and by a new social element, young working women, many of high social status, forced into poverty by social and political unrest and yet with no real voice of their own.

The novel exposes the glitter of high finance along with hopeless poverty. The woman of the title, Teresa Hennert had been 'a kept woman', bought and betrayed. It is a novel of crime rather than romance, of obsessive love that is tragically destructive. The recent translators point out that, alone of any other literary work at the time, the novel describes the symptoms of psychological distress suffered by soldiers in peace time, now known as Post-Traumatic Stress Disorder.[10]

A leading critic (who had been in love with Zofia, and perhaps remained so secretly all his life) wrote:

> The basic idea is huge and bold. Almost no other Polish authors have reached such a sphere. Here sociology and politics are intertwined with personal relationships, with the problematic of character; and emerge mutually from it. In my opinion all novels about social issues should be like this . . .'[11]

Zofia worked hard at characterisation and *The Romance of Teresa Hennert* reaches a new level of accuracy and engagement. She worked intensively on the novel, sending it in serial form to literary journals. Her only diary entry for the whole of 1923 begins:

> Grodno is far uglier than Vilnius. Jan is worse than last year and I'm a year older. I've already finished *Teresa Hennert*, written horribly from one number (of a literary magazine) to the next . . . Sometimes I tell myself with astonishment that in the autumn of my life I've found myself here, so far from the whole of my past life, that I came here with a man whose love for me is like some sort of frightful misunderstanding.[12]

Zofia was so cruelly restricted by Jan's despotic behaviour that she became withdrawn and timid, fearful of his disapproval. Always polite herself, she was terribly embarrassed by the rough way he spoke to her in front of their friends. A year later, on her return to Grodno after a visit to her mother in Warsaw, she wrote sadly:

> I have come back here, driven by Jan's loyal, remorseless and cruel love, a jealous love which doesn't want to understand anything. What does it matter that I'm now 39? Lacerated during these last years, torn away from my mother and my own world in Warsaw, tossed away here underneath the pressure of someone else's strength, held captive by this incredibly strong, though hysterical individual, squeezed between the pincers of his persistence, terrorized by capricious outbursts and frightful scenes – well, just the same I'm alive, I have found myself, I am! [. . .] But I have no memories, I am not allowed them. Even that short stay at *Meadow House* was a crime that must be paid for [. . .] Nothing connects me to this place, nothing except Jan.[13]

Perhaps she thought too of her sister Hanna's happiness newly married at thirty-six to Maximilian Bick (1882 – 1941), a genial, well-to-do man, Jewish and an official in the Polish Tobacco Monopoly (and both these facts would later impact the lives of the Nałkowska sisters). 'Mak' as he was affectionately called, was a generous man, loved by everyone and totally unthreatened by Hanna's artistic talents which he appreciated and encouraged – a complete contrast to Jan Gorzechowski who hated it when his wife affirmed herself in any way. Jan was a man of action, not of words. He couldn't enter Zofia's world – and also, given his whole ethos as a man who obeyed orders but also gave commands, he did not think that a husband should make concessions towards the woman to whom he had given his surname.

Zofia's sufferings were noticed by others. A young married woman, Princess Nadzieja, herself a published author and married to a landowner whose estate was just outside Grodno, admitted that Jan could be charming, great company, a 'good fellow' and kind to her children, chasing them energetically up and down the paths of her estate, even joining them on the swing, admiring their new pointer puppies and reading them stories, so that he won their hearts.[14]

'But I personally didn't like him. I sided with Pani Zofia because even in company her husband was rough with her and even impolite . . .' Nadzieja added.[15]

Although she was still in her early twenties, Nadzieja's life experience had already packed in enough drama to make an epic film. Nadzieja was Russian and thus even more an exile in Polish Grodno than Zofia. She had spent her childhood in St Petersburg, with a father she adored and an invalid mother who had died of cancer when Nadzieja was thirteen. Educated in the prestigious boarding school, the Smolny Institute, founded by Catherine the Great for daughters of the nobility, Nadzieja's life changed completely with the First World War. Small for her sixteen years, completely inexperienced, she became a nurse and soon headed for the front. The train came under fire and now became a makeshift hospital. Each nurse had 100 patients to care for, bedded in moving coaches without electricity. The bunks were three tiers deep, the most severely wounded and dying lay on the bottom tier. Despite these challenging conditions love blossomed for eighteen year old Nadzieja. The man in charge of the Red Cross troop train, Maurice O'Brien de Lacy fell in love with her. Maurice was Polish, of Irish descent, a passionate patriot who had joined the Red Cross to avoid having to fight in the Tsarist army. Fleeing from the Red Revolution, Maurice brought his young bride to his estate near Grodno and insisted that she should learn and speak only Polish. The estate had been possessed by enemy armies during the First World War and Maurice was busy day and night.[16] Feisty as ever, Nadzieja became an active member of various philanthropic circles, which is where she met Zofia.

After the meeting N came up to me and said a few pleasant things which she accompanied with her particularly endearing smile of her narrow lips revealing small white teeth. At once and for always she won my sympathy which later changed into sincere friendship, along with admiration for her talent, her refined thought and the harmony of her intellect and her external look.

She was attractive with her classical profile and her head weighed down with a heavy knot of hair pinned low. She spoke slowly, often beginning her sentences with the words 'well, exactly [. . .]' She moved without haste. She knew how to listen attentively.[17]

Zofia encouraged Nadzieja as a writer, while Nadzieja witnessed at first hand the tyranny to which this charming woman with her sweet smile, enormous talent and refined intellect was subjected at home. She saw how Jan's face changed when he looked at his wife. Once she happened to be visiting Zofia when Jan came home for dinner:

He kissed her hand, greeted me as always coldly and without a smile and asked if dinner was ready yet because he was in a hurry and had to go out again. Pani Zofia got up almost in a panic, assuring him that lunch would be served at once. She was never a good housewife and didn't know how to satisfy her husband's culinary demands, she always felt guilty in some way when she was with him and that made her uncertain. In fact this lack of self-certainty, unease and anxiety were features of Pani Zofia during her entire marriage.[18]

Zofia, not usually given to confidences, confessed to Nadzieja that Jan was sometimes cruel, a man of unbreakable will who had cut her off from her literary life, and did all he could to stop her writing. Nadzieja concluded that their marriage had taken place only because Jan had threatened to kill either himself or her if she refused him.

Years later, long after Zofia's death, her friend Zofia V also revealed in a letter that Jan Gorzechowski had threatened his wife with a pistol thrust at her temple.[19]

No wonder then that in Zofia's novel, the *Romance of Teresa Hennert* the tragic love affair of a vulnerable woman with an almost psychopathic lover ends with her murder, shot between the eyes. Zofia too knew the feel of cold metal against warm skin, a gun in the hand of a trained killer.

During their fraught and increasingly turbulent marriage, Zofia and Jan shared a love of animals. She particularly appreciated his gift of her grey-hound, Diana. Zofia had always accumulated pets and wrote about them in engaging short stories, so when a deer appeared their garden in Grodno, she delighted in the vagaries of this unusual visitor. The young deer features on a photograph from the period in which Zofia, dressed in white, seated in a wicker chair in the garden with Diana's nose on her knee is smiling, radiantly but nervously. She is obviously uneasy, while Jan, in full military uniform, loaded with medals, with a high collar cutting his lean jaw, stares grimly ahead, looking more as if he is sentencing a crimi-nal than relaxing in the garden with his charming wife and their pets.

The deer had been captured as a faun and had escaped to the Gorzechowski's garden. Zofia called her Basia, and noted that she never played although the dogs romped beside her. She ate Zofia's potted begon-ias, paper serviettes, newspapers, notebooks, manuscripts and a whole bouquet of pink roses. She chewed leather straps, belts and book covers and once, wrote Zofia, she 'immersed her little snout into an open box of chocolates, just like a horse into its nosebag [. . .] so I realised that she adored chocolates. After that she always ate them up from my outstretched palm, quickly and to the very last crumb.'[20]

Zofia included the deer in her collection of short stories about her friends the animals in her life; each story is a literary cameo, chiselled from precise observation. Here she describes how Basia made herself at home, settling to rest in Zofia's drawing room.

> You knelt on one slender foreleg first, then slowly on the other leg and stayed kneeling like this for a while before you took courage and finally bent your long, high back legs and crashed down on them heav-ily and clumsily.
>
> You settled yourself a few times until at last you felt comfortable. Your little head, solemn and peaceful, stretched high on your long neck. And after a while you began to chew, delicately closing your wonderful, soft eyes.[21]

This close observation and the chiselling power of her pen, along with attention to detail were essential tools in Zofia's careful craft. Such writing was not easy, and even at the end of her life it was noted that every word Zofia wrote was pondered over and re-written, 'like a potter shaping the clay,' as her friend Wanda Melcer had written (see chapter 6).

In the midst of her own fears and Jan's unremitting cruel love, Zofia made a brave decision and became a member of the Grodno Society for Care of Prisoners, a direct contradiction of her husband's police work. The next pages of her diary give an account of the prisoners and their needs which she would publish ten years later in a collection of short stories, *Walls of the World*. Zofia also used the prison experiences for a play, *The day of his return*. Both these works date from 1931 when Zofia was back in her own world in Warsaw, but in Grodno she was pleased to discover that her colleagues in the society for care of the prisoners were people after her own heart, socially active and anxious to improve the harsh prison conditions.

Zofia personally felt closest to a woman called Stanisława Choynowska, whose husband Piotr was the vice-president of the Civil Law Court in Grodno while Stanisława was involved in social work in the town.[22]

Like too many other friends of Zofia, the Choynowski family met a tragic fate in the Second World War. As a bloody reprisal for the killing of a German gendarme in July 1943 the Gestapo shot nineteen families, including Stanisława and Piotr, their 32 year old son, along with his wife and baby son, Piotr's elderly invalid sister and their domestic help. Only one son was saved because he was absent from home at the time.[23]

These horrific events were still twenty years in the future and meantime the prison visits brought Zofia a new sense of purpose. Women were imprisoned in a former monastery in overcrowded cells without daylight and up to their knees in damp and filth and separated from their families. These women complained that their soup was too thin. Zofia recalled that a soldier had once told her that officers never tasted the men's food and immediately asked if she might taste the prisoners' soup. She came to an agreement that the cooks should certainly lessen the amount of water even if they didn't add more peas![24] It was small thing, but it must have brought the women hope to think that they were being listened to, as indeed was the case in the female hospital ward where a pregnant women, bedded between two patients with venereal disease and due to give birth within two weeks begged to be released for the delivery.[25]

Zofia also tried to organise a bigger urn for water so that dying, consumptive prisoners would not go thirsty; and she and the group organised lectures for those prisoners who were not too ill to attend.

She noted their deaths, too many, in pain and with lack of any dignity, and although she felt an inward shudder at the crimes some of the men had committed, their need for better treatment outweighed her sense of revulsion and yet she knew that the thing the prisoners most longed for, she could not give them: freedom.[26]

Back at home after these visits, Zofia felt shocked by her own happiness.

> Look, a little greyhound puppy is running up, tottering on his puppy paws and sinking his sharp little teeth into my stocking. But I'm able to bend down, take him into my arms, cuddle him close and smell his incomparable puppy yawns. I can stand and water the flowers, sprinkling their leaves from the holes of the watering-can. And I dream: oh, if only I could take that little puppy to them so that his little life would bring them some gladness, or if I could give them some potted plants. Would it be allowed?
>
> Everything that we take for granted, the simplest things of everyday life – have all been taken away from them.[27]

As Zofia continued her voluntary work in prison she heard that prisoners, both women and men, were frequently beaten. She interviewed two Ukrainian women (at that point of time called Ruthenian) who had made a two day journey to Grodno to sell berries and eggs in the market where they had been accused of stealing cloth. Unable to understand Polish or the local Belarussian language easily, or to make themselves understood, they had been put into prison 'only for a few days'. One woman's face was swollen from blows she had received during the police examination – she was six months pregnant. The other, already an old woman had been beaten until she 'confessed'.

The women broke down in tears, desperately worried about their families at home who had no idea what had happened to them. The police inspector who had led Zofia and her co-workers into the cell tried to calm things down. 'Don't worry,' he told Zofia. 'Nothing bad will happen to them. They'll sit out their couple of months and if it turns out that they're innocent, we'll let them go.'[28]

Zofia told the story in *Women over There* in her collection *The Walls of the World* (1931).

Meantime, though, she confronted the prison commandant and asked whether prisoners were beaten during their cross-examination. She recorded his reply:

Ah well, of course beating is forbidden, but in some rare cases you can't do anything else to these criminals. I've beaten them myself. Otherwise they would just laugh at us and wouldn't confess to anything.

The chief explained that during cross-examination he always beat a prisoner expertly, with the edge of his hand curved around the ear in order to catch the flow of blood. 'The prisoners always answer differently after a beating,' he explained, and added by way of justification:

Each prisoner has to be in deadly fear of me, he must shake with fright when I look at him [. . .] In fact for a little while we did stop beating during examinations. And what was the result? Complete stagnation! They didn't manage to catch a single thief. After all that's what the powers above want from us but all that time absolutely nothing happened, and so we had to start all over again.

And Zofia commented:

Yes, this is exactly what this twenty-nine year old man said. He had a well-meaning, fat face above a gigantic accumulation of sickly obesity. Fat overflowed, moved and lived in a navy blue uniform. A row of shot glasses and tasty nibbles had been set in front of him. That's why he spoke so frankly. The situation was such that afterwards I was obliged to shake hands with him, to touch that hand whose edge knew how to beat expertly about the ear. And this is the way that statehood and Polish nationalism are confirmed here in the eastern Borderlands. Wild, stupid people find themselves in the hands of other wild fools. Bandits set fire to stately homes, they attack some small town or other with machine guns in their hands and loot it completely. They murder. And after that they come up for trial and go to prison. What a strange, incomprehensible world! You have to think: what is all this happening for, what is it leading to?[29]

Zofia's husband, a representative of 'the powers above' might well have told her what he thought the prison system was leading to. He might have given her his views about beating a prisoner during a cross-examination, but Zofia was not allowed to ask him such questions. From hints strewn throughout her novels, we know that there was almost no area in which Zofia was allowed to voice an opinion and almost nothing that these two people now shared with one another.

At this time, though, Zofia had the privilege of welcoming Marshal Piłsudski into her own home on three separate occasions. Jan was his close friend and Zofia noted that the great man was huge in every way, but had one overriding feature. 'He was a man of monologue,' she wrote, '[. . .] the most talented person in all Poland.'[30]

So, from meeting the leader of Poland, Zofia entered prison to learn the other side of reality in the Second Republic. Her work in the prison was a truly subversive step. She encountered men and women whom her husband regarded as criminals. She had stepped across an invisible boundary separating the haves from the have-nots, the people of power from the ones below. This would be the theme and the title of her greatest novel, *Granica, Boundary* (1935, translated Ursula Phillips 2016). Here in Grodno the boundary went right through Zofia's own home: petitioners seeking her protection and help came to her back door, while the Chief of Police, her husband, demanded his dinner in the front of the house. Thus the divisions that existed in Poland at large during the brief years of the Second Republic (1918 – 1939) were repeated in Zofia's private life as well as in her work, but she still honoured Jan's love, even though she knew it to be a vicious circle of love and cruelty.

A colleague in her prison work observed the discrepancy between husband and wife. Invited to their home he realised that Zofia seemed preoccupied and as they discussed political repression in Poland, she told her guest about shocking news she had just heard. Following a shoot-out in Warsaw in which several policemen and a student had been killed, three Communist activists had just been executed. The President had refused to grant them mercy.

'And just as well!' Jan interrupted.

'How can you say something like that, Jan?' Zofia exclaimed. 'A former freedom fighter like you!'

'Well, what do you think the President should have done? Come out in defence of criminals like them? Protect these delinquents who, having sold themselves to our enemies, shot the person who had uncovered their diversionary work?'

Zofia looked at Jan straight in the face with her cold eyes. 'You surprise me!' she said, her voice sounding choked.

Infuriated, the Colonel leapt up and left the room without another word.

Their guest added that Zofia had turned to him sadly:

'You see what power does to people. A few years ago he fought in just the same way and today he calls them criminals, although he knows that they were fighting for their ideals.' [31]

An unexpected event rescued Zofia from Grodno. Jan, always the picture of health, despite his war wounds - and in contrast to Zofia's almost constant indisposition – developed tubercular spondylitis and was in severe pain. The couple returned to Warsaw where Zofia shared Jan's sleepless nights, 'with deepest but hidden compassion' – only to bear:

the most incredible ignominy, the most burning injury. That's exactly his way – and there is no way out from it. Injured feelings and the most tender compassion lived simultaneously within him and even today I don't know what our relationship is really about, what the truth is in all this. And I never want to know the very worst things and certainly never put them into words.' [32]

'Never put them into words.' The remarkable thing is that despite the frankness and acute analysis of her life, and the lives of others, Zofia, a woman who finely tuned her words, found that some things, 'the very worst' could not be expressed on paper. Jan was openly betraying his wife with other women, he was drinking heavily and may well have been physically abusive too. Close friends read between the lines as the truth of the marriage came out in a fictional way in Zofia's next books.

For example, the opening of her next book, *Choucas* (1927) set in a sanatorium in Switzerland, offers a hint of the difficulties within her marriage.
The unnamed narrator and her equally anonymous male companion are
clearly at odds with one another as they prepare pieces of bread to feed
the Alpine birds. A brief dialogue shows that even this shared activity
provokes an argument, yet Zofia had no thought of leaving this most difficult husband, charming but jealous, brave and aggressive.

She was living on the edge of her world, on the edge of her nerves
often afraid for her own life, never sure where Jan's rages would end, but
she still believed in her marriage, still felt she should be in unloved Grodno
and endure her husband's 'unkind love.'

CHAPTER 8

Unkind love – and a curtain impossible to name[1]

> Youth isn't a state of being, it's a value given to everything else while old age takes that value from everything. And in addition to age that other thing is coming upon me, far worse, far more shameful which falls like a thick curtain between me and the world. But I don't want to name this thing in words.[2]

On their way to the sanatorium in Switzerland, the couple spent a few days in Vienna, where Zofia wrote in her diary a telling comment, 'Jan was kind.' They then travelled by train through marvellous mountain scenery to stay in the resort of Leysin, in a sanatorium for patients with TB – many of them incurable.

Here Zofia garnered experiences for her 'international novel', which she called *Choucas*, the French name for the Alpine choughs that flew around the sanatorium and settled in the balcony to be fed. Their visits symbolised the arrivals and departures of patients and visitors from many nations who, along with hopes of a cure, brought their own agendas of hope, prejudice, love and suffering. *Choucas* is enjoying a new readership thanks to Ursula Phillips' translation which won the 2015 Found in Translation Award.[3] The book is now much admired for its critique of the hatred which underlies nationalism. Zofia's accurately drawn pen portraits show people, mainly Europeans who make up a complete 'League of Nations'. The underlying theme that nations should no oppress one another is voiced by an Armenian woman, one of two refugees from the terrors of the Armenian massacres in 1915.[4] that nations should not oppress one another.[5]

Choucas shows that however friendly individuals may be, racism is deep within human beings. Immediately after hearing Miss Hovesphian talk about the suffering of her nation in the Turkish genocide, one of the

French guests comments coldly, 'These Armenians are unbearable. They bore us all with their misfortunes [. . .] The occupation of Cilicia has cost France billions.'[6]

'I hate the Irish,' declares English Miss Nora happily,[7] while Monsieur Verdy hates Germans, but when he explains that his only son had been killed in the War, Zofia understands, but comes to the conclusion that union between nations inevitably means that states outside the union are regarded as enemies:

> And so it looks as if the brotherhood of all nations, all peoples, is impossible. Because *whom* will they unite against?[8]

This profound issue, so succinctly expressed, is typical of the way in which *Choucas* explores deep questions of nationality, love, suffering, God and war, revealed through the words and actions of the characters. A twenty-two Armenian girl, terminally ill, says, 'God can't give one nation victory in its fight against another. I think that we're not allowed to pray for that.'

Referring to the genocide she had experienced, she comes to the conclusion that God is 'powerless against evil' precisely because the Incarnation of Christ means that God absorbs evil into himself:

> 'God suffered in him – because he was powerless against evil. After all he took suffering upon himself. He accepted not only his agony but also the evil of those who caused it. Would it have happened like this, if he had been able to do anything else?'[9]

The narrator makes no comment but the book ends – surprisingly from the pen of someone as completely without religion as Zofia – with a prayer from the Armenian liturgy:

> O Lord, have mercy upon us, O Lord have mercy upon us, Holy Trinity send peace to the earth; give health to the sick and relief to the suffering.[10]

And so Zofia returned to Grodno, to her own suffering where she shaped her notes from Switzerland into her novel, *Choucas*. Writing about the patients in the sanatorium, many of whom, like the prisoners in Grodno, knew they would never leave alive, Zofia constantly thought about her deafness, coupled with tinnitus. 'In bed at night it's just the same, and each early morning is filled with the same thing,' she wrote sadly.[11]

Here she found a new way to console herself. Now, for two hours each day she went out riding with her husband's second-in-command and another military man. She rode a chestnut brown horse called Icarus and her beloved greyhound Diana ran alongside. Overhanging branches brushed against them as they rode through the forests along narrow tracks and then out into the open countryside where Zofia delighted in the rolling landscape, and then homewards along the river bank. Then back at home, Zofia settled at her desk to write 'that thing about Switzerland' where 'the rough drafts stacked separately make up a pile six times higher than the final manuscript lying beside them.'[12]

Marshal Piłsudski visited Jan and Zofia once again in October 1925. These were difficult years in Poland when a kind of terror initiated by the regime reached its height and dissenters were imprisoned, beaten (as Zofia had discovered during her prison visits in Grodno) and tortured. Piłsudski, arguably the most important figure in Polish early twentieth century history, had been side-lined from political events. Talking to Jan and Zofia he described himself as a man whose glass had not yet been drunk to the dregs. They sat in a threesome long after midnight with Jan and Zofia absorbing the Marshal's every word, while his glass of unfinished tea stood beside him. Watching him, Zofia felt his enormous energy and huge will-power and sensed him to be a tragic figure who was hemmed in by lesser men. Piłsudski was a soldier, not a politician, he governed like a military commander and his loyal men-at-arms, including Jan, remained faithful to the very end. In fact the great Marshal has left his mark on the Polish psyche and is still seen as an all-powerful saviour who would never have allowed the Soviets to take over Poland in 1944-45 had he been alive.

> Hard, brusque, extreme, paradoxical, profound, himself being his own truth, pure, all of a piece, and forcibly lifting everything from top to bottom, from evil to good, to his own level. His faults pale into insignificance in the light of his character.[13]

Jan remained as jealous of his wife as ever. Zofia was allowed to receive only women visitors and the only outings permitted were her excursions on horseback with her two military chaperones. She formed a small reading group for women and although she was on a different level from the other participants, she enjoyed these discussions as well as her literary talks with the landowner's wife, young Nadzieja from Russia who asked her about the art of writing.

'It comes from within,' Zofia told. 'It's an inner compulsion to give some sort of shape to the world, and that can never be taught. Form is another matter, though. Form can and must be discussed. However,' she added with her charming smile, 'I only know one thing. You must only write when you can't help but write.'[14]

Right after *The Romance of Teresa Hennert* (immediately praised as a masterpiece), Zofia saw the publication of *House above the Meadows* (1925) In these stories Zofia takes the reader into the lives of poor, uneducated people, her neighbours in the Mazovian countryside that she knew so intimately and loved so well. The women are the workers, digging in the garden, growing their own fruit and vegetables, bearing the burden of multiple pregnancies, losing their babies and trying to nurture the ones that survived. The men are mostly drunkards and wife-beaters, or if they are well-doing, they are stingy and mean. The life of these simple villagers is so vividly told that it keeps the reader turning the pages and it is still a much loved book. It also included motifs that would appear in other books. As Zofia visited neighbours she noticed that one family had a dog that was never allowed off the lead:

> Near the kennel lay the saddest dog in the world who was never let off the chain, neither by day nor by night. When you went up to him he barked terribly at first, but then he even allowed himself to be stroked and he cuddled up to your knees and sobbed in a strange doggy way.[15]

She had noticed another dog kept permanently on a lead opposite her house in Grodno and wrote about it in an article published later, in 1934:

> Opposite the balcony on the other side of the street was a dog that was always kept tied up. I would leave home, go away and return. I might be absent for whole hours, even for months and when I got back I would

always find him in the same place – deep in the yard, under the fence, on a chain. In summer heat, when the street was completely empty and sad and nothing happened and in winter when frost and deep snow transformed the whole town into the most beautiful spectacle – he was always there.[16]

A dog kept on a lead day and night will become an important symbol in Zofia's most acclaimed novel, *Boundary* (1935). Once again, the reader sees how scenes are repeated throughout Zofia Nałkowska's work, each time with a new resonance, so that, as her friend commented, it is important to 'read her whole'.

Rave reviews greeted *The House above the Meadows*. A distinguished critic noted the universality of the simple stories, in which small events and people become profound and timeless, 'wrapped around with eternity,' as he put it:

Zofia Nałkowska loves life in all its forms and manifestation, with all the senses of her refined individuality. She loves the secret tangles that connect the soul of each person with the soul of the world.'[17]

Zofia also learnt that she had been voted the most popular woman writer in Poland. Her lack of self-belief and the lifestyle she was leading far from the literary scene made the honour seem superfluous and took away some of its meaning for her.

How can I benefit from all these connections? I am alone here, far away, quiet, and very poor [. . .] cut off from my past as if I had died.[18]

Even her house, that home of her own she had longed for, her books and pictures, the flowers she tended could bring little comfort because the environment was so destructive to her innermost being; finally life in Grodno with her volatile and dangerous husband became so unbearable that in April 1926 Zofia returned to her beloved *Meadow House*.

When I clutched the bank, drowning, the man closest to me trampled on my fingers with his heavy boots so that I had to fall.[19]

Her life in Grodno was physically over – but would continue to feature in her short stories, dramas and novels. We can hear her sigh of relief as she writes in her diary:

> I have come here, as before and as always, to lick my wounds which my misery and my happiness have given me. The moon has moved across the sky beyond the branches and leaves of the tree tops, outside the window is the blackness of the garden. I am alone with the oil lamp, with books on the table, a new novella just begun, fresh ink covered with a glass dish instead of a lid. I have come here, as always, to lift myself up once more, to recover and conquer again, to consider the great evil and the great good of my life, to understand it and receive it.[20]

Exhausted and defeated, Zofia tried to recover as she went for walks in the Warsaw parks alone or with her closest woman friends, Zofia V and another friend from her childhood, Hela Boguszewska. Above all she immersed herself in the healing wonders of nature before she started to believe in herself once more,

> I don't want to go back there, where everything contradicts my values, where everything pushes me towards death. My Diana is still there, my books and things dear to me, the prison I loved, which was always forbidden to me as well, along with people I was fond of and everything that was good. Four years living outside my own environment have shattered me and disorganised my life. Love no longer calls me there, only resistance, anger and threats.[21]

In this oblique way, Zofia referred not only her husband's infidelity and cruelty, but also to her deep disillusionment when his position at the head of the police had made him betray his former ideals. Later evidence indicated that Jan Gorzechowski may well been responsible – and certainly would have known about – the beatings and torture of political prisoners in the town of Brest (now in Belarus). These men had opposed Piłsudski's coup in May 1925 when, as a result of political instability, corruption and economic failure, popular opinion favoured the Marshal's return to power. The leaders of the failed coup were arrested and imprisoned in the fortress in Brest under Gorzechowski's jurisdiction. They must have known they could not expect any mercy from one of the Marshal's most loyal men.

Zofia never formally divorced her husband and in a re-run of Leon Rygier's machinations, she found herself constantly the butt of his ill-humour and was financially fleeced by him. Jan visited Warsaw in August 1926, 'and dragged me back into his strange circle of cruelty and love'.[22] The couple travelled to Kielce for the annual celebration of the Polish Legionaries. Still an officer's wife, still at the mercy of her husband, Zofia happened to pass the house where she had lived during her first marriage. She found the countryside around Kielce green and charming (unlike the bleak marshes around Grodno) and also felt an upsurge of her long lost youthful self. She was interested to see Piłsudski again after their long talks in Grodno, but the political mood concerned her. She recalled the coup that had occurred barely three months earlier, in May 1926 when a grenade had torn apart the ceiling and one of the walls of their Warsaw flat. Zofia's first diary, written when she was only twelve, had gone up in flames.[23]

Now, aged forty-one a new life was beginning for her – or the old one was flowering once more. She took up where she had left off, always short of money, never letting it show, always writing and now, right in the centre of the literary and the diplomatic world, she was admired, feted, desired. *Choucas* was completed and sold, Zofia was invited to start a literary salon but Jan was posted to Warsaw and showered his usual disapproval on the scheme.

In spite of this, Zofia had clearly returned to the place where she truly belonged. A photograph shows her striding out along Warsaw's elegant Nowy Świat (New World), a stylish, confident woman, smiling happily and obviously engaged in animated conversation with the mother she loved so dearly. She describes her new clothes in her diary: silk stockings, a modish suede hat and a brown coat trimmed with marabou down, all bought with payment from her publishers; Zofia supported herself life-long with her pen, her books provided her only earnings.

She gradually liquidated her old life in Grodno. Books and papers were returned to her and Jan eventually brought her back her beloved grey-hound Diana – though in between times a little stray dog had attached herself to Zofia, showered her with doggy love and refused to leave her side – to appear later on the pages of Zofia's books.

Never mind the dog, Zofia Nałkowska was now meeting all the big names of Polish and European literary talent – and was recognised as being up there with the best of them, feted at literary lunches, at breakfasts in foreign embassies, in balls in the President's residence, and finally, perhaps the highest honour of all, she was chosen as part of the procession to accompany the remains of a great Romantic poet, Juliusz Słowacki (1809 – 1849), through Warsaw to the train which would carry the silver casket to its resting place in the Royal Chapel in the Wawel Castle in Kraków. Cheering crowds lined the route between Warsaw and Kraków. Zofia, the only woman among the male literary greats in the solemn procession, felt caught up in this national fervour. 'No act of reason can spoil the beauty of that moment,' she wrote. 'I gave myself entirely to emotion and submitted unreservedly to its beauty and greatness.'[24]

Now, in the full flower of her literary life – with her greatest work about to appear within the next five years. Zofia felt her sense of humour return, she enjoyed friendship with other writers, including Maria Dąbrowska (1889 – 1965). Maria came from an impoverished landowning family near Kalisz, in western Poland, a town she celebrated in her four volume epic, *Nights and Days*. Maria was small and dumpy with short hair cut in a mannish style, Zofia was tall and statuesque, a frigate in full sail, as she was jokingly referred to. Their writing style was very different too. Maria painted on a large canvas as she explored the life of several generations of a family while Zofia sought an ever more simplified form, increasingly honed to the barest details. Zofia was both an engraver and a composer who created both counterpoint and harmony by unravelling the 'knots of life'.

Zofia cared about her appearance and cultivated her image. Eventually Maria was to mock her for this, but in the early stage of their friendship she simply noted that when she had arrived at Zofia's flat:

> she was powdering her nose and painting her lips. She told me that she feels healthier when she is made up and more able to face life. I find it interesting how such things are seriously important for women just like a glass of vodka for men, as a pick-me-up for mood. I've got nothing against make-up for women, so long as they do it well, which unfortunately they rarely do. I think that this is a one of these customs which nothing and no one will ever combat, it will always come back. Since

such things never change, you have to simply take note of them. Classical art made poetry out of this whole business.'[25]

Always generous to younger writers, Zofia appreciated the early drafts of Maria's epic – 'what I have seen is excellent' she wrote. She also told Maria that she was separating from her husband,[26] but in fact, Jan wouldn't let Zofia make the final break, even though it was clear to all their friends and acquaintances that the couple were living in total discord. Instead, as Jan commuted between Grodno, Brest and Warsaw, Zofia found herself covering his financial costs. Jan, she complained, lived like a lord, way beyond anyone's budget, let alone her modest means. She even paid the alimony he owed his first wife.[27]

In 1928 Zofia escaped from some of her Warsaw pressures to France, holidaying with her 67-year old mother Anna. They stayed in Nice where she noted that 'the horses wear hats, but the people don't'[28] – a humorous observation which she would put into her novel *Boundary*. In Nice too she bought her first fountain pen[29]; mother and daughter then moved on to Paris, the city Zofia most loved, 'the capital of the world' as she called it. On the journey home by train – two nights and a day in a crowded compartment, Zofia chatted to a young Polish student and was amused to discover that 'he didn't read Polish literature, especially women writers and couldn't bear Nałkowska! Luckily,' she added wryly, 'he didn't like Proust either.'[30]

Marcel Proust (1871 -1922) was an important writer for Zofia who read and re-read his great seven-volume epic *In Search of Lost Time* and, having finished the last volume, found that Proust had 'put into words all my unspoken truths.'[31]

The other great influence on her writing, whom she also constantly revisited, was Fyodor Dostoyevsky (1821I – 1881), particularly *Crime and Punishment*, but also his shorter works, *Poor People* and *Humiliated and Insulted*. She read both authors, the Russian and the French in the original languages.

Zofia put her new fountain pen to good use, writing the last two chapters of her next novel, *Unkind Love* (*Niedobra miłość*). It was first published in serial form – she was forced to work in this way because she needed money so desperately, and also, she explained, because deadlines helped her overcome what she described as her natural laziness. She once quipped that 'it's easier to read Dostoyevsky than to write Nałkowska.' *Unkind Love*, subtitled 'a provincial romance' was published to great acclaim in 1928. The basic plot is very simple: a love triangle, but the book works on much deeper levels. Zofia uses her own marital unhappiness to show the complicated twists and turns of human relationships. Her deepest question in *Unkind Love* (which was voiced in *Choucas* and would later be the basis of *Medallions*) is 'why do human beings oppress one another?'

Far from being an act of revenge against her violent husband or a piece of writing therapy, Zofia's novel offers a psychological analysis of human behaviour; she is particularly interested in the question of identity: how is our sense of self influenced by other peoples' opinions of us? By setting her novel in a 'provincial town' she also explores sociological issues which she first raised in *The Romance of Teresa Hennert*, including the treatment of ethnic minorities in those territories which had recently returned to Polish rule. In *Unkind Love* she used material she had first recorded in her prison diaries to describe the brutal murder of a young aristocrat by local partisans and its impact on his mother.

His widowed mother, Pani Osienienecka, justifies her harsh treatment of her farm labourers:

I never visit their homes, I can't. I know they live in awful conditions, I simply cannot get into this. The children sit there in the damp and cold. The walls are full of holes and the roofs let in the rain. I can do nothing for them in these terrible times when our whole existence is unstable. I can't do anything to help them just on the spur on the moment.' She looked gloomy as she said this. She was truly sensitive. She pursed her narrow lips sadly but firmly [. . .]

There was a time before the war that Pani Osieniecka visited their cottages, brought medicine to the peasant women and took an interest in their children. But no longer. She now knew that they were wicked, foolish, ungrateful barbarians – a nameless mass from which her younger son's murderer had emerged [. . .]

Restraining her annoyance, she said that our government is building schools so that they can be taught in their own (Belarussian) language and local teachers are paid from the national purse.

'Can you imagine, is it possible to believe that England for example would do something like this, that anyone other than Poles would do it

[. . .]?' Over there in Warsaw they don't understand, they don't know that only a strong hand, strict authority can somehow keep them contained. They don't know the local conditions here on the border. Here a good master is despised. If peasants are lent tools or are given grain and don't have to pay for grazing their cattle, they think that the master is clearly not sure of his position in charge of his land, that he only wants to butter them up. That's why it's essential to beat our peasants if we catch them damaging our property, we have to contain them by threat and fear – then they will be loyal and humble and no murderer will emerge.[32]

Zofia in her author's voice makes it clear that she does not support these illiberal views, yet she allows the reader to sympathise with this woman who lives literally on the edge of Europe, right on the Polish/ Soviet border amongst 'peasants whom she views as murderers, and Jews, whom she views as enemies.'[33]

Unkind Love is situated in Grodno, though the town is not named in the novel. The Jewish population at that time was just under 50%, but there are no Jewish characters in the book. However, through the windows of Pani Osieniecka's town palace we see 'a corner of Poland that was not Europe.'

A blue dusk was falling. From the palace window you could see on the other side of the market square, a row of dirty old buildings, crammed from the cellar to the roof with Jewish families. Every window was lit up, illuminated everywhere with that characteristic warm light of the Sabbath candles in the milky-blue festive evening.[34]

In *Unkind Love* the main protagonist is Agnieszka, a beautiful, bright, young wife, newly arrived from Warsaw and 'the world.' Agnieszka radiates a joy so infectious she transforms the dull life of the small town. Her husband, Paweł Blizbor, by contrast is a withdrawn, gloomy character, whose love 'exceptional, jealous, wild, gloomy, sensitive and boundless' cuts his vibrant wife off from the rest of the world. People were astonished that a girl with the world at her feet had chosen such an introvert, gloomy husband – or that he would betray her for a mousy quiet woman, Renata, married to a much older man, dutifully bringing up his two sons and always committed to doing the right thing.

Within this framework, the novel raises issues of power, of crime and punishment, of the relationship between a landowner and the people, issues too of our helplessness in the face of love, both cruel and kind. Zofia sets up a magnificent skating scene in which the first hints of the love triangle are delicately suggested and the interaction of characters is as sharply observed as the cutting edge of their skates. The skaters fly along the frozen river, trying out lively dance steps and figure skating leaps – best and most daring of them all is Agnieszka. At one point the ice is so transparent that they glimpse the river bed far below and see 'sleeping stems and ragged scraps of marshland plants'[35] – a moment drawn from life, when Zofia, her mother and sister took to the ice during winter evenings in their beloved *Meadow House*.[36]

Unkind Love met with a warm reception. Critics praised not just its artistic worth and carefully constructed dynamic – that was already a foregone conclusion about anything from the pen of Zofia Nałkowska. They also noticed the sociological aspect of the book – all this praise and even a financial award for the book came at the same time of the drastic ending to Zofia's marriage.

Two years after the publication of *Unkind Love* Zofia's first stage play, *House of Women* (1930) revealed to audiences the cruel love of Jan Gorzechowski when one of the women says:

> You don't know what he demanded from love [. . .] he was so severe, so implacable, he had such an innate contempt for evil. In his love there was torment which alone is the measure of its depth. Yes, he took my love, took it in silence, without a whisper, without a word, roughly and briefly [. . .] I wasn't a source of happiness and peace for him, I was a source of torment [. . .][37]

Posted to Warsaw, Jan insisted that Zofia should move into his Warsaw flat. She duly did, and sank most of her prize money into decorating and furnishing the apartment that was to witness some of the most humiliating moments of her marriage. At the end of *Unkind Love* Agnieszka's father removes his daughter from the marital home. In real life Zofia's mother hired a removal van and took Zofia and her possessions back to Anna's flat on Marszałkowska 4.

The Gorzechowski couple were still seen together at official events at which Jan 'hasn't changed at all'. He told Zofia that she was to blame for the breakdown of their relationship while he continually abused her verbally in public, even gate-crashing her literary soirees and creating havoc. He openly romanced with other women. Zofia used her diary to analyse the morass of injury and extinguished love.

> I'm going mad from stupid despair. I have no little corner in my life where it would be good to be . . . My so-called fame, my various admirers, mean nothing to me at all. I don't sleep at nights just thinking about that, I plan revenge. I have to deal with an evil man and whatever I try to do, it's all a failure, a mistake and a curse. In a frightful state both financially and health-wise, where can I draw strength from in order to overcome? I can't make any plans [. . .] It's way below freezing, life is poor, there's no hope.[38]

Maria Dąbrowska also recorded that the cold was frightful, there was a shortage of coal, with terrible queues outside coal depots and ordinary people were helpless in the face of this catastrophe.

> We have enough coal for one day, only for today and tomorrow. Nałkowska nobly offered me half her supply which she had received today.[39]

In her diary Zofia summed up her terrible marriage:

> So I have finally parted from my second husband at the cost of unbelievable effort, of humiliation and suffering so frightful that they were like martyrdom or lunacy. For nevertheless in a moment of illusion I moved into his apartment. Those four small rooms to which I moved all my things – Diana, books, papers, the mahogany furniture, the old mirror, and which I reconstructed, cleaned out and decorated so that they became nice and comfortable – those four rooms became the place of my worst disaster, despair and shame. Only there he revealed himself completely, only there slowly and with amazement I realised who he is, And in the face of that reality I still asked: how did it happen? Did he become different, has he changed? Is it that through all those years I didn't let myself see him as he really is? Was I so blinded by his love for me?[40]

1. Zofia and her sister Hanna with their parents and grandmother.

2. Wacław Nałkowski, Zofia's father, who researched and defined Poland's physical boundaries: portrait located in the Nałkowski Museum in Wołomin.

3. Works on geography by Wacław Nałkowski.

4. Page from the collection of poems *Pierwocin*, written by a teenage Zofia, with one of her drawings.

5. Page from *Pierwocin* with later comments.

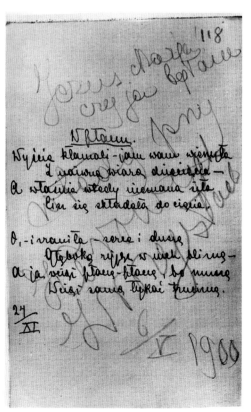

6. Zofia Nałkowska, 1903.

7. Zofia's first husband, the poet and school teacher Leon Rygier, 1922.

8. Zofia with some major writers of the time, Nałęczów 1907.
Seated left to right: Stanisław Bryliński, Zofia,
Ignacy Matuszewski, Władysław Tatarkiewicz.
Standing left to right: Adam Nagórski, Wanda Malinowska, Stefan Żeromski,
Adolf Nowaczyński, Stanisława Malinowska, Kazimierz Wroczyński.

9. Ludwik Liciński, a friend of the Nałkowski family, political activist, writer and revolutionary, 1904.

10. Edmund Szalit, young lawyer Zofia fell in love with in 1909. Their affair was unconsummated as he was married and had a little girl.

11. Zofia Villaume, Zofia's closest friend who supported her during her divorce from Rygier, c. 1903.

12. Zofia Nałkowska, portrait first published in her fifth novel *Narcyza*, 1910.

13. Family piano Zofia played for one of the Russian officers who occupied her *Meadow House* during World War I.

14. Disarming Germans on the streets of Warsaw. Zofia witnessed Poland gaining independence in the German controlled areas in 1916.

15. Jan Gorzechowski, Zofia's second husband, 1914.

16. Janusz Korczak's memorial stone in Treblinka extermination camp. Korczak was a doctor, writer and close friend of Zofia's father who dedicated his life to the care of children, and features in Zofia's youthful memoirs. He was killed in Treblinka in 1942.

Or was there some deeper need in Zofia Nałkowska that made her seek destructive relationships which were going to be repeated in the next years of her life? Maria Dąbrowska wrote: 'I'm sorry for her. She's chasing after something – seeking – in a kind of shining emptiness.'[41]

She was seeking for love as well as for the fame which was rightfully hers. And she was about to fall in love with a man with whom she could be her full self, with whom she did not need to hide her intellectual abilities or her innate finesse, did not need 'to be simple in order to be understood.'

Alas, he could not reciprocate, he was a man who 'loved differently.'

CHAPTER 9

House of Women

This timidity, this dissatisfaction with myself doesn't indicate modesty. It is actually that I expect myself to achieve something unusual, desiring some kind of maximum, as much in the area of appearance, dress and impression as in creative and intellectual values

The death of Zofia's nonagenarian grandmother in December 1927 became the catalyst for a new literary event, a play called *House of Women*. In December 1927 Zofia wrote in her diary:

Her death was so peaceful [. . .]. Just a few quiet breaths, each one becoming weaker. She was ready for death [. . .] but we weren't at all prepared for it. There was something indestructible in Granny, something so unchangeable. We were so proud of her long life. We thought that she was well. She knew she was loved [. . .] but as soon as she died huge remorse of conscience exploded inside us, we were so sorry for all those things we hadn't done, the little things we'd neglected which could never now be done.[1]

This text would be lifted almost unchanged into *The Impatient Ones*, the novel Zofia wrote before the Second World War. When Zofia writes 'we' she means her mother and sister. These three women's lives remained intertwined to the very end. Zofia featured their relationship, along with that of her grandmother and widowed aunt, in her play *House of Women* (1930). Writing for the stage was a new departure for Zofia. This particular play brought her accolades, foreign travel, fame and at least two love affairs.

In writing for the stage, Zofia found the right outlet for her particular talent and technique. She always wrote in scenes and the

momentum of her novels comes from the interaction of her characters, so the theatre was an ideal setting for her work. She enjoyed
watching the audience's reaction, though she was always fearful of
negative criticism and condemnation.

House of Women has been described as a great gift to Polish and European
theatre, not least because it gives women serous acting roles. Recently
adapted for Polish television, the drama proved to be as relevant – and as
challenging – for the actresses as it was almost ninety years ago. The
recent dramatization, also heralded as a 'triumph' shows the timelessness
of the interaction between three generations of a family. Grandmother
on stage sits in an armchair with her back to the window. She has her own
little table beside her, a tartan blanket around her with a footstool and an
extra cushion for comfort. From this location eighty-two year old
Grandmother offers words of wisdom, much as Zofia's real grandmother
must have done in *Meadow House*.

In the play, the women, who are either widowed or divorced, circle
around Grandmother with warmth and affection as they reflect on the
loves they have lost, on their betrayals and grief. The twist in the drama
comes with the arrival of an eighteen year old girl who reveals a secret
that shocks the women and leaves an unanswered question.

Maria Dąbrowska attended the premier in Warsaw in March 1930, and
shared Zofia's box. She noted that Zofia had achieved a huge success and
added that the dramatist was so tense throughout the play that she was
'barely conscious'. The drama hinges on the young girl's revelation to the
newly widowed Joanna about the kind of man her supposedly heroic
husband Krzysztof really was. In Maria's view this revelation should have
been the starting point and not the end of the drama, but she recognized
that, 'Pani Zofia is too great and excellent a writer to have done that sort
of thing by chance.'[2]

Zofia was amazed at the warmth of the play's reception. The next day
her telephone never stopped ringing and 'the press was phenomenal,
simply phenomenal.'[3] The theatre director, Arnold Szyfman (1882 – 1967)
who had seen the play's potential from the beginning, was delighted at its
success. So now Zofia took on a new life – the life of her play. She toured
with the drama from Poznań to Lwów (now L'viv,) the city where her
mother had been born. She stayed in the elegant Hotel George.[4] She
appreciated the applause that greeted each performance, but returned to

her hotel desolate because she was always alone. It was a new experience for her to sit in a theatre and not see a single familiar face – but wonderful to see strangers watching the stage with complete attention, deeply involved in her words and her work.

Her itinerary included the historic town of Lublin where she met relatives of her father, Wacław, although she didn't have time to travel out to the country and see the estate which her grandfather had allowed to go to ruin. She recalled that *Meadow House* had been built very much as an echo of her father's lost childhood home.

House of Women was also performed in Kraków, a city with so many memories for Zofia; it had been home to her mother and grandmother and had also been the scene of the trial of Stanisław Brzozowski. Her special memories were of Edmund Szalit whose love Zofia had 'stolen' – in her words – from his wife for one happy year when her marriage to womanising Leon Rygier had foundered, a love which Zofia had refused to allow her lover to consummate for the sake of his wife and small daughter. Edmund had died in 1915. Wounded on the battlefield he had dragged himself through marshes attempting to reach to a first aid post but was too weak and had drowned. Zofia, now a famous author, visited Edmund's widow who had attended a performance of the play:

> I saw his photographs, his wonderful eyes, his mournful beauty, first loved twenty years ago. I read his last letter and the little note which he wrote in pencil as he was dying [. . .] stained with his blood [. . .] He died alone at night, in the November night, knowing that no help would come. The letters are full of his boundless love for her and her daughter. He asks for forgiveness that his death will take him from them [. . .] Even today I believe that he was my only true love; twenty years on and fifteen years after his sad death I weep tears of gratitude, rapture and terrible grief.[5]

In June 1930 an international conference of PEN Club was held in the Tatra mountains in the popular ski, mountaineering and summer holiday resort Zakopane, much visited by writers and artists, many of whom had built handsome wooden villas, carved in traditional styles. The town had not been wrecked in the carnage of the First World War nor in the Polish-Bolshevik war; its picturesque chalets had become a visitor attraction.

The local Highlanders still wore their distinctive dress and spoke in dialect. Folk art was made and displayed in a museum and the town also boasted a theatre. On the recommendation of her doctor Zofia decided to stay on after the PEN Club conference and enjoy the mountain air.

And so she witnessed a tragic death – and received a personal shock.

She had been invited to join a merry company of writers and artists for a picnic at Morskie Oko (the sea's eye), the name of the deep lake in the mountains that she had depicted in one of her earliest stories, *Heavenly Night*. The group had picnicked a little too well and on the way back to town the car in front of Zofia's, plainly going too fast, crashed on a steep bend. The noisy picnic changed into a tragedy. The car had turned on its side. The driver lay spread-eagled in the road – he had ignored shouted warnings to slow down. Two other passengers were hurt while a third, Julian Ejsmond, a thirty-eight year old author and poet, was fatally wounded with a fractured skull and died in hospital two days later. The bend where the accident happened is now named in his memory.

It fell to Zofia to telephone Ejsmond's widow, Janina, who motored to the Hotel Bristol in Zakopane where Zofia too had taken a room. Janina did not come alone. She was accompanied by Zofia's husband with whom Janina was having an affair. To Zofia's chagrin, the couple actually stayed together in her hotel. At the funeral Jan Gorzechowski walked arm in arm with Janina Ejsmond and acted like a close member of the family, while his rejected wife could only look on in silent pain, grieving too for a life cut short in the full flower of its literary endeavour, in the midst of fun and good company, beautiful scenery and glorious weather.

After the funeral Zofia took a room in a guest house and eagerly awaited the coming of a famous theatre company who were to perform *House of Women*. Meantime she went for walks along beautiful mountain pathways with no one to talk to except a random horse, or a bee that she carefully shook off her clothing, anxious lest she do it harm. She reflected bitterly that she was still married and hadn't tried to wriggle out of the yoke of matrimony and be like 'other women', seeking love affairs, much as she longed for that one special person.[6]

Soon afterwards she happened to meet Poland's greatest composer of the era Karol Szymanowski (1882 – 1937) – and now her Zakopane experience took wings. Zofia was accompanied by a writer and artist, a genius and an eccentric, Stanisław Witkiewicz, or Witkacy, who drew her portrait in pastel. In return she gave him chocolates and a book. Witkiewicz introduced Zofia to his friend, the anthropologist Bronisław Malinowski. They all found Zofia charming, a sparkling intellect, witty and ready to flirt, but she wrote bitterly that it was just a pose. 'I am an unhappy wife, abandoned by my husband, a woman who is always alone.'[7]

She was short of money too, but at least she had her return ticket to Warsaw, paid by PEN Club. Szyfman, the theatre director finally sent her money that was owed to her and when the actors arrived the performance was very well received. Karol Szymanowski attended the performance and warmly complimented the dramatist. Zofia privately admired his looks and his charm – and soon she was writing in her diary that Zakopane was doing her good. She now met Karol nearly every day, sometimes in the company of other people, but often alone. Her hopes soared as she fell in love. There was a little sourness in this onrush of sweetness: Karol introduced her to his 'secretary' a charming young man who, as Zofia noted with surprise, used the familiar form *thou* when he spoke to his employer. The back story, though, showed Karol in the best possible light. The composer had helped the young man financially and thanks to Karol's generosity he was able to continue his studies and also have treatment for TB.

Something in the interaction between the two men puzzled Zofia. 'I sort of know – but I can't really imagine this, so I'm not going to believe it,' she wrote and soon was in raptures as if she were twenty all over again.[8]

Karol invited her to his beautiful wooden villa and showed her his manuscripts, explaining that the folk music of the Tatra Highlanders had influenced him greatly and he had absorbed its tonal patterns and rhythms. Interesting though this insight into the art of composition was for Zofia, even more absorbing was the composer himself. A photograph shows Karol with the ubiquitous cigarette between his fingers and Zofia with her gaze riveted on him. In his company she could be entirely herself. There was no need to make herself simple as she had done with Jan, no need to stifle that scintillating wit. She could be clever, charming, feminine, witty and feel at ease with a man just two years older, a man who was not married and who, she was sure, felt deeply for her, though she was troubled by his slightly indifferent manner, troubled too because he didn't say the words she most longed to hear and soon Karol – who was feeling tired

– had to return to Kraków. He been diagnosed with acute tuberculous, his throat and vocal chords were affected. He was a heavy smoker in an age when no connection was made between smoking and the conditions that arose from this habit.

Karol left behind another young protégé, Michał Choromański (1904 – 1972). Like Karol, Michał came from territories in Ukraine that had been incorporated into Soviet Ukraine. Karol generously helped refugees from those eastern regions. Michał's father had been killed in the First World War and he had been left to support his mother and sisters. He spoke only Russian but soon became one of the greatest writers in Polish in the inter-war period. On one occasion, as they travelled together in the back of a car Zofia felt full of sorrow for this talented young man who had suffered a leg amputation. However:

[. . .] having my head and heart full of Szymanowski – I lazily permitted this and that in the kindly darkness and speed. The first kiss for two years (not counting the insulting, always burningly humiliating things with Gorzechowski). I was sincerely moved and very surprised at myself.[9]

Michał read his new novel to her – Zofia was always ready to encourage younger writers whose manuscripts she read with focus and full concentration. It would later be said rather unkindly that the way to literary success was through Zofia's bed.

Michał, twenty years younger than Zofia, told her he was going to 'break her life.' Another despot? Luckily, her heart was too full of Karol to take things further – for the moment at any rate. She pictured Karol's face, 'handsome, charming, noble, filled with sad benevolence. And how he smiled!'[10]

Karol returned to Zakopane before Zofia's departure in mid-September and spoke in a way that she understood as a declaration of love, although he kept to the formal mode of address. He met in her hotel, bent towards her and timidly confessed:

I love talking to you, madam, I come here every day after all and I never usually do that. I don't know, I can't describe it to you, can't explain but my instinct pushes me towards you. After all you are a charming creature.

Zofia returned to Warsaw with the taste of honey in her mouth and joy in her heart. She went over these words again and again, weighing them up and balancing them against the other things she knew about him – his coldness towards women was legendary. No woman – and he had many admirers, was able to get beyond his polite but weary indifference, which she too had felt from him, but those words changed everything for her. She felt herself caught up in a 'storm of happiness' to think that where other women had failed, 'I'm the chosen one.'[11]

Karol had talked to her of his loneliness and Zofia felt this confirmed his 'otherness".

> This blemish on his perfect beauty – so fanciful and weird that I disbe-lieved it, has now been confirmed. I saw that this is a drama for him, that finally **this thing** is his own drama. The thing that stands out is his disagreement with happiness, struggling with himself rather than with the world. He only said 'loneliness' but in the torment of his smile, in the sadness of his eyes there was a plea for forgiveness or perhaps even consent or, I hardly dare think, for rescue [. . .] My delight for this man has no bounds [. . .] Our mutual understanding – our words mean the same thing, and the way we look at the world is the same. How much this means to me, after all I lived for so many years with a man without any real conversation. I still can't believe it. His words continue in me. I chew on this delight for hours and days and in no way do they lose their flavour, but keep renewing this spasm of happiness.[12]

Zofia saw Karol's inability to reciprocate her feelings as a blemish. Her fellow writer, Maria Dąbrowska, took a different view. Towards the end of her life she wrote:

> Why call homosexuality an 'impure desire', 'dirt' etc? That same love like all others might be 'pure' or 'impure', depending on the circum-stances, it could be dissolute or enormous happiness.[13]

Incredibly, Zofia deluded herself that she could 'rescue' her beloved Karol and be the woman in his life; Karol had his own reasons for not disabusing her. Next winter, in Warsaw, they were often seen together. Karol introduced Zofia to his family and at New Year 1931 they exchanged their first kiss – but it was only a gesture of friendship and Zofia began to understand that she could expect nothing more.

In any case, she was kept busy. Her increasing fame cost time and money as well as time from the writing which brought her all too little money, while balls, breakfasts and presentations required fashionable clothes, visits to a hairdresser, train and taxi fares – and a man's arm to lean on.

She toured with her play to Croatia and to Czech and enjoyed hearing these languages on stage in the mouths of her created women characters, particularly Czech, the language her own grandmother had spoken. On the way to Zagreb she travelled via Vienna and bought 'a nice little hat with feathers hanging over the ear.'[14] She loved Zagreb and was warmly welcomed, less so in Prague, though she reminded herself that Czech blood flowed through her veins. But even surrounded by people she was always alone. 'How different I am from Gorzechowski's women who humiliated me in his house,' she wrote, able now with hindsight to recall some of her past bitterness.[15]

In November 1930, having allowed her forty-sixth birthday to pass without notice, Zofia was invited to the President's Palace, Belweder. She managed to exchange a few words with Piłsudski, 'not about politics, unfortunately.' And she was presented with a medal, the Order of Polonia Restituta (of Poland Reborn), an award for her literary achievements.

These were troubled, uncertain times. Piłsudski quarrelled with Parliament and there were calls for the end of his dictatorship. The repression – and torture – of political dissidents in Brest provoked a nation-wide outcry and, said Zofia, 'the best people in Europe have the worst possible view of Poland.'[16] The world economic crisis hit Poland hard and the response of the government was to become ever more illiberal. Prices fell everywhere, the jobless took to begging in the streets and in order to counteract the worldwide economic depression, the government in Brazil ordered tons of coffee to be thrown into the sea, while in America wagons of corn and sweet corn were burnt. This provoked another outcry. Antoni Słonimski, the poet and literary critic who had written a warm review of *House of Women*, attacked these actions in a poem, *Burning the corn* (1931) and wrote an angry piece in his *Weekly Chronicle*.

The people who do this are ill clad and ill provisioned, acting on the orders of people who are well clad and well provisioned. Both those who give the order and those who carry it out know that the produce they are destroying is essential for the life of those who stand by and watch this modern execution.[17]

The economic crisis affected widowed Anna Nałkowska too. *Meadow House* was falling apart, way beyond the strength of Anna and her daughters to repair. It was no longer an attractive proposition for summer visitors who usually rented the ground floor. In any case, summer holidays were an unaffordable luxury for most people now, and in this time of financial hardship no one was likely to buy a house which lacked even the most primitive sanitation. Zofia got busy in the overgrown garden and found relief from the affairs of the heart amongst her many pets while her mother picked raspberries, dried truffles and spread green tomatoes on the window sill to ripen, glad that there was plenty of dill and that they could eat green beans and peas from the garden.

Then, said Zofia, she sat down at her little desk and wrote geography text books, just as she had done when her daughters were children.[18]

Unfortunately Zofia's beloved greyhound Diana, now old and infirm, needed veterinary care. Zofia didn't want to transport her in a cage in a railway goods wagon, so she asked a friend to give them a lift in his car. It turned out to be an expensive expedition because the car got stuck in the sandy roads. Zofia had to pay a large sum of money to get a farmer with horses to pull the car out and thereafter, along with her sister Hanna, continued the journey perched on the back of an open cart along with a barrel of coal tar and packets of nails for repairing a bridge further along the road.

Hanna, who didn't enjoy an easy relationship with her older sister, told Zofia that she was reputed to be haughty and unapproachable, particularly at the performances of her plays. People gossiped about her, a beautiful woman, a real Messalina.

Zofia turned this into a joke – yes, so sexy, jolting along next to a barrel of tar! They were both laughing over this when a large limousine overtook them with Jan Gorzechowski in the passenger seat. Hanna froze, horrified for Zofia's sake that she should be seen in such a humiliating position.

Zofia said she didn't care, she was so far removed from that world of big cars and high-up dignitaries. She reflected in her diary that she had always thought that her innate uncertainty that made her embarrassed at approval, although she sought it and needed it, was to do with her discontent with herself. If she was not well dressed or looked tired she turned away from people and did not acknowledge their greetings, which gave her the reputation for being cold. Having read a French psychologist, Ludovic Dugas (1857 – 1947), however, she found herself 'demasked," and concluded that she 'belonged to the great family of *timides*"; this timidity, said Dugas, is a characteristic of artists and writers which has nothing to do with shyness, but stems from an inner dissatisfaction.

> This timidity, this dissatisfaction with myself doesn't indicate modesty. It is actually that I expect myself to achieve something unusual, desiring some kind of maximum, as much in the area of appearance, dress and impression as in creative and intellectual values.[19]

As poverty hit harder, Zofia and her mother lived on the margins of destitution in their tumble-down house. She reflected on the line that divides the haves from the have-nots which runs right through the world. It is not a clear dividing line, though, because sometimes the same person can be on first one side and then the other. Zofia gives two examples.

She was among the have-nots when her publisher told her he couldn't pay her because there was simply no money. And yet the owners of the publishing house had several cars, enjoyed luxury trips abroad, the women were splendidly dressed and their children were well fed while –

> Mother and I sit here with a washer-woman instead of a maid, in a shabby house which no one wants to rent this year, we are living off borrowed money in fear and worry and our living expenses are 4 zlotys daily. We save on water to wash with because we have to fetch it from someone else's well, we save on butter and meat, we drink horrible weak coffee. We wear old clothes [. . .] But lodging here in the kitchen and in the little house made out of a barn – and obviously not paying anything – are two different unemployed married couples. The ones in the kitchen survive along with us somehow, she helps out while he sometimes works in the garden. The other ones have nothing at all. If I sit out in the sun in the deck chair in my old costume and that green wrap from Nice which I finally brought here, with a book in my hand, a pencil and notebook,

worrying what we will do when I spend our last 100 zlotys and I look at myself with their eyes, I see how privileged I am.[20]

Thus, the boundary line that had divided her house in Grodno, also ran though in her tumbledown *Meadow House*, separating her, financially squeezed as she was, from her neighbours who had nothing.

She had expressed the thought about the boundary line in her Grodno diary. Now, in a story in her newly published collection of stories, based on her prison visits, *Walls of the World*, she wrote:

The thinnest line ran through the middle of the house. It divided the whole world on one side or the other [. . .] One of these worlds reached us from the street. Automobiles and carriages drove past the gate. Good-natured, nice women and good-hearted men came down the bare stone steps [. . .] In our little drawing room, seated on the red sofa we talked about the things we had in common – about horses, travel, sometimes also about love [. . .] From this side from to time people with important surnames and unforgettable deeds entered [. . .]

But that other world squeezed through the kitchen doors, down steep dark steps from the yard. It didn't mix with the first world at all, it was its opposite and sometimes – unfortunately! – its explanation. People came for money to this side, for rescue, they came out of destitution or despair. They said that they had been here and there, that they had been everywhere and had nowhere else to go. They looked at me with eyes that no longer held any expectation. They had simply come here. I listened to their words to the end and often I didn't do anything either. And even if I did do something, in no way did I change their need.

They said goodbye and went away while I returned though those doors and found myself on the other side of that line that divided the world between one side and the other [. . .] And both those sides were our Polish reality [. . .] (But) in every place on earth and at every moment we are either on one side or the other of this line which breaks the world apart and which goes through every house.[21]

This boundary line would become the foundation of Zofia Nałkowska's finest novel, *Boundary* (1935).

Despite the economic hardships, 1931 was a good year for Zofia in her writing life. *Walls of the World* was followed by a new play, *The Day of His Return*. This play, like the stories, dealt with the problem of evil, it was widely performed and received good reviews.

Zofia Nałkowska, the so-called Messalina, supposedly sex-driven and indifferent, could write about crime and punishment precisely because she had visited the dark places of society. She had sat with the dying, had spoken to criminals as well as to those who were the victims of crime. She had also looked deeply into herself and seen the sources of potential evil there. She expresses this in the longest story in *Walls of the World*, *Marcjia's Family*.

Zofia visits an impoverished family. The house they live in is no more than a tumbledown hut. An old man is dying, but as Zofia sits beside him she finds herself not thinking about him, but about his bed: this destitute family had a beautiful mahogany bed. The wood was scratched, the polish rubbed off, but in the hands of a furniture restorer the bed could have become a real jewel, as once it had been in someone's stately home. And Zofia confesses:

> So what was I thinking to myself as I listened to Łoński's complaints and saw how he suffered? I was stubbornly thinking that if I wanted to pull his sleeping place from underneath him and give it to a refurbisher, I would see for myself how the golden red mahogany sun would shine through the fine enamel of the subtle lacquer.

> So it seems that it is not in our power not to be bad. We can only not want it, can try not to express it. The most we can do is not commit evil, but that is not yet all.[22]

Zofia's play, *The Day of his Return*, looks at the impact of crime on a family whose son has just returned from prison having served a sentence for murder. His father takes an unforgiving stance – only God can forgive evil. He expresses the thought that we long for what is good but love what is bad, and he makes a statement that Zofia will pick up in *Medallions*, that:

Each one of us is a potential criminal, Yes, yes, Everyone is a criminal even if he has not committed a crime, And that is never obvious to anyone – until they do something wrong.

The Day of his Return was widely performed, including in England, where it was staged in Birmingham as 'the play of the season.'[23] It was still staged in Poland after the war and more recently, since the publication in Poland of a major biography of Zofia Nałkowska by Professor Hanna Kirchner who had brought the diaries to publication, there has been renewed interest in her life and work. A recent performance of her play was found to be as relevant as ever.

Everything Zofia wrote was the product of deep thought. And almost everything was the result of her own lived experience. However, one important experience never found its way into print but stayed locked within the pages of her private diary, only revealed to the world after her death. And that was her unrequited love for Karol Szymanowski whose sexual orientation prevented him from taking the affair further. Like Zofia, he too longed for a home of his own, warmth and some sort of family life. He later said of Zofia that he valued her too highly to try to live a pretence with her, although gossip connected their names together.

Zofia was fast becoming acknowledged as the literary voice of Poland and was invited to represent her country abroad. She wrote in her diary on 4th November 1931:

> I've just got back from a journey which lasted five weeks. I've been to Greece. I was merry and happy. On the road through beautiful, friendly Yugoslavia, so well known to me, and in this strange marvellous land, between the changing worlds of the living and the dead, among mountains and the sea, olives, cacti – I preserved my image, sometimes ill, but strong, enduring, active.[24]

She wrote eleven travel articles on the way, to help fund her journey. These were published in various Polish journals and several were also included in a collection of her work published after her death, *Views near and far* (1957). Her journey was in the company of younger women writers and journalists:

[. . .] thriftily, with hardships and self-denial, I wrote in the company of one or two companions in tiny shared hotel rooms without hot water [. . .] So it turned out that I can do that too. I too could go out in crumpled dresses and torn heels and, dressed like that, still look good and present myself well at receptions, banquets and interviews. Finally, I was allowed to be old.[25]

Aged 47 when she wrote this, Zofia only allowed herself to age in her diaries, never in her public life. She had just been nominated as President of the Polish Writers' Union and the younger women had asked her to travel with them as their representative. Wanda Melcer, who had worked under Zofia in the short-lived Office of Foreign Propaganda in 1920, had booked the hotel rooms on their tour and tried to do it as cheaply as possible. Unfortunately one of these cheap hotels was the sort where men booked rooms for an hour, so all night long, the Polish women were visited by drunk sailors. In the end they barricaded their door with the wardrobe. The younger women in the delegation all moaned like mad, wrote Wanda, but, 'Pani Zofia never complained." On the other hand, Zofia got up late, didn't like the food and pulled faces as she ate, to show her displeasure. She somehow couldn't cope with packing and unpacking. Her hat box never seemed to shut properly and she wanted the younger women to help her carry her things.

However, despite her natural tendency to command, and very firmly demanding attention, she never failed to care about our rights. Highly educated and cultivated to her very core – she would never behave improperly, she gave everyone her due and so from this point of view she was a pleasant companion.[26]

Their journey lasted two months – and Zofia worked intensively all the time. Wanda's memoir mentions that, seeing the younger journalists working on their correspondence with their papers propped on their laps, Zofia had exclaimed in surprise, 'How can you write as quickly as that?" Wanda also recalled a reception at which:

Zofia appeared a little late but not at all out of breath, more corpulent than us, older, a little withered, but majestic, wearing a turban and a silver lamé wrap trimmed with white fur and a collar turned up in the style of Maria Stuart, which was fashionable at that time. Her entrance and the way in which she stood at the table spread with hors-d'oeuvres was really and truly lovely.

This word portrait fails to show the red lipstick, the even teeth and those forget-me-not blue eyes that were Zofia's most beautiful feature. No black and white photographs show them either and indeed it has been said that no photograph ever did full justice to this woman whose charm came from her fascinating personality and her carefully cultivated style.

One important moment during the two month journey came in Vienna where Zofia was delighted to see new social housing equipped with bathrooms, kitchens with gas cookers, shared rooms for laundry and ironing, sports halls and swimming pools, which she contrasted with wretched housing conditions in Poland. These Viennese workers' housing developments would form an important element in her novel *Boundary*.

Her return to Warsaw brought the lady with the silver stole back to reality. She wrote to her dear friend Zofia V:

> What a comedy! I'm surrounded by people rolling in money, who don't guess at all the way things are with me when I wriggle out of invitations and other nice proposals with stupid excuses about not feeling well.[27]

And yes, she was meeting with the highest of the land: ministers of state, diplomats, even the President. She saw how far the government had fallen from its early ideals, especially after the shabby affair when political prisoners had been arrested and tortured in Brest. All the important people, former legionaries and brothers together in the fight for independence were now the subject of jokes in the press. Zofia saw all these figures, known to her from her marriage to Jan, when she was invited to the ceremonial opening to a Pavilion of Art – a hotel stands on the site now on the large open square which has reverted to its pre-war name, Piłsudski Square. Military music and the national anthem which greeted the arrival of the President sounded hollow to Zofia who wrote sadly, 'it all means something different now and awakens different emotions.'[28]

This falling short of government and Ministers of State from their first promises is woven throughout Zofia's books from *the Romance of Teresa Hennert* to her last novel *Knots of Life* – a theme as relevant as ever today.

CHAPTER 10

My highest level

I have decided not to pay attention to the reader this time, not to seek simplicity, not to try to be engaging and understandable. I am allowing myself to be on my highest level. Everything that I have just lost will come to my aid.

1932 began with the first kiss from Karol Szymanowski, but it was only to drink 'Bruderschaft', a gesture of friendship and Zofia recognised it as such.[1] She was now enjoying time spent with Michał Choromański, the young man to whom she had 'lazily permitted this and that' in the back of a taxi in Zakopane. She admired his writing talent and enjoyed his jokes, loved his company too and felt sorry for him as he struggled to earn a living and support his widowed mother and family. He telegrammed her from Tarnów, a historic town 80 km east of Kraków, with a magnificent Renaissance Market Square and an important Jewish quarter whose splendid synagogue was later torched by the Nazis. Michał told her that he had been summoned to Tarnów because his invalid mother had fallen from a moving train and had laid injured on the tracks – an event that would later be transmuted into another woman's story in *By the Railway Track*, one of the best known Holocaust stories from *Medallions*.

Zofia had plenty on her agenda. She had just been chosen as President of the Polish PEN club and had been invited to Zagreb to a performance of her play, *The Day of his Return* in its Croatian translation. She went out to the Yugoslav embassy for her visa on a bright day in early January, walking through a Warsaw made lovely by the pearly mist, frost and the rosy wintry sun. And then she was on a train, travelling south, alone in empty carriages, noticing two luxurious sleeping cars with hardly any passengers. The whole transport system was still working, she wrote, but 'lacking its human component.'² People simply didn't have money to travel; Zofia herself had found funding for her journey thanks to a chance conversation with the relevant minister at a ball at the Romanian Embassy.

In Vienna she bought a hat and a cheap day dress – she couldn't afford a new evening dress for the premier of the play – while in Zagreb, a city she loved, she found a small hotel, her room fragrant with a laurel wreath donated by the women who acted the roles she had composed. She reflected on the possibility of a romance with the director, whom she found terribly attractive, handsome, beautifully attired and 'fiery like a tiger.' But her 'elderly virtue' triumphed. Zofia resisted the 'fires of love' to enjoy the platonic company of a man who, like Zofia herself, was 'free from all that Slavonic brotherhood and banal patriotism.'

Back in Warsaw, though, her 'elderly virtue' succumbed to the charms of Michał Choromański (1904 – 1972), twenty years younger than Zofia. They went to watch *City Lights,* a Charlie Chaplin film. This poignant silent film about a tramp, a millionaire and a blind flower girl, written and directed by Chaplin himself was shown in Warsaw exactly a year after its premier in America. Besides the film, though, Zofia was only too aware of her much younger companion, enjoying his 'hot, but not binding' kisses. She studied his profile in the flickering light from the screen, a short nose and full lips – and her heart told her that she was in danger.

And then – 'who would believe it', there followed two weeks (but they were like two years) of love just as he demanded it, 'indecent and mad':

> Trapped in the pincers of sensuality I experienced once again that leap from pleasure to the most severe suffering [. . .] I gritted my teeth in order to bear it, I took that feeling into myself, it swelled like an avalanche. I was only a woman, a woman . . . I think I'll have enough strength this time to last this out. I had to cast aside layers of mind-set to agree to this, to embrace happiness and insult in a single act of forgiveness, to drown everything in my immeasurable affection, in a sea of tenderness. And I didn't last out. ³

After those two weeks of mad love Michał arrived forty-five minutes late for a date with no explanations or excuses and Zofia broke off the relationship with her young lover with her 'heart breaking with agony and yet with a smile on her face.'⁴

Reflecting on the affair, Zofia realised that, unlike her friendship with Karol Szymanowski, Michał's 'demonic individuality' had intimidated her to such an extent that she thought she would no longer be able to write. Now, happily, 'I have returned to my true self.'

Zofia was soon on her travels once more. In February 1932 she toured with the theatre company who were performing *The Day of his Return* in towns in Volhynia, a part of eastern Poland hitherto unknown to her. This area now belongs to Ukraine.

Rehearsals took place in an unheated cinema. The actors rehearsed intensively although they were tired and cold; two went down with flu and Zofia was required to fill in as an understudy during rehearsals and thus entered the world of her play in a surprisingly intimate way.

Although conditions during rehearsal were primitive, Zofia enjoyed considerable comfort staying in the residence of the governor of Volhynia, Henryk Józewski (1892 – 1981). The bath water was yellow, and the maid apologised, but everything else, including the host himself, far exceeded Zofia's expectations. The Governor's residence had once been a convent and then in the 19th century had been turned into a splendid palace for the Bishop – so resplendent indeed that Tsar Alexander I (1777 – 1825) had stayed there several times in his capacity as the first ever Russian King of Poland; in later years the Russian powers-that-be turned the once-gracious building into a prison. With the advent of Polish Independence the building then belonged to the Polish Government. Zofia appreciated the luxurious surroundings, including beautiful semi-circular vaulting that adorned the ceiling on the ground floor.

She found the historic town, Łuck (Lutsk), very pleasant and enjoyed her conversations with Józewski, an artist, a former spy, a freedom fighter and politician, one of Józef Piłsudski's most trusted men, who cared deeply for the cause of Ukraine. Henryk Józewski survived several attempts on his life; during the Second World War he organised and edited many secret journals. Henryk actively supported the Warsaw Uprising, was injured and was finally imprisoned by the Communist authorities in Poland from 1953 – 1957, when he immediately resumed his career as an artist.[5]

Zofia was pleasantly surprised to discover that Henryk had devised the scenery for a production of *Hamlet*: the tension between thought and action was a highly relevant issue for the leaders of the new Polish State. Henryk Józewski, as Zofia observed, was a man of action, totally engaged with the needs of all citizens of Volhynia, no matter what their ethnicity happened to be.

Zofia admired Henryk's political and social ideas as well as his intelligence, although she noticed something not quite genuine in his smile. Maria Dąbrowska, a personal friend described him as:

> An uncommon man, entirely absorbed in politics, but in politics in the high style, beautiful, cold, noble, devoted to ideas, yet as crafty as they come. I see in him a phenomenon very rare in Poland, perhaps aside from Piłsudski he is the only such.[6]

A man who had been a spy would certainly not lay all his cards on the table, as these two great Polish writers noticed, each in her own way. Zofia also noticed his beautiful grey eyes and his confident, optimistic manner. His wife whom Zofia doesn't name in her diary, 'quiet, serious, seemingly inconspicuous, but in fact knowing her place very well,' was also an artist. Julia Józewska showed Zofia her paintings and invited her to return next year and use their home as a quiet place to write.

The Governor's house was certainly a helpful place for Zofia's creativity. Reading Freud, she reflected on her sexual experiences, believing that her despair over lost happiness in love had been sublimated into joyful thought that set her creative juices flowing once more. And as proof of this, Zofia recorded that she was feverishly writing in pencil notes for her next book.

> I have decided not to pay attention to the reader this time, not to seek simplicity, not to try to be engaging and understandable. I am allowing myself to be on my highest level. Everything that I have just lost will come to my aid.[7]

These words, of immense importance to students of the literary work of Zofia Nałkowska, refer to the genesis of her greatest novel, *Boundary*. Perhaps it's significant that this work had its beginning in a town that was very much a boundary place. Łuck/ Lutsk had grown out of the Kingdom of Rus', the Mongol invasions and the emerging Lithuanian state (11th – 14th centuries). Its historic castle still bears witness to the clash of mighty powers, while the First World War had seen six different enemy armies fighting in the streets of the quiet town.[8]

When Henryk Józewski became Governor the infrastructure of all major towns in Volhynia was almost non-existent. Jewish water carriers brought water to the homes in the towns, fire engines operated with horse-drawn carts and buckets of water – and fires were frequent in closely crowded wooden houses. The main industries were sugar beet, forestry, the growing of hops, brewing and tobacco production. With her Czech ancestry, Zofia might have enjoyed the taste of beer brewed by the Czech firm Zeman, and would have been gratified when the Governor told her that Czech settlers in Volhynia were the best and most productive farmers, better even than the Germans who had also settled there.

The ethnic mix was reflected in the places of worship. Łuck boasted a magnificent synagogue, richly decorated in the style of the Polish-Italian Renaissance and so strongly fortified that it still stands today. Zofia would also have seen a wooden temple belonging to the Karaite sect of Judaism, which has not survived, as well as Roman Catholic, Greek Catholic, Russian Orthodox and Protestant churches and schools where the curriculum was taught in at least five different languages.

Primitive though Volhynia was, Henryk Józewski had already managed to make positive changes and Zofia was very impressed. When she left by train on 16th February 1932 she noted how important this work of integration was – and how precarious. All too soon Polish right-wing politics swept Józewski's reforms away. Ukrainian culture was suppressed, and burgeoning nationalism went underground – only to result in ethnic violence and murder later, especially in 1943 / 44, carried out with extreme brutality by Ukrainian nationalists against their Polish neighbours. Finally, the traumatised Polish communities were 'resettled' in former German territories between 1945 and 1947, by which time the Western Powers, along with Stalin had incorporated Volhynia into the USSR.

Despite the kind invitation of the Governor and his wife, Zofia never returned to Volhynia. In spring 1932 she was invited to Estonia where *House of Women* was to be performed in two cities. She wrote about her experiences in three travel articles 'which were torn out of my throat' by her editors and as a result of this she came to a personal ground-breaking decision: 'I won't write anything I don't want, and I shall write only the way that I think.'[9]

This decision, she wrote, was forced from her by demands from her publishers and her own lack of self-confidence; it was also made against the background of a new love affair, 'young, wild and deep'. Would this affair support her and bring happiness or hinder and negate her?

She noted his name: Miroslav Krleža.

Miroslav Krleža (1893 – 1981) was a leading literary figure in his Croatian homeland. He had come to Warsaw at the invitation of his friend Julije Benešić, a translator of Polish literature. Miroslav and Zofia conversed in French and in Russian and, Benešić commented with satisfaction that both parties were charmed by one another.

And for Zofia, spring, her favourite season, had truly blossomed. The month of April was cold, but she was reborn. She invited Miroslav and Julije to *Meadow House* – always a first step towards deeper acquaintance. From then on those days of April and May were given over to scintillating conversation, in spite of the language difficulties, to walks and visits to the Zachęta Art Gallery. At last she had met a man with whom she could be fully herself both as a woman and as an intellectual being.

> My days are full of hours heavy with happiness and worth. I write in bed in the morning, making notes in pencil for this *Boundary*, which ought to be different, better than all my books. This comes into the whole business with MK.[10]

She found delight in everything she shared with him: their jokes, their deep discussions about literature strangely unhindered by language. He had read two of her novels in Russian and could compare them with her plays. She read his books in Croatian, battling 'through the darkness of the Croatian language', and felt that she had returned to her real self in a relationship that was complete in every way, something she was experiencing for the first time in her life. This man had no need to use her as a platform to further his own work nor as a show-piece to support his egoism.

> As I writer he is a phenomenon I could never get tired speaking about, as a man, as a philosopher, as an academic – these are all

territories to be explored [. . .] 'I could write a whole book about your face,' (he said to her). We live in complete isolation, there's almost nobody else except us. So the most important thing in the whole world just now is this.[11]

The day of parting had to come. Miroslav had to return home to Croatia to his work – and to his wife. Zofia went back to her beloved *Meadow House* and started to send instalments of her new novel to literary journals, to resume the usual grind of fighting for money and paying off debts, but this time with an inner sense of certainty. 'I know who I am.' Her inner self, which had been so taken apart and trampled upon during her marriage to Jan Gorzechowski was renewed, restored in a return to well-being after the chaos and confusion of her recovery – and for that she was deeply indebted to 'M.K.'.

She spent the beautiful summer months in *Meadow House* visited by friends old and new. Michał Choromański, paid her a visit and told her that Karol Szymanowski had said, 'She's so charming, you know, so unbelievably charming, it's so extraordinary. Such femininity with such an intellect – only it's strange: she doesn't react at all, she's a-erotic.' And Michał confessed that both men had agreed they could love Zofia 'homosexually.'[12]

But Zofia still had her 'M.K.' on her mind with hopes of a meeting in Paris; indeed her next diary entry on 11th November 1932 finds her in a hotel in Paris, the day after her forty-eight birthday.

Her living conditions were far from ideal. Her little room on the third floor had no private facilities. Zofia spent long hours working with her pencil and those long strips of paper, lonely but feeling more confident in her own skin, honest and 'almost naked', free of illusions, 'old as the hills' as she wrote in a letter to dear Zofia V., while the life of Paris buzzed by outside and, finally 'M.K.' arrived.

She kept on writing, hoping too that her play *The Day of his Return* would be staged in Paris. A Polish poet and diplomat, Jan Lechoń (1899 – 1956), working in Paris as cultural attaché showed great interest in the play, and added in a letter:

I'd like you to think that Pani Zofia Nałkowska's new play is as deep and splendid as it seems to me. I know from letters and reviews that it made a huge impression on stage, but even just reading it, it

seems as passionate as moments in Żeromski (1864 – 1925, a major
writer J.R.), and theatrically considerably more logical and concise
than his dramas. It's so strange that Pani Zofia Nałkowska, that subtle,
discrete, philosophising lady should speak in those passionate, brutal,
sincere words.[13]

Zofia's hopes of this stage performance in the cultural capital of Europe
were, alas, unfounded, as were her attempts to gain money from new
publications of her previous novels which had been badly translated in
French. Instead she spent hours correcting the poor translations as well as
getting involved with meetings with PEN Club in Paris and seeing people
– and all the time regretting those wasted moments that she could have
been spending with Miroslav.

Their affair was as meaningful as before and she continued to see
herself in a new light – or rather to affirm the real self that had been
suppressed for so long. But Miroslav had to return to Croatia. Alone in
Paris, living on rations brought to her room by the hotel staff, smitten
with flu, edging down three flights of stairs to the wash room wrapped in
her fur coat, Zofia kept on writing her 'accursed' *Boundary*, and finally
returned to Warsaw to rainy, cold spring weather which did nothing to lift
her spirits. She was plunged into deep depression, doubting her talent and
worth as a writer, while bringing to birth the book that has been acclaimed
the greatest of her works, deserving European recognition and fame.

Back home in *Meadow House* Zofia took her manuscript apart and
reworked many passages, while she was constantly visited by young hopefuls who wanted her to read and assess their manuscripts. One such writer,
Witold Gombrowicz (1904 – 1969) appreciated the fact that she took these
fledgling authors seriously and didn't act in a condescending way to their
new, more radical voices.[14] This was high praise from a controversial young
writer and shows Zofia's intellectual flexibility and her readiness to embrace
things that were new and unorthodox. Plagued with lack of money, she
lamented that even in her mature years at the height of her fame, she was
still struggling with poverty, while at the same time heavily involved in the
often unpleasant politics of literary life, with constant demands on her time
and oppression from an increasingly illiberal government.[15]

Suddenly, though, a new talent appeared on the scene, a most unlikely
source of inspiration 'too delicate and weak to be my salvation but his

thought world gives me courage to resist oppression and inspiration.'[16]

This almost crippling shy young man was Bruno Schulz (1892 – 1942) a high school teacher and artist from Drohobycz (now Drohobych, West Ukraine). Encouraged by friends Bruno Schulz made his way to Warsaw and on Easter Sunday 1933 appeared at a small guest house in Warsaw's Nowy Świat (New World Street). Here a sculptor, Magdalena Gross (1891 – 1948) who knew Zofia's sister Hanna, telephoned the great literary lady on Bruno's behalf and Schulz arrived, nervously clutching his briefcase and told Magdalena that the fate of his book depended on Nałkowska's goodwill:

> Magdalena rose from the table and went to telephone to Zofia Nałkowska [. . .] I don't know what arguments Magda used to persuade Nałkowska to see Schulz, but a few minutes later she returned and announced triumphantly: 'Grab a taxi right away and go to this address.' Schulz left, practically pushed out the door by Magda and myself [. . .]. Poor Bruno was pale, his hands trembling. The taxi took off and after about an hour later Bruno returned, calmer [. . .] 'Nałkowska asked me to read a few of the first pages, then she interrupted me and sent me out, asking me to leave the manuscript with her. She wanted to read it through herself. It was an encounter between a comet and the sun. The comet burned up [. . .]' Schulz paced back and forth, refusing even some tea . . . Finally, around seven o'clock in the evening the longed-for call came. 'This is the most sensational discovery in our literature!' Nałkowska exclaimed to Magda. 'I'll run tomorrow to Rój (the publisher J.R.) so that this book can be published as quickly as possible!' when Magda repeated Nałkowska's words to Schulz, he stood as if rooted to the floor, paralysed. We started to shake him, to hug him in order to revive him.[17]

The 'most sensational discovery in our literature' was *Cinnamon Shops* a collection of short stories, now known in English as *The Street of the Crocodiles*, the title of one of the stories in the book set in Schulz's multi-cultural, multi-ethnic native town Drohobycz. These stories open up a world that, as Zofia saw, is 'full of surprises', a world that is universal. They are now much studied and admired world-wide, but the breakthrough came when Zofia Nałkowska, so used to having the works of young writers thrust at her, saw at once the enormous worth of Schulz's stories and hurried them into publication. As awards and acclaim followed, Zofia took almost as much pride in Bruno's achievement as if it were her own. Her review of *Cinnamon Shops*, places it in the forefront of Polish (and indeed world) literature:

> The style of this book illumines and penetrates reality as if from its underside, revealing it deformed and true, like a cross-section of tissue under a microscope – a reality that is intensified and threatening. It is an immensely interesting book to which one returns for new surprises that can be read anew in different ways, at different depths.[18]

Bruno and Zofia became close friends, and, briefly, lovers. She enjoyed his letters – he was a great letter-writer, which were 'creative, deep and of the finest thought.'[19] In these letters Bruno expressed his profound adoration. He gave Zofia an album of his drawings, done uniquely for her with a long dedication, and bound by himself with brown silk. He brought her 'a quiet, sad happiness.'[20]

From then on Bruno Schulz, the self-effacing genius from Drohobycz took his place at the forefront of the pre-war Polish literary scene, but politically these were dark days in Poland. A peasant uprising near Brest (and therefore in Jan Gorzechowski's previous jurisdiction) was blamed on the local Communist Party; activists were tortured and threatened with the death penalty. This caused a huge outcry and Zofia was one of many protestors. Her mother Anna added her signature to the protest. The protest resulted in the death penalty being commuted to life imprisonment and a female activist, Regina Kaplan, being tried in a civil court.

Zofia was never a political activist but she started to receive leaflets and information about political prisoners. She brings this into *Boundary*, where Elżbieta, one of the main female characters, also secretly receives such forbidden literature.

Her diary, however, makes no mention of a major event in her literary life, a huge personal and professional honour. On 29th September 1933 Zofia Nałkowska attended the inaugural meeting of the prestigious Polish Academy of Literature where she was the only woman member for the next years of its existence, a huge accolade and public recognition of her place in the Polish literary canon. A photograph shows her in full evening dress, seated next to Pani Mościska, wife of the President of Poland.

So now there was even more reason for emerging writers to seek Zofia's approval and support for their own writing. Her diary is full of names of senior, illustrious writers alongside young hopefuls who sought the company of this woman who was, as noted above, discrete and subtle, full of finesse and above all someone who encouraged others. All this came at tremendous cost in terms of time, and also the need to keep up appearances when 'poverty regulates our life (mother's and her own) here in Meadow House and in Warsaw.'[21] Her room in her mother's apartment on Marszałkowska 4 was a salon on European scale. Maria Kuncewiczowa (1895 -1989) whose novel *Foreign Woman*, published in 1936 was a profound exploration of the experience of being a foreigner, uprooted and unaccepted, acknowledged that she owed a lot to Zofia who 'encouraged you to love life.' Zofia's greyhound, Diana was always present at her literary gatherings. Maria recalled that an ardent revolutionary prophesied that the day would come when 'bitches will lap blood in the gutters of Warsaw.' Zofia replied, 'Will that be good for Diana's health?' And Maria concluded, as so many others emphasised:

> You brought flowers to her. Floral tributes were very much the thing because that apartment was situated if not in Paris, at any rate on Parnassus [. . .].

> So one arrived with flowers and found Pani Zofia in the drawing room, sitting erect on an old-world sofa, looking through the window or else somewhere beyond the lamp. Looking sharply, attentively, not at all dreamily. A quick turn of her head, a few easily spoken words, a movement of her hand – and right away you felt at home, and yet at the same time, somewhere far away. On her ground-floor flat, in a building situated in a European province in a country downtrodden by history, by-passed by tourists, Zofia Nałkowska offered her guests tea and little cakes from Wedel, but from a horizon no narrower than that of Montparnasse or of London's Bloomsbury.[22]

Witold Gombrowicz too appreciated the European stature of Zofia Nałkowska:

> Her house was one of the literary centres of Warsaw [. . .] Pani Zofia was seated on the sofa and conducted the conversation like a

distinguished matron from the days before the Great War [. . .] There's no question but the intelligence and culture of this distinguished woman was reflected in the level of the conversation. She coped trium- phantly with the hugely different groups of people who took part in those sessions. More than once I admired the skill with which this lady was able to revive a spark even from notorious oddities, off-beat people, stammerers and non-speakers [. . .]

And that's exactly what Nałkowska loved most, she loved to sniff out talent, search out the good stuff, even if it was something you'd never notice without a magnifying glass. They'd bring her the manuscript of some unknown poet and three days later we'd be discussing it at her tea-party. And more than once her sense for new things bore fruit: she discovered Schulz [. . .] she didn't refuse to help me and give me advice. No wonder young people clung to her. And she too clung to young people, being amazingly lively for her age, making other women jeal- ous, so that some said ironically, 'Literature rejuvenates.' [. . .] She loved to receive guests, she loved elegance, she herself was both elegant and world-class – and those features which are so normal in Paris seemed almost indecent and provocative in some social settings in Warsaw [. . .] In general you have to say that this woman didn't suit either Warsaw or Poland, Her place was Paris, or at any rate Western Europe.[23]

A lover of life, Zofia loved human relationships, despite their knotty compli- cations and the heartaches they often brought. When Bruno Schulz left Warsaw to return to his roots in Drohobycz, 'leaving such a large empty space behind him, although he is so small,' Zofia wrote from Zakopane, adding:

I answered his greatest need, I gave myself to his adoration. Grateful and kind, I didn't forbid him to idolise me. But the way he thinks of me is different from the way I think about myself. I don't find anything in me that's worthy of attention. I can't write, even though that's why I came here, not skate or ski.[24]

Three months later she met 'my new talent'
He was twenty-six, tall, blond, unsmiling, a young man from the prov- inces, living in great poverty, doing his own cooking and laundry. The

manuscripts he brought to her smelt 'of dampness and poverty'. Some, Zofia noted, were brilliant, others were patchy. His name was Bogusław Kuczyński and he would become Zofia's lover, agent, secretary and tormentor until the outbreak of war saw them fleeing from Warsaw, only to part and go their separate ways, Bogusław to Romania and thence to London, while Zofia returned to dangerous, war-torn Warsaw, caught within the pincers of a tyranny far more cruel than anything she had ever experienced from any of her lovers.

CHAPTER 11

Literature rejuvenates

The Jewish district spread out under the castle [. . .] Three synagogues stand close to each other where at dusk by candlelight Jewish men sit on their benches, bent over their books [. . .] The men here wear hats, not caps and beautiful long side locks. On the Sabbath many appear in lacquered slippers and white stockings, in shining satin tunics, their hats are then velvet edged around the brim with beautiful brown fur [. . .] In the evening they all process in groups across the down-trodden grass beside the river [. . .] But the younger boys go down the bank, toss off their clothes and jump into the cool water in their underpants [...] they chase each other, calling to each other and do gymnastics before getting dressed.

It was her fiftieth spring. Her Warsaw flat was full of the scent of lilacs, a heavy cluster brought from *Meadow House*. Her accounts were dismal, debts were mounting, she had to borrow money from Mak, her good-natured brother-in-law.

Back in Drohobycz, Bruno was sending charming letters, full of adoration, while Zofia went on a 'date' with three promising young male writers, a stroll around the Old Town at night, and along the banks of the Vistula River, provoking an acquaintance to try to persuade his fifty year old mother to go out on a date and 'charm young men like Pani Zofia.'[1]

One of the three was Bogusław who 'is growing ever greater in my eyes, revealing his perspectives and depths.'[2] Zofia found him a puzzle, he was both timid and proud, young, bitter and with something threatening in his manner which gave her pause for thought.

'Do I want this? I'm not sure,' Zofia confessed to her diary. 'That scene, reminding me suddenly of Gorzechowski's stormy love. His stubborn resistance and rebellion. 'Pani is my enemy.'[3]

She invited him to *Meadow House* to celebrate her name day and they discussed their affair, certain of their mutual attraction along with disbelief that this could really be happening. Meantime, Bruno Schulz, knowing nothing of Zofia's new situation, sent a bouquet of dark red roses along with a typically beautifully worded letter. But, Zofia thought, what he was expressing was not love, but a kind of cult stemming from his own needs. She well understood that the shy genius from Drohobycz craved humility in his erotic life – his drawings bear witness to this sense of abasement as a man before women who strut large and often naked across the page while men prostrate themselves before these vast goddesses.

Their affair had lasted a year but they had only gone to bed once, Zofia reflected, and although sadness overwhelmed her at the thought of the injury she was doing to Bruno, she was now in a different place, one that filled her with fear that grew as the new relationship progressed.

The issue was not merely Bogusław's impatience, emotional hunger and lack of trust, it was the difference in age. Zofia reflected on French writers who had taken lovers much younger than themselves. She had the example of her friend Hela, just two years younger than Zofia, who was enjoying a relationship with a man half her age. She could also think back to her great cry of protest in 1907 when she had declared that women and men should be equal in consensual sexual freedom. But theory is one thing. Zofia was only too aware of the twenty year discrepancy and what this meant for the younger man.

'What can I say?' she asked herself. 'I am old. I am finishing, finishing. But in these torments are flashes of the same tremor of happiness as before. And dying with fear for myself, with sorrow for him (Bruno) and longing for the other (Bogusław) I exist in a state of constant elation.'[4]

In spite of her dilemmas she continued to read deeply and to list the books in her diary. She had also been invited to represent Polish PEN Club at an international gathering in Edinburgh.

The Polish group included the critic and writer Antoni Słonimski and his 'new, pretty, nice wife' as well as Joseph Conrad's niece and translator, Aniela Zagórska who occupied the bunk above Zofia in her cabin on the a new cargo vessel called *Lech* (an old name for Poland). They sailed from Gdynia – it was *Lech's* third journey and Zofia enjoyed this new experience, her first sea voyage. Lying in her bunk, she recalled her last days in

Meadow House with Bogusław, they had listened to Stravinsky and Chopin (*Ballads* and *Barcarolle*) on gramophone records and what passed between them had fulfilled all the promises contained in the music. And she kept on writing. The accounts of the sea voyage in Zofia's diary are so precise we feel we are with her as the ship dips out into the open sea, sails down the Kiel Canal and thence out to the North Sea.

From the deck she looked down at the engines and was amazed at 'the beating heart of the ship, which could be felt like a subtle trembling under the deck, under the straw mattress and the thin skeletons of the deck-chairs.' The machinery was 'like two bent legs of a mechanically galloping horse striking rhythmically on the pistons.' Later the group went down to the depths of the ship to watch the crew at work. The stoker was heavily tattooed. Zofia felt that his work four hours on, eight hours off must have been like working in some kind of torture chamber. She also chatted to a sailor who advised her to visit Madame Tussaud's waxworks museum and see large as life the figures of Hitler and Mussolini alongside those of the British Royal Family. It's certain that Zofia had no wish add that to her itinerary; however, the Polish guests were also invited to the captain's bridge. Zofia thought that the self-contained world of the ship and this voyage which demanded no effort, in the company of pleasant people with nothing but sea around her, was the height of passivity.

They sailed up the Thames and spent two days in London where Zofia worked on her speech for the conference 'which anybody else could have done in a single morning.' It was being translated into French and she was pleased with the result, though with her usual severe self-criticism she felt the speech was 'too heavy and boring'. She enjoyed the London parks and witnessed a ceremony at Buckingham Palace which included the arrival of distinguished guests in cars and 'two of the strangest carriages with ladies in old-fashioned dresses and ostrich feathers on their heads.' These coaches on gilded wheels were drawn by two bay horses. Two coachmen in three cornered hats and red jackets, splendidly embroidered with gold, sat up front while two others identically dressed stood at the rear.

Zofia found London more homely and intimate than Paris, its elegance more discreet and life on the streets, in spite of the queues of buses, seemed quieter.

From London the Polish visitors travelled north to Glasgow where every day in this 'strange land' was filled with delight. Scotland seemed to have been etched from 'an old woodcut [. . .] full of romantic charm, castles everywhere, even ruins, monuments everywhere, memories and traditions.'⁵

Edinburgh reminded Zofia of Kraków with its sense of tradition and the way in which the skyline is dominated by the Castle on the rock, just as the Wawel Castle rises above the city of Kraków. The group visited historic Carberry Tower near Edinburgh, home of the sister of the then Duchess of York, Elizabeth Bowes-Lyon. The castle was 'modest and could hardly be called comfortable, but soaked in every kind of antiquity and a deep, pious respect for things of yore.'⁶

A reception followed where members of the Royal Academy wore black gowns while the Lord Provost and the whole Town Council were robed in red. Zofia found it strange that at such receptions the host was greeted first, and his lady only second.

The visitors attended a Garden Party in the grounds of Holyrood Palace and a banquet filled with 'mournful Scottish music' where they witnessed 'the strange entrance of a herald blowing a trumpet and behind him a cook with oatmeal sausage which was carried right up to the top table.' They were also treated to a military procession with the drum major twirling his mace 'frightfully' while the drummers made acrobatic twists and turns with their drumsticks.

After all that ceremony the PEN Club meeting might have seemed a bit of a let-down but Zofia's speech 'On internationalism in literature' was met with applause.

They visited Loch Katrine and sailed down the Clyde in pouring rain. Conrad had loved this river, his niece Aniela told Zofia, and the best ships in the world were built here.

But now Zofia had a problem. If she continued sightseeing with the rest of the group she would miss a meeting of the Academy in Warsaw, something she could ill afford to do. The others did not have the same pressing money worries and Zofia felt isolated her from her companions. 'I am famous, much acclaimed – and poor, but I pretend it doesn't matter,' she told her diary.

Back in London she found letters from Bogusław and thought about his poverty, chosen because he wanted to be a writer; she thought about her friends who were also poor and she longed to be back in that real world, away from career writers 'and their frightfully over-dressed women' whose shallow conversation reminded her of the atmosphere in Grodno that had depressed her so much.⁷

And so she travelled back to her real world overland through Holland and Germany but the experiences of her visit to the UK remain valuable as a documentary of the time, and as a footnote to them, Bogusław wrote in Zofia's diary (just as Jan Gorzechowski had done at the start of their ill-matched affair) a single word in Polish: 'I waited.'

*   *   *

Zofia returned to a difficult *ménage a trois*. Bogusław, officially her secretary, took up residence in Anna Nałkowska's large flat. This complex, irritable twenty-seven year old was now living with, as Zofia put it, 'two elderly ill women', while Anna, who did not like Bogusław, vied with him for her daughter's attention.

The plusses of the relationship were that Bogusław got Zofia organised both in her writing life and in her finances. He had a typewriter (who paid for it is not known, but we can guess). He typed out a timetable which he pinned on to Zofia's door and which she was obliged to obey.

Thanks to his iron discipline, Zofia finally finished *Boundary* in April 1935; she recorded her relief and gratitude in her diary[8]. The downside was that he became more and more obsessively jealous, kept her friends at bay and told her that a great person like her shouldn't be on familiar 'thou' terms with anyone. He cultivated her image and was loud in his disapproval if she wore something that didn't come up to the standards he had set.

He acted out the dominant, demanding male, prioritised his own needs and his writing life, tapping out a largely forgotten novel on his typewriter. Still convinced of his potential, Zofia read and edited his work and felt a deep kinship of a shared outlook, alongside an awareness of Bogusław's bitterness and negativity.

At first, she thought that:

'his gloomy, demanding youth is no barrier, it consists of joy and enticement, it builds respect, sometimes even terror. Isn't it strange that exactly here is certainty, that the future can be reckoned as long-lasting, 'there are no jokes' in this affair. It makes me want not to die. And I sometimes think that only death, and nothing else will mean the end of this affair. It would be good if I were able to show good measure here, if I turned out to be tactful (dying first). Bogusław, who doesn't like empty phrases, said, 'I'll climb on to the pyre after you.'[9]

These negative strengths were put to good use as Bogusław bullied publishers as well as Zofia, but if he increased her earnings by getting books reprinted and translations done, he also spent the money – after all, he was earning nothing himself.

That spring, as Zofia and Bogusław adjusted to their life together, two alarming events occurred.

The first was personal. Zofia's diary writing had lapsed for several months after her return from Edinburgh. She opened her notebook again at the end of April 1935 to record the scene at five a.m when her mother had screamed in her sleep. Zofia had rushed into her room to find seventy-three year old Anna only half-conscious, writhing in bed with fear and suffering on her face. 'It's the end of me,' she had moaned.

Bogusław had called for the doctor and for Hanna and her husband Mak, who lived close by, and after medication was administered and poultices applied Anna had calmed down. This brush with mortality sobered Zofia. Her mother was so dear, so reliable, always there – and now Zofia realised that Anna Nałkowska was old and becoming frail; this was the third such attack within the last five months and Zofia feared that her mother might not withstand another like it.

It was in fact the beginning of the dementia that was to cloud Anna's last years and draw out from Hanna and Zofia their most tender, devoted care, as Anna became increasingly unlike herself, angry and demanding, losing control.

The next event shook the nation. It happened at Zofia's name day which she celebrated with a crowd of guests, including ministers of government and their wives, the Chinese Ambassador and a host of writers, not all close friends

Like a whispering game, wrote Zofia, the news was passed from group to group, from room to room: Marshal Józef Piłsudski had died.[10]

It was the end of the name-day party. It was also the end of an era. Days of mourning followed, as a result of which a literary event in Barcelona to which Zofia had been invited, was cancelled – and unfortunately Zofia had already bought an expensive evening dress and the payment that she had budgeted for would not now materialise.

Later that year Bogusław, who had been a member of the prestigious Cadet Corps, was called up for military training. Zofia followed him to Nowy Sącz, a beautiful, historic town, once second in importance only to

Kraków, situated between three rivers in the mountainous countryside with the Beskidy range close by and the Carpathians on the horizon.

This was new terrain for Zofia. She delighted in the harmony between the historic buildings and the peaceful landscape. She describes it minutely in her diary and later in a beautifully written travel piece which ought to delight everyone who loves this picturesque area.

Left alone in a modest hotel room while Bogusław was involved in his training course, Zofia tried to write. She had to do a piece on Piłsudski, whom she had of course known personally. And, a complete surprise and something she was not well suited for, she had been paid to write a film script for a Bible-based film about Mary Magdalene, as well as a radio play, *Teresa's Nights* – a huge task, which she found just as difficult as writing a stage play.

Early mornings were always difficult for her. This is when she felt her most unwell and her darkest thoughts haunted her. Money, of course. The fee she received for attending the Polish Academy of Literature had just been lowered. *Meadow House* was unsustainable and probably going to have to be sold. And Bogusław!

In a fit of jealous rage he had seized the beautiful album which Bruno Schulz had given her, the text of *Cinnamon Shops* with Schulz's original drawings, bound in brown silk, with a long dedication to Zofia. Bogusław had ripped up the precious book and burnt it in the stove so that absolutely nothing could be saved from it.

Always painfully able to understand the other person's side in any argument, Zofia had forgiven Bogusław, realising the depths of his jealousy were not only because of her relationship with Bruno but also because Bogusław must have known that Schulz was by far the superior writer, a man of genius, whose work was unique.

Yet in the dark morning hours the deed haunted Zofia – what right had Bogusław to give vent to his anger in this way, especially when Bruno and Zofia were no longer lovers, when she had given him up for Bogusław? How could he allow himself to stoop to such barbaric, wild behaviour and destroy something so unique, so precious, so very strange and different? And why was it that Zofia had to put up with all this, even when she felt she could not suffer his rages any longer?

However, the beautiful surroundings of Nowy Sącz far from Warsaw and its busy traffic brought her tranquillity.

In her diary (and later in the travel piece) Zofia describes the people she met out on her walks or as she sat on a bench watching the River Dunajec flow peacefully by.[11]

She was pleased to see people out in canoes and small boats, young people swimming and sunbathing – all these things which previously belonged to foreign travel were now happening in Poland. She glimpsed soldiers marching, training and exercising their horses along the top of the railway cutting and over the little bridge across the line and spoke to a woman selling wooden goods, a widow who had given birth to eighteen children, of whom eleven had died.

Her husband, she said, was a good man and didn't really drink, just a glass or two occasionally. 'He hit me across the mouth because I keep getting pregnant. As if it was my fault! So I say to him, 'For God's sake, man, why are you hitting me, after all, giving birth to a child isn't the same as eating a sweetie.'

Too poor to pay for a midwife, she gave birth unaided. So these children were born and then they died.

'But in tears she told me only about one boy who died when he was twelve and a half. Because he had a beautiful death. He was only ill for three weeks, with a cough, like them all. His eyes were full of merriment but he dried up, And when he was about to die he asked her to dress him all ready for the coffin. She took cloths, washed him and dressed him. And he reminded her, 'Will you give me trousers, Mum?' 'Yes, yes, you bought them yourself already.' 'And a hat?' 'Yes.' And when he was dressed he sat on the bed and waited peacefully, making sure I hadn't forgotten anything he'd need for the coffin. Then I burst into tears and I said to him. 'My little son, I thought that you would lead my funeral procession and now I'm having to do it for you.' And he said, 'Thank you, Mum for these kind words. Pray for everyone who brought food for me, may they live for a long time.' Then he lay down and died. And the priest said that such an easy, conscious death was a great grace from the Lord God.[12]

Zofia also spoke to two Jewish ladies, one a young mother with a little girl, the other an old lady, bowed with age but wearing a wig that was surprisingly youthful. She had two splendid diamonds in each ear, each pair linked with silver claws. A long piece of red cotton threaded through each ear-ring and attached to the old lady's neck showed how precious these diamonds were. A third lady, who covered her head with a hat instead of a wig, dressed in black in spite of the heat, also wore diamonds. She chatted to Zofia, telling her how nerve-wracking she found it when young people dived into the river from the diving tower that had five levels, so that they could choose different heights. Each time one of the boys dived in she turned away and hid her face in her hand.

Zofia described the Jewish quarter:

The Jewish district spread out under the castle [. . .] Three synagogues stand close to each other where at dusk by candlelight Jewish men sit on their benches, bent over their books [. . .] The men here wear hats, not caps and beautiful long side locks. On the Sabbath many appear in lacquered slippers and white stockings, in shining satin tunics, their hats are then velvet edged around the brim with beautiful brown fur [. . .] In the evening they all process in groups across the down-trodden grass beside the river [. . .] But the younger boys go down the bank, toss off their clothes and jump into the cool water in their underpants [. . .] they chase each other, calling to each other and do gymnastics before getting dressed.[13]

Seven years later in August 1942, the lady with the ear-rings, the young woman with the little girl, the men with their elegant Sabbath dress and the boys who enjoyed themselves in the cool river water were herded along the river bank with machine guns trained upon them. Over the next three days without food or drink in the heat of the summer sun, they were marshalled in groups to trains that were waiting in the railway cutting where Zofia had watched the Polish cavalry exercise. The Jewish communities of Nowy Sącz and the outlying areas were transported to the death camp of Bełżec and murdered.

Thus Zofia's finely observed description records a way of life that was totally annihilated in the Nazi genocide, a crime of such magnitude that Zofia would sum up in a phrase so concise that it is almost untranslatable, *ludzie ludziom zgotowali ten los* . . . People prepared this fate for their fellow human beings.

The five Polish words quoted above have become one of the most famous sayings in the Polish language. They introduce *Medallions*, translated into English by Diana Kuprel (North Western University Press Illinois, 2000).

Returning home to Warsaw, Zofia helped Bogusław launch a new radical literary magazine, *Studio*. She contributed work to it; a section from *Boundary* as yet unpublished as a book, appeared in the first edition, and other illustrious names, including Bruno Schulz, contributed to the first editions. At the same time Zofia noted that the world situation was becoming more perilous. On 3rd September 1935 the Italian armies took Abyssinia (present day Ethiopia). Zofia heard the news on the radio as she awaited the broadcast of her radio play, *Teresa's Nights*.

The theme was the age old story of a young girl selling her body to support her family – her fiancé leaves her in disgust. It did not go down well with the intelligentsia. Maria Dąbrowska described it as a fiasco, but Zofia was comforted that her live-in maid, Mania, wept over it and so did the other domestic helps in the building. In any case the next month, October 1935, an event occurred which eclipsed the radio play: the publication of Zofia's masterpiece, the novel she had called *Boundary*.

CHAPTER 12

Boundary and beyond

Telephoned with congratulations to Nałkowska who has received the State Prize. The maximum amount of earthly successes are heaped upon this woman, which is what she deserves and which she also needs very much.

Zofia doesn't record the date of publication of her new novel, *Boundary*. Deeply distrusting her writing abilities, she notes on 8th October 1935, two days before her fifty-first birthday, that the book had been met with a 'cold kind of recognition.' Soon, though, she's able to say that *Boundary* is being recognised as a phenomenon, 'even a masterpiece.'[1]

Her previous novels, *The Romance of Teresa Hennert* and *Unkind Love* sharply critiqued the way that the powers-that-be in the new Poland had lost their earlier vision for democracy, particularly with regard to ethnic minorities in the Eastern territories. *Boundary* gives an even more searing account. The novel charts the main protagonist Zenon's downward slide from youthful idealism to entangled compromise as he rises in the ranks of the town's elite.

Boundary offers a profound sociological and psychological analysis of the contemporary scene. We can say of *Boundary* as Zofia herself said of Bruno Schulz's work, 'It is an immensely interesting book to which one returns for new surprises that can be read anew in different ways, at different depth.' (see chapter 10).

Each new reading of *Boundary* offers a greater appreciation of the 'knots of life' that this mistress of style unravels and re-ties in ever more complicated patterns. Patterns of family life, of social behaviour, of compromised and compromising response to other people's expectations are exposed in this novel, along with class structures. The dividing line between the people at the top, the 'just managing' middle layer and the people at the bottom who are not managing at all is just one of the many boundaries in this intricate book which also highlights the day to day drudgery of the maid of all work and the coldly disparaging way her employers take it all for granted and cast her aside when she becomes too ill to work.

A book published in Poland in October 2018 supports Nałkowska's searing account of the two worlds of the mistress of the house and her maid. Domestic servitude was the lot of a third of all workers in Poland on the eve of Independence, and most of those employed were women. Even relatively poor people could afford a maid who carried heavy loads, ate the left-overs from the food she had cooked, slept at night by the kitchen stove that she had to clean each morning, carried out the refuse, did the laundry, darned torn clothing and could be dismissed at a moment's notice.[2]

Time shifts (following Zofia's interest in Proust) play an important part. The book begins with a sentence that Polish adolescents who read *Boundary* as a set book at high school know by heart:

The short and splendid career of Zenon Ziembiewicz, which finished so grotesquely and tragically, could now be completely re-evaluated from the standpoint of its preposterous end.[3]

So the beginning introduces the end – while the end re-opens the beginning . . .

Other boundaries are between youth and age. Elderly women left alone in the world after the First World War had robbed them of their sons and political change their possessions are viewed through the pitiless eyes of fifteen year old Elżbieta as she passes them cake at her aunt's tea party. Zofia believed (and expressed this thought in her diaries and in *Choucas*, her novel set in the Swiss sanatorium) that youth is a positive attribute while age is negation.

Small wonder then that Zofia felt wretched about the imbalance in her relationship with her young lover Bogusław, so aware of the twenty-two year age gap between them. Age, particularly of women, is dealt with in depth in *Boundary*.

Underlying this multi-layered novel is a love triangle. Zenon, the son of an impoverished landowner, has an affair with his mother's nineteen year servant girl, Justyna – just as Leon Rygier had once seduced Zofia's own maid. This sexual entanglement was, said the good citizens of the town:

'A tasteless affair which he hadn't had the wits to handle decently or sensibly like a man.'[4]

'*Like a man . . .*' A world of lies and subterfuge lie behind those words, and Zofia exposes them. Zenon's father is a serial adulterer and his mother knows how to 'handle' her feckless husband by forgiving his many lapses and maintaining a public face of high moral and religious conduct.

Zenon steadily becomes more and more like the father he despised; another boundary he fails to cross even as he tries to delude himself that 'other men do worse.' His career is on the way up and the last thing he needs is a love-scandal. He gives Justyna money and this highly capable young woman, whose naïve trust has been so cruelly betrayed, thinks that this is meant to pay for a backstreet abortion. Filled with guilt, with sorrow for her lost motherhood, with grief for what she has done to her child, Justyna crosses yet another boundary, plunging into apathy and psychosis.

Justyna is an outstanding character. Zofia captures her simple, uneducated language in a way that doesn't talk down, but expresses her honest personality. Her lament for her lost child is simple and deep as a folk song, profound as the great Polish elegy, *Treny – Threnodies*, by Jan Kochanowski (1530 – 1584) one of the best-known and most widely translated Polish poems. In an essay on Zofia's work Bruno Schulz affirms Justyna's place in European literature, pointing out that she is almost a re-incarnation of Goethe's Gretchen, the tragic young woman who sings out her woes as she sits at the spinning wheel. Schulz concludes that 'Nałkowska finds no justification, no balm for the incurable wound in our existence.'[5] In Justyna's lament, we hear the young woman's own helpless, sorrowing voice:

> Most of all she remembered [. . .] how when she was lying in bed at night after those pains, quietly so that she wouldn't wake anyone up, that she had moved. And it had it had slipped out of her, like a little mouse. The whole world hadn't wanted it, its birth father hadn't wanted it – only in her alone it had a hiding place. She alone in the whole world could have looked after it, so that it could have made its way in life. In her alone it had salvation and shelter. But she too, its own mother, had turned against it. So where was that infant supposed to turn for rescue when she herself, she too had done this to it?[6]

Zofia never became a mother. Her childhood friend, Wanda Melcer suggested that she may once have had a miscarriage.[7] Children do not feature much in her novels and family life is seldom shown to be happy. Elżbieta in *Boundary* yearns for a family, mother, father and child seated around a table in the lamplight – just as, after the unexpected death of Wacław Nałkowski, Zofia, her widowed mother and sister had sat in a sad threesome around the lamp lit table in *Meadow House*. Although Zofia deeply respected her father and adored her mother, she rarely portrays parents in a positive way. Fathers are either tyrannical or feckless, mothers, as in *Boundary*, abandon or reject their children. Yet in *Boundary* there are two fiercely maternal women, both unmarried. Justyna's mother works day and night as an underpaid, unappreciated domestic servant for her child, while a lodger in Elżbieta's childhood home refuses to give up her out-of-wedlock son even though she cannot look after him herself.

Boundary is also concerned about the ways in which we adapt our personality to suit the opinions others have of us. We watch Zenon as step by step he becomes corrupt and compromised. Yet another boundary passes through the very house where much of the action takes place, the childhood home of Elżbieta and her aunt Cecylia. Sub-let rooms under the roof and rooms in the unlit basement are occupied by the impoverished and by the desperately poor and these lives too intermingle and act upon each other. Thus Zofia Nałkowska creates worlds within worlds within the setting of a provincial town. Incidents and people are densely interwoven in 'knots of life' that are ultimately destructive. Seemingly insignificant or unrelated details interlock in ways that make the structure of this intricately layered novel resemble a musical symphony.

One scene above all highlights the genius of this composition, showing the boundary between our public presentation of ourselves and real inner motives. It comes near the end of the book, linking the ending with the sentence that opened the novel. Zenon's plans for creating better housing and working conditions in the town of which he is president have failed. The local factory has gone on strike with harsh responses from management and prison staff. And now, in the dimly lit street, Zenon feels threatened by a crowd, coming ever closer to the town hall where he works and as he tries to escape this apparent menace he finds the door locked. He rings and as he waits for the door to be opened he sees in the dark glass his own reflection, his fur collar, his bowler hat and right behind him, comes the crowd, their faces picked out in the street lamp, as though Zenon himself is leading the very people he is trying to escape.

This masterly twist encapsulates the complex situation of Zenon's working life – and of the unstable, angst-ridden Polish government at both local and national level. Zenon, the mayor, whose mission should have been to improve the lives of working people is now desperately trying to escape the menacing crowd (though Nałkowska explains that in fact this was actually just a small group of people). It was a scene that would be repeated in the Gdańsk shipyards in 1970 and again in 1980 when workers in a worker's state demanded better conditions and the fearful, vacillating authorities backed away from these rightful demands.

However, to all readers of Polish literature this scene, like an optical illusion, completely reverses a key moment in an important novel that preceded *Boundary* which deals with events on the eve of Polish Independence in 1918. Called *Przedwiośnie On the Eve of Spring*, this novel by Stefan Żeromski (1864 – 1925), published in 1924 and considered one of the masterpieces of Polish literature, ends when the young hero seizes a red flag and marches with it at the head of a crowd of demonstrators, a gesture of triumph and hope. Zenon's image in the glass makes it seem that he too is at the head of the crowd, leading to freedom the very people he does not want to meet.

There could be no better comment on Polish political reality during the fraught years of the Second Republic than this reversal which turns all the rhetoric, bombast and empty promises of hard-won freedom upside down. The publication of *Boundary* occurred during the continuing world-wide economic crisis. Zofia lamented that in the whole publishing indus-try the author was the most redundant person whose needs for an income were met with astonished embarrassment because, after all, nobody is buying books now. *Boundary* was selling well but the author, with two successful dramas, a range of highly praised novels and articles in leading journals still had no money!

She was not alone. Karol Szymanowski, increasingly frail and unwell, had no money to pay instalments for his hired piano.[8]

Zofia continued her work with PAL – the Polish Academy of Literature, still the only women among men, some of whom were bending to the political winds of the time, making sessions at the Academy another torment for Zofia who was not prepared to see major writers side-lined because they were Jewish. Her relationship with Bogusław too was fraught but still seemed essential. 'It would be cruel to split up,' she wrote on her fifty-first birthday.[9]

She was working as hard as ever. Two plays based on *Unkind Love*, described by one of Zofia's readers as 'the most splendid contemporary novel'[10] were in progress, one was already being rehearsed while Zofia 'ruined' herself by buying new clothes for luncheon with the wife of the increasingly unpopular Polish Foreign Minister, Józef Beck (1894 – 1944). She bought a velour hat, a suede handbag with matching shoes and a fashionable scarf to add a touch of colour to a new dark blue dress.

As 1935 wore to a close Zofia went down with a cold, following a frosty walk in the evening with Bogusław through some of the most beautiful parts of Warsaw. As she tried to persuade herself that she simply had a bad cold and nothing more serious, she reflected on the on-going trial of young Ukrainian nationalists and recalled that not so long ago young Polish freedom fighters were on trial, refusing to speak Russian in the court, just as these young dissidents refused to speak Polish, but only Ukrainian.

It's an easy and banal idea that borders have been shifted but nothing changes, the same relationships still continue and in the same places, probably in the same buildings and halls, the same words are repeated only in a different language.

She reflected sadly on the fate of these young patriots who:

are normal people, young boys and girls, They go to university, make friends with one another, fall in love, study together and of course they want independence for this Ukraine of theirs. Someone just has to say the word and these young people commit themselves to an underground life, deluded that they can change the world, 'that 'wrongs' will disappear and 'freedom' will reign' while all that actually reigns is death, young peoples' death, death they that they have waited for in the loneliness of prison.[11]

So December wore away. Mother was always active – working away at her desk, writing her geography text books, trying, like her daughter, to earn some money, anxious, just like her daughter, about debts and unpaid bills, while Boguław's 'organising spirit' and despotism dictated a strict regime: no one was allowed to visit before four pm and Zofia was only allowed to answer the phone in the afternoons. Zofia saw that this was useful for her writing life although Mother didn't like this regime at all. Anna started to spend the weekends with Hanna and her kindly husband Mak. In her increasing dementia Anna had become as greedy for entertainment as a small child. She demanded to go out to a café, to have a little walk, go to the theatre. Zofia indulged this behaviour as much as she could – it would become not just difficult but actually dangerous when Nazi terror visited Warsaw's streets. But for now, Zofia wrote sadly:

> I'm not always kind, sometimes her obstinacy, criticisms, her advice and her grievances make me angry. But I always apologise and take back whatever was bad. I really give her great satisfaction. She knows that she is loved. But of course it's about something else. It's because she must have peace and harmony, so that she thinks that everything is fine – she, the one who is always the best, self-giving, still charming even when she's wrong and presumes too much, more able to feel pity than to be angry.[12]

Anna grieved for the unhappiness Zofia experienced in her increasingly difficult relationship with Bogusław. She had disapproved of the relationship from the start – and made it obvious as well, but she steadily lost insight despite her efforts to drive the darkness of dementia away. So Christmas passed. Bogusław bought and dressed the tree. Then on 29th December 1935 Zofia learnt that *Boundary* – and its author – had been awarded the prestigious State Literary Prize for Literature.

Now there were many phone calls (perhaps Bogusław waived his afternoons-only rule on this occasion). Zofia learnt that the jury had been unanimous in giving her the award. Her book was a huge literary success, a phenomenon, an undisputed masterpiece, yet her immediate response was to feel guilty that the other short-listed authors hadn't won, and she felt particularly sorry for Józef Wittlin (1896 – 1976) whose novel *Sól ziemi*,

The Salt of the Earth, missed out on the award but was later put forward for a Nobel Prize. An English translation has recently been published by the Pushkin Press.

Banned in Communist Poland and only now being rediscovered, *Salt of the Earth* is a lyrical account of a way of life shattered by the outbreak of the First World War. However, in contrast to *Boundary,* Wittlin's novel celebrates the dying world of the Austro-Hungarian Empire, while Zofia's novel bravely critiques contemporary Poland. Zofia liked Wittlin and said of him, 'You can only say 'nice Wittlin'.' And indeed 'nice' Wittlin telephoned to congratulate her on her award.

Maria Dąbrowska phoned as well, but there was a sour note in her reactions which she recorded in her diary on 30th December 1935:

Telephoned with congratulations to Nałkowska who has received the State Prize. The maximum amount of earthly successes are heaped upon this woman, which is what she deserves and which she also needs very much.[13]

Deserves . . . and *needs* . . . It was an astute observation, but if Dąbrowska had been party to her rival's complicated home life she might have shown more understanding. Zofia had defied convention in her scandalous affair with a much younger man. She had followed logically the demands for female sexual freedom that she had put forward in her speech in 1907, but had chosen an insecure, despotic, neurotic man, who asserted his rights to be head of the house, though never its breadwinner – that doubtful privilege belonged to Zofia. She wrote day and night, despite her ill-health, the onset of her menopause, the demands of her young lover and her ageing mother. She lived an outwardly successful life, charmingly hosting foreign guests, while at home she faced conflict and violent quarrels as Bogusław smashed windows and yelled childishly, 'I hate your mother, I hate your sister and your brother-in- law, I hate all your friends . . .'

So, 1935 finished with a huge literary success for Zofia, with domestic turbulence and political and social unrest in Poland, with mounting tension on its borders and in much of Europe, while to celebrate the New Year she bought her mother a splendid warm dressing gown and a fashionable shawl.

CHAPTER 13

Storm clouds near and far[1]

Just as distant hills and forests appear closer before a storm, we live in
the aura of a new war. We go round in circles – as though waiting for a
catastrophe in some nightmarish antechamber. The peaceful, sometimes almost jocular tone in which daily letters to the press mention the
coming war, that it will be such and such – only intensify the nightmare
situation in which we needs must live. This reckoning on the coming
war as an accomplished fact, this resignation from any resistance to the
business concerns of the arms manufacturers who seek to persuade
nations that war is in the people's interest – all this fill sme with deep
revulsion.

The New Year, 1936 saw Zofia being 'permitted' by Bogusław to receive
Bruno Schulz 'for a short visit'. On 11th January she records that she
spent the morning writing a children's book, then at two o'clock she
was at the dressmaker's, being measured for an evening gown to wear
to the premier of her new play, *Renata Słuczańska*, based on *Unkind
Love*. Lunch followed the dressmaker, then more writing and in the
evening she was invited to dinner at the Hungarian embassy.

I wore my London lace dress with two roses and I enjoyed success
from many different viewpoints. All this after a sleepless night because
of one of Bogusław's scenes. But let me not think about him or write
anything bad here. I am moved by and grateful for this bad and great
love of his, which can't be explained by his youth but only by his
unusual, powerful bitter nature. Just think how, after everything he
told me about his hatred yesterday, today he stood outside in the rain
and the mud waiting for me while I wasted time in stupidly superficial

chatter with men in tails. This spring downpour has lasted two days now and today the wind simply tore your head from your shoulders. Ach, *Busiu, my Busiu*.[2]

The swings and roundabouts of this affair, good bad, bad good, tormented Zofia for the next three years until a greater evil separated the unhappy couple.

The next diary entry records an outing with Mother 'so delicate and frail.' They went by taxi to a café which Anna had previously visited with Hanna and Mak, who were both on holiday in Zakopane. Zofia immediately wrote to reassure her sister that their mother was well enough to go for a short outing. The return journey was by taxi as well. 'I save her from too much movement or any kind of decision.'

With loving delicacy and tactfulness, Zofia tried to support her mother who, no matter how tired she was, immediately seized her pen with green ink and her endless slips of paper to work away at her geography books, trying to battle her ever increasing weakness and the disintegration of on-going dementia.[3]

The next big event was the premiere of Zofia's new play. Unfortunately, it wasn't performed in the intimate small theatre where the rehearsals had been held but in more grandiose National Theatre – and the impact was rather lost. At the same time Bogusław was receiving poor reviews for his first novel. He launched a new literary journal, *Studio* and thanks to Zofia, many established writers, including Gombrowicz, Witkiewicz (Witkacy), Schulz, and Zofia herself were represented. This journal with its left-wing tendencies lasted only a year and each issue was a millstone around Zofia's neck for she had to do the bulk of the work in getting it ready for publication and also had to fund it.

Bogusław himself was becoming ever more despotic – the very feature Zofia had looked for in 'her one and only man' her youth. Zofia was always at pains to note his good points and rare kindnesses and pass over his 'scenes', his tantrums and cruelties which would nowadays be classed as domestic abuse. Probably as a result of this daily tension she was plunged into a whole series of illnesses while at the same time she had to cope with her mother's whose 'life is becoming cramped and shrunken, from day to day her life is growing smaller,' as Zofia wrote sadly.[4] Amidst all these cares she attended receptions with the highest in the land, struggled with nastiness in the Polish Literary Academy, of which she was the only woman member, wrote articles and reviews and started a major piece of work, never to be fully realised, on her father.

Reviews of *Boundary* continued to affirm and depress her. On the one hand it was acknowledged as a masterpiece, but two critics, who had previously been in love with Zofia, took revenge by writing negatively about her work, while a third, an extreme misogynist, with nothing good to say about any woman writer, simply tore the book to shreds in his review. However, the general impact of the novel was so huge that a film was planned and literary Warsaw staged a 'trial' of Justyna. This 'trial' was played in front of a packed audience in main hall of the Warsaw Conservatory. The verdict that Justyna was innocent was viewed as an enormous triumph for the author herself, and also for the voices who demanded social change in contemporary, illiberal Poland.[5]

In the midst of domestic tantrums and trauma as Bogusław, stressed by his lack of literary success, demanded peace and quiet for his writing, Zofia began to doubt her place in the literary scene. Nevertheless, she embarked on a new novel. She had the title already, *The Impatient Ones*, but when she asked for an advance she was told, discouragingly, 'And suppose you die before publication, madam?' Zofia, taken aback, managed to smile and joked, 'Oh well, that will get you out of the contract.' But her publisher was serious and demeaned her further by mentioning a minor writer whose sales had fallen off as soon as his obituary notices had appeared in the paper.[6]

Being written off as dead did nothing for Zofia's morale. She managed to go away to a spa and health resort but Bogusław plagued her by sending bad reviews and making demands for her support of his journal. Feeling no better, she returned to Warsaw where she put plans in motion to move from their large flat at 4 Marszałkowska Street, which was noisy, cold and expensive to heat, to a smaller, sunnier flat overlooking Łazienki Park with its mature trees, lovely walks, and charming red squirrels who are so tame they run up to strangers and eat nuts from their hands.

As Zofia looked around the empty flat she contemplated the eighteen years she had spent there and the numerous people who had enjoyed her hospitality, many of them the most eminent names in pre-war Polish cultural and political life: literary critics, artists, musicians – Szymanowski included – ministers of state of both left and right wing parties, diplomats and distinguished foreign guests – as well as young writers, some doomed forever to be forgotten, others whose talent she had encouraged.[7]

Karol Szymanowski telephoned and arranged a meeting. He had aged, Zofia noted:

> He is still having a difficult time financially in spite of his recent success in Paris, but his appearance – a most beautiful grey-blue dressing gown, an amazing shirt underneath, even the quality of the handkerchief tucked into the breast pocket – all seemed to contradict that fact. Roses on the table, flowers everywhere, one elderly unexpected guest brought three large creamy chrysanthemums. This kind of fame, his greatness and these accessories are actually not quite up-to-date. None of our colleagues is able to create this kind of aura. Wherever he is, he surpasses his surroundings with a somewhat old-fashioned elegance, a kind of Wildean aestheticism [. . .] along with his noteworthy culture, the charm of his conversation, his truly good taste and his kindly intelligence.[8]

A month later Zofia, Hanna and their mother attended a family wedding in the Gothic Cathedral of St John in Warsaw's Old Town. Their route took them past the Baroque Church of St Alexander on Three Crosses Square where nineteen year old Anna had married Wacław Nałkowski, evoking many memories. Anna's sister Janina had been married there too and the bridegroom of this wedding in the Cathedral was Janina's much loved grandson Tadeusz Wróblewski, whom she had brought up after this mother's death.

Zofia noted that her seventy-five year old mother, whose plentiful brown hair had hardly a thread of grey, simply radiated beauty, surrounded by the loving care of her two daughters, while Aunt Janina's own son, Zofia's cousin and father of the bridegroom turned up at the wedding smelling of drink. Zofia later used this scene in her new novel *The Impatient Ones* where the good-for-nothing father leaps from the pages of her novel, an impossible buffoon who, unbearably, becomes a larger than life character.[9]

As the year went on Zofia was caught between her mother's needs and overwhelming love and Bogusław's increasingly impossible demands, his anger and temper tantrums, behaviour more like that of an angry teenager than a man approaching thirty. Zofia plunged deeper into ill-health;

Bogusław and her mother fought like tigers over her care, calling a doctor who treated her with cupping, kaolin, and all manner of injections while she worked on a translation of *Madame Bovary* – anything to bring in much-needed money, for the care of this impossible triangle fell upon her shoulders.

Zofia ended the year by comparing herself to Maria Dąbrowska who sneered at Zofia's *grande dame* behaviour. Zofia retorted in her diary 'I shall keep my complexes, illnesses, lack of money and my inferiority complex, my writing is my stubborn and 'heroic' conquest of all of this.'[10]

It had been a hard year for Zofia, a feeling that she was being surpassed by younger writers in spite of her obvious fame, feeling like a pauper in comparison with European writers she met at international gatherings, the taxing care of her increasingly infirm mother who was slipping ever more steadily into the nothingness she valiantly tried to fight by writing her geography books. 'I've got to finish this because if I die I'll never know if anyone liked it,' was Anna's constant plaint – and Zofia knew that this endless non-writing was her mother's resistance against the engulfing darkness of dementia.[11]

Outside the home war clouds darkened the horizon. In an article in a Warsaw journal, Józef Wittlin, whose book *The Salt of the Earth* had been shortlisted along with *Boundary* for the Polish State Prize in 1935 wrote:

> Just as distant hills and forests appear closer before a storm, we live in the aura of a new war. We go round in circles – as though waiting for a catastrophe in some nightmarish antechamber. The peaceful, sometimes almost jocular tone in which daily letters to the press mention the coming war, that it will be such and such – only intensify the nightmare situation in which we needs must live. This reckoning on the coming war as an accomplished fact, this resignation from any resistance to the business concerns of the arms manufacturers who seek to persuade nations that war is in the peoples' interest – all this fills me with deep revulsion.[12]

Zofia's diary entries for 1937 continue to be full of complaints about Bogusław's impossible behaviour, yet she also expresses her amazement that this young man still loves her. She records a scene when he returns all smiles after a few days away, enters the flat ready to embrace Zofia like a lover. Unluckily, just at that moment Anna happened to cross the little hall between the kitchen and her room – and Bogusław immediately turned on the old lady with icy rage for being in the way and impeding his love life.

Reflecting on her difficult marriage to Jan Gorzechowski (from whom she never formally divorced) and now her relationship with Bogusław, Zofia writes sadly: 'I don't know if it's my fault that emotionally I choose people who are so damaging to my life, or if the fact is that they choose me.'[13]

Zofia's almost constant ill-health ate up her money – but when she was unwell Bogusław was her mainstay and support, making it harder than ever to think of separating from him. On the one hand he acted like a tyrant, forbidding poor Anna from listening to concerts on the radio because it disturbed his peace, on the other helping Zofia with correspondence and her translation work. Their relationship was now in its fourth year, as Zofia reflected when she went away to recuperate in the spa town of Krynica in the beautiful Beskidy mountains – passing Nowy Sącz on the way, with memories of the time she had spent there with Bogusław two years before.

As well as drinking mineral waters and enjoying walks among tall fir trees in health-giving fresh air, Zofia appreciated talks with a young writer friend, Halina Maria Dąbrowolska which she reflected on as she took the train back to Warsaw.

Discussing Zofia's fraught relationships with Bogusław and her mother, Halina had pointed out that Anna Nałkowska might have been just as dissatisfied with any other husband or partner of Zofia's – even someone as kind and worthy as her son-in-law, Mak, Hanna's husband.

'How strange to think that my beloved mother is a little vain and despotic and loves flattery so much,' wrote Zofia, recalling that it had been her mother who had 'rescued' her from Jan Gorzechowski, coming personally to transport her then forty-five year old daughter back to her own flat. She recalled her mother's constant refrain, 'I'm only thinking of your happiness. Don't be angry with me because you're going to be unhappy (with Bogusław) so don't say that I didn't warn you.'

'She treats me like a child,' Zofia told her diary. 'She's the one who always knows best.'

And yet, and yet . . . 'She's the person I love more than anything else,' she concluded.[14]

She returned to Warsaw to find the first chapter of her latest novel, *The Impatient Ones*, already in print in a literary journal –without any of the corrections she had toiled over during her stay in the spa.

Ten days later came the news that Karol Szymanowski had died in a sanatorium in Switzerland. The papers were now full of articles about the composer whom Zofia had believed herself in love with, the man who had said of her that she was the only woman he might have been able to love. She recalled his polish and style, his charm and wit – and his voice becoming ever weaker, until at the end, at their last meeting, it had been little more than a whisper. However, she was too unwell to watch the funeral procession when his embalmed body was brought in a glass-topped coffin to Warsaw, nor could she attend his burial, which was to take place in Kraków. Yet, she wrote, a little surprisingly, considering the enormous passion she had felt for him: 'I can't think of his death as a personal loss since he was lost to me long ago.'[15]

A month later a charming young friend from Grodno days, Zhenya Exé (1899 – 1943) took Zofia by car (a small new Ford) to Zhenya's uncle's fish farm north east of Warsaw. Zofia planned to set part of her novel *The Impatient Ones* in this area whose famous fish ponds are still much visited today.

The fish ponds were only about thirty eight kilometres from Warsaw, but the whole area seemed to Zofia like another world, lit by a full moon. The dark pine trees gave a melancholy impression, the Ford car ploughed through sandy paths; the whole place was deserted without sight or sound of human habitation – a good sign, for this is where Zofia was planning to set a murder.

The house they were to stay at seemed gaunt and unwelcoming, with vines intertwined around barred, shuttered windows. The owner, Zhenya's uncle Gabriel Makedoński (1883 – 1957), was Russian of Greek descent. Zofia thought he looked like an Englishman and noticed that he had something rather unpleasant in the expression of his lips. He related the ins and outs of his work with the fish farm and Zofia listened, fascinated. Fish for her were often a symbol of darkness and death. Teresa Hennert had gone fishing with her lover Omski before he murdered her and he then took her body out to the middle of the lake in the same boat. Fish took on sinister connotations in *Boundary* too, so, now, ready to write about a murder, Zofia absorbed the stories in depth.

And now Zhenya, delighted that Zofia was so pleased with the unusual expedition, sat down on the edge of the bed – and told the whole story. So Zofia heard about a murder that had taken place fifteen years ago one dark November dawn in this deserted landscape, somewhere amongst those sad pine trees – exactly where Zofia planned to locate her next crime.

'Yes, well, but who was the killer?' Zofia asked, feeling that something wasn't quite right, that perhaps she hadn't heard it all correctly.

'Who do you think?' Zhenya said triumphantly, jerking her head towards the door. 'It was him, of course! My uncle. His victim was young and very attractive. Uncle was crazy about her, although she was married to his own brother who had been fighting the Bolsheviks – he was due home that very day. The court let my killer uncle go free because he said he had been acting in self-defence. The woman had chased after him into the forest, he said, and it was so dark he didn't know who was sneaking up behind him, so he took a pot shot.'

Truth being stranger than fiction, Zofia carried the story in her mind all night and in the morning when she opened the shutters and watched the sun come up through the bars in front of the window she thought about the murder and the betrayed wife who had lived through it all, and, so recently dead, had already been supplanted by a 'fiancée.' No wonder Zhenya had called this strange house a 'submarine.'

The sun came out, the sky was blue and the fish ponds sparkled in the sunlight, while bees buzzed around lilacs fragrant with scent. The forest still seemed dark and ominous, ghostly, without shape, only towards evening, illuminated by the setting sun, it suddenly seemed alive, almost as if it were holding its breath.

Zofia used this scene in her novel and meantime recorded happily in her diary that although she had spent all day out and about, getting her feet wet in the marshy ground, she hadn't caught a cold or felt unwell.[16]

She returned to storms in the Polish Academy where right-wing literary figures had taken over the leadership and were trying to impose anti-Semitic decisions on the rest. There were storms at home too. Mother was being moved from Zofia's apartment to Hanna's which meant constant phone calls and shifting of luggage while Bogusław, who demanded these changes, fluctuated between moments of enormous energy and attacks of bad temper: everyone had to do what he wanted, everyone was guilty except him. Depressed, indeed oppressed, Zofia drew delight from nature, the view from her window was a source of joy. Lying in bed and feeling unwell, Zofia rejoiced in the glimpse of sunlight on the budding trees in a way that was almost mystical, and recorded her response in words that were a kind of prayer. She also took equal pleasure in a huge bunch of her favourite marigolds from her friend Halina which, refreshed in the water, smelt wonderful.

Later she and Bogusław visited the Lublin area where both had family. Zofia, gathering materials to write a book about her father, met elderly relatives and heard stories of Wacław. Her old aunts who lived in deep poverty were delighted to meet their famous niece. 'They're always writing about you in the papers,' Zofia was told.

She saw the land where her father had spent his childhood, where he had ridden bareback – and where he had kicked over the water buckets of the little girl whose silent acceptance of the injury he had done her became a matter of shame for the rest of his life. From these relatives, and also from her father's childhood diaries, Zofia learnt that Wacław had been treated cruelly by his own father, beaten, kicked and denigrated, she guessed that perhaps that was why he had taken out his boyhood traumas on the defenceless child.[17]

More travels followed: to Gdynia, on the Baltic, to Copenhagen and finally to Paris for six weeks where Zofia stayed in a luxurious hotel and enjoyed the company of international writers, including James Joyce, 'sad, thin and delicate.'[18] However, international tensions made for uneasy relations. The Jewish delegate from Palestine accused the Poles of anti-Semitic actions, the Polish Jewish writer Antoni Słonimski accused fascist governments of murdering poets and the Italian delegate annoyed everybody.

After the conference, which Zofia found artificial, she moved to a cheaper hotel and explored Paris. She enjoyed an exotic night club where the dancers were all black. Zofia was in the company of a poet Jan Brzechwa (a weak poet, but an attractive man, she said)[19], and his wife. Meantime, she awaited the arrival of Bogusław, worried how her unpredictable young lover would behave. However, once he got over this usual fault-finding – he didn't like her shoes – Bogusław instantly negotiated the Paris Metro and embarked on publishing deals for Zofia. One thing Zofia found worthy of mention was that for the first time in their four year relationship, the couple enjoyed a large double bed.

They travelled back through gloomy, fascist Berlin. The whole dark atmosphere, unpalatable food and exorbitant prices reminded Zofia of the German occupation of Warsaw in the First World War.

Sorrow awaited Zofia in Warsaw – Mother had decided to sell *Meadow House* while Hanna had developed what seemed to be breast cancer. Weeks of worry ended with the good news that the tumour had not been malignant but the New Year brought war ever closer until in March came the shocking news that Germany had invaded Austria, while in the Polish Academy two of Zofia's former lovers, now old men, made life difficult.

'You are a monster, madam,' declared one. 'I've hated you for a long time – as a woman.' And he added a slighting allusion to her relationship with Bogusław, while the other, a major literary critic demanded that she return his love letters from long ago.[20]

Worse still, a critic wrote an article entitled *The Twilight of Nałkowska*. Deeply wounded, Zofia felt that she had one foot in the grave and was barely cheered by the immediate response from a younger writer and admirer, Tadeusz Breza (1905 – 1970), who wrote an article entitled 'Nałkowska's Splendour.'[21] Plagued with ill-health, even taking opium, Zofia kept writing *The Impatient Ones*, the darkest of all her books and, with no *Meadow House* now, found a new refuge deep in the countryside in the hospitable home of her friend Zofia Villaume, and Zofia's husband Gustaw Zahrt. Their house, Adamowizna, would become a refuge and sanctuary for Zofia and for many other beleaguered people in the dark days of the Second World War.

CHAPTER 14

Taken to the gates of hell

> Each of the figures of the novel is burdened with heavy luggage from
> the past and retreats into family memories [. . .] The whole gallery of
> rejects is brought together by the oldest of the clan whose funeral is the
> knot which ties the whole story together.

As the thunder clouds of the Second World War drew closer and the
papers reported ever more threatening news, Zofia felt as though she was
living through a re-run of events of 1914, only she was now twenty-four
years older and her life seemed to be slipping away.

'I'm like the old women in *Boundary*, tossed to one side, left on the
shore,' she wrote sadly as she struggled with *The Impatient Ones*.[1] Writing
never came easily to her, her books always went through many drafts, but
this particular book filled her with fear.

> The gloom and defeatism of *The Impatient Ones* contradict my own
> basic sense of harmony with life [. . .] I'm afraid for this book and its
> fate. I can't get on top of it, I know it's bad. These are not the usual
> writer's doubts [. . .] The whole process of writing fractures and
> deforms my original plan, nothing stays put within this broken frame
> (12.9.1938).[2]

This broken frame . . . having written these unwittingly prophetic words
Zofia went for a walk through Warsaw's Old Town and, in the dusk and chill
of that October evening viewed rebuilding work on Bonifraterska Street:

> The window frames of all four storeys had already been torn out and
> look like empty eye sockets, black and unspeakably threatening. Unseen

people were throwing piles of rubble from broken roofs down on to the pavement. It was all so astonishing, I didn't want to go away. I found the Arsenal on Długa Street, it had been restored long ago [. . .] Ach, and the Krasiński Gardens, the facade of the Palace, the water with swans, the marvellous perspective in the darkness, a jewel set against that dreadful district, a place which I've by-passed many times – and was in it for the first time in my fifty-three years.[3]

'That dreadful district' was the poor area in the north of Warsaw that was predominately working-class Jewish and two years later would become an overcrowded ghetto, eventually housing up to 450,000 people. Those 'empty eye-sockets' and piles of rubble would soon typify the city which would become one 'broken frame': Warsaw, the city Zofia loved and where she truly belonged. 'Why haven't I written about this?' she wondered. 'This is where my real patriotism lies.' Not in military slogans or in nationalistic cant, but in the streets and splendid buildings that were so soon to be blown sky high. Completely unaware of what was to come, Zofia captured her city in words before it disappeared for ever.

She returned from her walk to discover that Bogusław had finished his third novel. Zofia thought it was good; however, a phrase from the book haunted her, *ruins, ruins, everything is finished!* – more prophetic words which she recalled when Bogusław's younger sister, now a frequent visitor, said that she was studying for an exam on 'the means of defence against gas' and even 'against bacteria warfare.'

Zofia's fifty-fourth birthday in November passed without recognition. She attended the film of *Boundary* with her mother and was relieved to read good reviews and to hear that crowds queued outside the cinemas.

The New Year (1939) which was to bring such horrors began in the usual way with the enormous stresses of this difficult relationship between the eminent writer who was beginning to feel fame slip from her and her jealous young lover. Zofia lamented that books were all that she had left to her (soon people would be burning them for firewood). Bogusław had cut her off from her mother, from her friends and from fellow-writers. She couldn't listen to music on the radio because Bogusław wanted peace to write. Zofia lived in 'perpetual terror, in silence and frightened to make a single move.' She wondered why she put up with it. And yet Bogusław wouldn't leave, and even though they were deeply in debt Zofia continued to finance them both. Bogusław embarked on home improvements and still looked handsome when he shaved and was well dressed – but none of this mattered to Zofia any more. All her feelings, even negative ones were dead.

The terrors of her relationships with Jan Gorzechowski and with Bogusław, the imbalance between lust and love, desire and despotism were worked into *The Impatient Ones* and took Zofia and her readers 'to the gates of hell', as one critic wrote after 'It's a terrible thing . . . it opens an abyss in the place where no one looks for it, in everyday life.'

Domestic violence, love turned to terror, family life gone wrong do indeed open an abyss in everyday life; all these are present in *The Impatient Ones*, a book that baffled critics when it was first published, as it was so new and different they did not know how to place it within the literary canon.

'It made my head spin, I was so shocked,' said a critic, while another opined, 'It's a unique book, and not only in Poland, shocking and great.'[4]

The timing of the publication date of *The Impatient Ones* was unfortunate, right on the eve of the cataclysmic events of the Second World War. Small wonder that it was largely ignored on publication and was later by-passed by the Communist regime. It was ahead of its time, predicting post-war French novels, yet also harking back to Dostoyevsky, an author whom Zofia re-read repeatedly. The tightly controlled story is seen through the main characters without the author's comment, while Zofia was not afraid to write ungrammatically if need be, and to use startling metaphors and aphorisms.

Bruno Schulz, who reviewed the book in a literary magazine, wrote that Zofia had gone to the very depths of her being in her latest novel. She had exposed the roots of her consciousness both as a writer and as a woman for whom sexual pleasure and suffering were always necessarily linked. Schulz correctly saw that this new book, startling though it was at the time, is part of the complete symphony that is the literary output of Zofia Nałkowska, of whom her friend Wanda Melcer had said, 'You have to read her whole.'

In *Boundary* Nałkowska had turned time on its head, starting with the ending; in *The Impatient Ones* time is played out within a spiral. Schulz noticed that the novel breaks with chronological order in such a way that: 'Freed from the mechanical knots of time, Nałkowska [. . .] harmonises different parts of her novel and creates a mutual resonance.'

Schulz goes on to say that although the plot is slight and uncomplicated:

> Each of the figures of the novel is burdened with heavy luggage from the past and retreats into family memories [. . .]. The whole gallery of rejects is brought together by the oldest of the clan whose funeral is the knot which ties the whole story together.[5]

This novel is above all a family story. No one is rich or well-to-do, the characters are ordinary people who struggle with relationships and their sense of identity. It is the story of love and passion gone wrong. The keynote, as Bruno Schulz noted, is the baggage from the past that each of the characters, and especially the main protagonist Jakub, carries. Jakub says of himself, 'I am a sack stuffed full of the living and the dead, a collection of strangers.' And nothing could be more prophetic, for these words, written before the Second World War, exactly sum up the social and psychological trauma of Polish and Jewish survivors which the Communist Government did nothing to alleviate.

This core concept makes *The Impatient Ones* a novel of universal significance: in Europe two world wars had piled first trenches and then cities with unknown dead; in Eastern Europe too many dead lie in unmarked mass graves, while in the modern world we watch cities become bomb sites as unnamed bodies are washed up on alien shores. At the start of the twenty-first century Professor Maria Janion, a nonagenarian writer and critic, published a book with a highly significant title that shocked the Polish literary world, *To Europe, yes, but together with our dead*.[6] The dead here are the Polish Jews whose absence went unnoticed throughout the years of Communism. It is still a largely unvoiced fact that the loss of so many of one's nearest and dearest has left unhealed scars in almost every family both in Poland itself and among those of Polish descent living all over the world. The losses are territorial too: sorrow for eastern territories appropriated by Stalin in 1945 also haunts many hearts, a ghost that has never officially been laid to rest.

All this gives the problems woven through *The Impatient Ones* a very modern ring; it is only now that some Polish writers are trying to deal with the dead that haunt the memories of sensitive souls and bedevil the national psyche.

The twisted knots of family life, misunderstandings and love gone wrong make up the story of *The Impatient Ones*. The sins of parents are most truly visited upon the children – Jakub, an unloved son, fails his own children, while his second wife, Teodora, damaged as a child after her mother's suicide, cannot give herself unreservedly to Jakub. Her love changes to hatred and his to despair which in turn leads to murder and suicide – domestic crimes still reported almost daily in the media. Zofia confronts these desperate realities and draws the reader ever more deeply into their tragic truth. An English translation is underway, while readers in Poland, rediscovering Nałkowska have also come across *The Impatient Ones*. Many find this neglected novel a greater book than *Boundary*.

Zofia, however, had already started a very different novel that would take her ten years to complete. This book, later called *Knots of Life* opens with a splendid ball attended by the dignitaries of the Polish government who were shortly to flee from the gates of hell, first to Romania, then France and thence to the UK. The supposed 'twilight of Nałkowska' was in fact the nightfall of the Second Republic which she had first witnessed as it emerged from the political chaos at the end of the First World War. When the complete book was finally published, it was Zofia's swan song to the literature and the failed society of the nineteen twenties and thirties in which she had been a brilliant and sharp-eyed participant.

The account of the ball in *Knots of Life* developed from one that Zofia had attended in February 1939 in the splendidly renovated eighteenth century palace of the Ministry of Foreign Affairs which would be blown up five years later. Although clouds of war hung over the occasion, elegant crowds flowed beneath crystal chandeliers. Medals glinted in the lights which gleamed on the bare shoulders of women whose backless dresses made them seem half naked. The guest of honour was the Italian Minister of Foreign Affairs, Count Ciano, but it was his wife who attracted comment. She was Mussolini's daughter (his natural daughter, it was whispered). In the room where the distinguished Italian guests sat with their Polish hosts, Zofia noticed three Polish dignitaries, a vice minister (fat with slack jowls) and two aged, hugely rich countesses all staring frozen with horror at

> the unattractive, thin Italian woman [. . .] in whose dry body, under
> the skin of her bare shoulders flows the blood of the man who invented
> fascism and who seized Ethiopia [. . .], the natural daughter of a

political *arriviste*, a stone mason's grand-daughter and now a princess, countess and Minister's wife'

Having delivered her broadside at the guests and the ageing Polish aristocrats, Zofia turns her pen against herself and adds, 'As I left that room I saw something in the mirror above the long staircase took my breath away: that stout elderly lady was me.'[7]

Three weeks later, on 15th March, having heard the shocking news that 'Czechoslovakia no longer exists', that the German armies had entered Prague, Zofia went to visit her mother and her Aunt Janina, newly arrived in Warsaw from Lwów. Aunt Janina, said Zofia, was grey-haired, thin, very ill and old, but always good-humoured and charming. Janina shared some family stories and Zofia learnt for the first time that she had French blood, as well as her mother's Moravian genes in her veins. It turned out that Zofia's great-grandfather, had been a soldier in the Napoleonic Army who, bedridden with a leg wound, had never returned home. As a lover of France and widely read in French literature, Zofia must have been glad of that French connection, but for the moment the news from Prague was too shocking. Zofia recalled the sunny days she had spent there the previous June as part of a Polish delegation. She recalled a young woman who had translated her books and had been so kind to her and young people who had put on a gymnastics display, while the whole city was plastered with slogans, 'We'll never submit to anyone! We were, we are and we will be!'[8]

Four months later Zofia escaped from her critics, including that emerging talent, Czesław Miłosz who cruelly attacked *The Impatient Ones*,[9] from the conflicting agendas of Bogusław and her mother and travelled by train to Truskawiec, a spa in the eastern Beskidy Mountains, now part of Ukraine, to drink the waters, have a massage – and be plagued with bad dreams. Plunged into depression, she decided that this 'twilight of Nałkowska' was about to become night.[10]

A well-meaning acquaintance, Gizella, who had attached herself to Zofia and desperately wanted to write her biography, and also to rescue her, from Bogusław (who naturally hated her) had travelled to Truskawiec with her. Drohobycz was only a few kilometres away and Bruno Schulz came to visit. Zofia enjoyed hours of stimulating chat with Bruno who took her to visit his home town. Listening to Bruno's fluent, intelligent conversation, knowing how much he loved her, Zofia could hardly believe that she had given him up for Bogusław.

When she left for Warsaw Bruno came to the sunlit station to bid her farewell with a splendid bouquet of flowers and a cake baked by his sister; neither Zofia nor he could possibly know that they would never meet again.[11]

Zofia spent the month of August 1939 with her friend Zofia V, enjoying the peace of the Mazovian countryside, simple country people, sophisticated neighbours, wild flowers, twelve cats and hours of talk with her closest friend. She worked on her novel and was delighted when her mother Anna was also received in Adamowizna, Zofia V's hospitable home. As well as constant concern about the imminent war, the other blot on the horizon was the unexpected arrival of Bogusław, full of himself as usual, totally unaware of the bad impression he made on his hostess and her neighbours, spinning enormous plans, always just starting to write something really interesting – and with a huge negative mood swing if things weren't working out the way he wanted.

His stay had a damaging impact on Zofia's health, psychologically and physically. Her temperature soared, she shivered despite the lovely sunny weather, couldn't sleep. 'And all this was because Bogusław had made me get up at dawn and go down to the river barefoot in my swimming costume through the freezing dew just as the first rays of sunlight slanted through the trees.'[12]

Zofia returned to Warsaw on the eve of a war that was to take her and the city she loved to the gates of hell and thence into an inferno. Yet one thing always kept Zofia from total despair. Life. Zofia loved nature, she loved all living things and constantly wrote that it was a great privilege to be a human being on planet earth. Through thick and thin, in ill-health, sorrow and even despair, Zofia was always glad to be alive – and therein lay her endurance and her joy.

CHAPTER 15

Bombardment

If there were a Warsaw cultural prize for the best upholder of intellectual atmosphere during the five years of Occupation I would award it to Nałkowska without any hesitation.

'Strong, united, ready . . . we won't let them take a single button from our coats . . .' These slogans falsely reassured people all over Poland that war would be brief and Poland would win.

September 1st was always the first day back at school. School uniforms were neatly ironed, shoes were polished till they shone, text books, carefully covered in brown paper, were packed into school bags. The weather was glorious, but the long summer holiday had come to an end.

And then – it happened. Radios and loudspeakers announced the shocking news. The first bombs fell at dawn on the Warsaw suburbs. An astonishing array of well-equipped German soldiers, armoured cars and gleaming motor bikes crossed the Polish border at 5.45 am. Fighter planes flew so low that terrified villagers could see the swastikas on the wings and even the mocking faces of the pilots and crew who aimed machine guns at people working in the fields or driving a cart along country lanes.

Soon new notices appeared: 'The President of the Republic of Poland announces that our eternal enemy has today has commenced offensive actions against the Polish State, and this I affirm before God and before history [. . .]'[1]

In Warsaw people dug anti-tank ditches. Air raid sirens sounded. People were warned about gas attacks, although, as Zofia commented, they had no masks. She had a small first aid box with gauze, cotton wool and some medicine. Bogusław taped down the window panes. He was expecting to be called up, but no word came. Zofia was glad that her mother and sister were staying with friends in a manor house out of town. 'I intend to stay here in Warsaw, no matter what happens,' she declared, although she was dismayed to discover that the Academy had called off its scheduled meeting and with it the only hope of getting some money.

The next days were filled with uncertainty and contradictory news. The only constant feature of life was the wailing of the air raid siren and a warning voice, 'I announce an alarm for the city of Warsaw, an alarm for Warsaw.'[2]

At 11 am on 3rd September Great Britain went to war. France announced its decision at 5 pm, but the bombardment didn't stop. Friends telephoned or braved the air raids to visit one another, take counsel together and make plans. The big question was should they leave the city – or stay?

By the fourth night of bombardment Zofia decided not to go down to the cellar, and along with Bogusław, his young sister and her friend, sat in the hallway of their flat with their cases packed. Bogusław had even brought his typewriter. Bombs detonated, the typewriter click-clacked and Zofia marvelled that at moments like this Bogusław became dear to her again and she to him, in spite of all the scenes and tears. It was unthinkable that they might part now, so although Zofia would have liked to have gone out to the country to be with Mother she decided to stay with her lover in this strangest, hardest test.

Hearing that the Academy were offering lunches, Zofia went there, only to find that the place was empty. Cars were full of exiting dignitaries and streets were packed with pedestrians, laden with bag and baggage, all fleeing the bombarded city. There were no taxis or buses and on her way home on foot Zofia witnessed an appalling sight. Seven silver fighter planes, lit up by the sun, flew above her head and machine guns shot randomly – soon, she noted sadly, there would be not seven but seventy bomber planes blasting the city.

On 6th September the President of Poland Ignacy Mościcki (1867 – 1946) abandoned Warsaw and headed south-east towards the Romanian border with other government officials, adding to the sense of shock and betrayal, not just of the citizens of Warsaw but of the small provincial towns that suddenly hosted these dignitaries whose expensive cars clogged country roads among horses and carts and peasant farmers armed with pitchforks.

However, the Mayor of Warsaw, Stefan Starzyński (1893 – the place, date and manner of his death are unclear but it was certainly cruel as this courageous man was arrested by the Gestapo) stayed at his post, encouraging citizens with daily broadcasts which have become the stuff of legend.[3]

Zofia and Bogusław decided to leave. Zofia was worried about her caged birds, but managed to contact her sister's housemaid who agreed to take them back to the shop. This maid also promised to phone Hanna and her husband Mak to let them know that Zofia was joining the evacuation, along with another writer friend, Pola, and of course Bogusław, leaving behind all her letters and manuscripts, her father's papers, her new manuscript *Agata's Children* (later re-named *Knots of Life*), clothes, possessions and a second fur coat (she took one with her). Carrying this heavy coat, a suitcase, and of course a notebook and pencil, she set off towards the railway, along with Bogusław, to meet up with Pola Gojawczyńska (1896 – 1963) whose writing Zofia had encouraged to the extent of putting Pola forward for a scholarship.

The station was jam-packed – yet oddly enough no one gave way to fear as they watched bomber planes chasing like hunters through the reddened skies. People shook their fists at the enemy in a gesture of defiance. A new brand of satire and black humour sprang up – laughter was also a form of resistance, and Warsaw resisted the horrors of Occupation until the city was a smoking ruin.

So now, in the first bombardment which cost over 20,000 lives, jokes were bandied about:

Bombs exploded, houses collapsed in Warsaw and this chap got a bad attack of hiccups. Finally he begged his friend. 'I can't stand these hiccups, just give me a fright, old man.'[4]

Humour, yes, and solidarity. Zofia and her companions boarded an overcrowded train. People rested their heads on the knees of strangers and dozed in shifts but daylight brought more danger. The train was an easy target for bombers. Passengers dispersed to seek refuge in villages or hid under bushes while the driver tried to mend broken tracks. The glorious sunshine persisted, the sky was achingly blue and the aerial bombardment continued for hours without pause.

Seated beside the motionless train, Zofia met a highly placed acquaintance, unwashed, unslept, who calmly invited people for a game of bridge. Zofia felt happy that Bogusław was kind and caring, looking after her, asking her to stretch out on the grass, putting something under her head while she rested. She was happy too that wild flowers bloomed in the fields about her and she felt that she could almost forget the appalling crime that was taking place in those oh so clear late summer skies.

And so it went on, a little forward movement, then bombardment, hasty evacuation from the train while explosions burst along the track.

Zofia took refuge in a potato field and, flattened against the ground, covered in dust, unwashed and wearing the same clothes that she had left Warsaw in, she felt that her heart was literally beating against the bare earth, something she had only read about before. She only knew that she wasn't afraid.

People finally abandoned the bombed out train – many just dumped their luggage. Zofia and Bogusław were setting off on foot when, 'Suddenly, from out of a copse close by, an enormous bomber, travelling so low that it was like a car going along the road, flew right above our heads, shelling us with fire, It didn't do any harm except make a noise but the impression was weird.'[5]

Zofia and Bogusław joined a group of refugees who were walking for safety through a bombed forest where fallen trees had left enormous craters, trunks were split in half. A fellow-passenger shared some milk, they rested and had just set off again when a villager appeared from behind her fence and offered coffee. Overcome with gratitude, Zofia drank the sugarless weak brew. The woman refused any payment so they left something for her children. They sat in the yard on chairs that the family brought out for them and shared news and views about the war until nightfall when they managed to hire a cart and drive off into the darkness. The horizon was lit with the fires from burning villages, so the driver took a path through the forests until the next small village where he left them. Wrapped in her fur coat, lying on the ground in front of a little shop, Zofia dozed, while passers-by grumbled as they stirred up dust around her.

This incident went into *Knots of Life*:

At the edge of a burnt out village stood a small grocery store, all its goods almost completely sold out. People gathered outside, went in and out. At their feet, just in front of the little shop a large woman, dressed in a fur coat, lay motionless on the ground, resting on one elbow. Passers-by tramped close to her face. She must have fallen deeply asleep, exhausted, or else she had felt unwell after her journey, or perhaps she was dead. Nobody bothered to check.[6]

Zofia's war-time wanderings lasted for a month. On September 9th she and other women were given refuge in a parish priest's house where she parted with Bogusław. The decision she had agonised over for so many years was finally made for her in the teeth of terror. Bogusław begged her to escape from Poland with him, but Zofia refused. Her manuscripts, her father's archive, her flat and possessions (if they were still intact) and her ageing mother drew her back to Warsaw, so in the darkened hallway of the village presbytery, the lovers whispered their farewells. They were not to meet for another seven years.

The bombing continued. The skies remained pitilessly clear, refugees travelled by night and farmers ploughed after dark. The shocking thing was the state of barefoot, hungry, soldiers and disorientated depressed officers. Everyone wanted to fight – there had been victories, but no one gave orders and no one knew what to do.

Shedding more of her possessions, Zofia battled on, grateful for the chance to wash herself and her travel-stained clothes in streams or rivers, grateful to the country people who gave the refugees hospitality, hiding her own sorrow at parting from Bogusław and her worry about her mother. The grand lady of the literary salons was an asset to her travelling companions, never complaining, even when she had to camp out under the stars, wrapped in her fur coat, using her bag for a pillow, longing for a hot drink; when she was given some boiled water in a kettle she used her small supply of precious leaves to brew tea for the others in her group, which now included a married couple and their little daughter who shared this long trek.

Zofia wrote her diary in rare moments of solitude. Occasionally the company managed to hire a country cart. Once the driver was completely drunk and the horse was lame. Zofia noted the sorts and conditions of the refugees: the poor carried bulging bundles in bags made of hand-spun flax, the intelligentsia and officials had briefcases and smart little suitcases. The headgear was as varied: headscarves, hats, berets, caps, military uniform and the distinctive black hats of Orthodox Jews. People wore normal shoes, tennis shoes, ski boots or went barefoot, but all were alike in being hungry, exhausted, anxious and they all needed somewhere to sleep, and something to eat and drink.

People applauded Zofia's good humour, her social skills and seeming lack of fear. She charmed reluctant villagers into giving the tired refugees a bed on straw and a pail of water. This woman who had graced the company of aristocrats and diplomats, who was acknowledged to be one of the top three literary giants of pre-war Poland, could chat sincerely to simple villagers and listen to the stories of hardship of the people whose kindness she accepted with heartfelt gratitude. When a peasant woman, having made a large potato pancake for her unexpected guests, then offered Zofia and her companions a room and brought in straw for bedding, one of the refugees stretched out to sleep – and jumped up in alarm. 'We can't lie on that!' she whispered

'What, is it fleas?' Zofia asked.

The shocked woman shook her head.

'Bed bugs?' Zofia suggested.

'Not bed bugs, cockroaches . . . huge, enormous.'

Oh dear, Zofia thought. We've just been offered such good conditions, a roof over our heads, a room to ourselves and clean straw, and now this.

At this point their hostess came in. 'Well, so what? At least they don't bite.'

Zofia laughed, 'What a good thing they're tame,' she joked.

The man of the house thereupon removed the straw. The travellers wrapped themselves up in whatever they could – Zofia's fur coat had definitely come in handy – and lay down on the bare ground.[7]

Next morning Zofia got up early. The September heat wave was over, the morning was chill and Zofia didn't feel well, but she chatted to her hostess who was milking the cow and complimented her on the beautiful countryside around the village and on her garden. The woman smiled and became, said Zofia, completely charming and anxious to please. She told Zofia that the Germans had occupied the nearby town of Łuków one hundred and twenty kilometres east of Warsaw and on the main railway link. Zofia would have often passed through the historic town on her travels to and from Grodno, but there was no hope of a train now. Just the same, Zofia decided to return to Warsaw bombed and ruined as it was. Her writing friend Pola received an invitation to stay with local landed gentry. Their old manor house been a bishop's residence and was built in such a way that it shared one wall with the Baroque church. At Pola's insistence Zofia stayed with this family for the next six days, all the time hoping to find some way of getting back to Warsaw.

The house was crowded. Thirty people sat around the table: family, relatives, friends and refugees. Soldiers camped outside on the lawn, hungry, stupefied by the terrible turn of events and exhausted. People arrived and left, refugees in their own land. The hospitable landowning family fed as many people as they could and Zofia soon made herself the right hand woman of the lady of the house, who got up before dawn to start yet another day's work, bandaging the injured, many of whom, it was clear, would not make it home.

The cook told Zofia, with tears in her eyes, how she had brought some grateful soldiers fresh buttermilk – they were very thirsty. One officer refused to drink. A bullet had shot through his tongue and the roof of his mouth. Pus and blood trickled out of his mouth; the cook had then offered him raspberry juice and had cried as he drank. He had tried to thank her by stroking her head. 'Are you married?' she had asked. He nodded. 'Any children?' He held up three fingers.[8]

Zofia reported the story in the simple detached way that was becoming a feature of her writing.

Next day, though, she patted a 'gloomy brown pointer' and got her finger bitten in exchange. The wound became infected and she too needed first aid.

On Sunday 17th September Zofia joined the group of guests and the family from the manor house and, unusually for her, attended Mass in the seventeenth century church where, amidst the music and the prayers, she felt a whole ocean of tears rise in waves in her throat.

O, God, the things that have happened during these last few days! Our country seems non-existent now. There's no word from Kraków and Lwów, cities to which trains no longer run, to which you can't even send a telegram, from which no letters or newspapers come! Warsaw . . . I see it all from afar like impenetrable darkness, like a piece of space taken from centuries gone by. I try to think of small things, closely related to the affairs of this little corner. But at once I realise how frightfully alone I am among these people and how indecent it is to burden them with my presence.[9]

That evening appalling news shattered everyone who clustered anxiously around the radio. The Red Army had just invaded the eastern territories. Poland had become nothing more than a boundary line between Hitler and Stalin, between fascist and Communist rule, while in Warsaw the Royal Palace had been bombed along with the Gothic Cathedral of St John where Zofia had attended her cousin's wedding and the bridegroom's drunk father had caused such embarrassment. Civilians tried to rescue priceless works of art from bombed buildings in a city whose streets had become graveyards, while the Mayor encouraged his citizens with his daily broadcasts: 'Warsaw has given proof of its great character. To the splendid memory of the past we add the present deeds of the defence of our city.'[10]

Nevertheless that night also came news from the Commander in Chief that all Polish armies should retreat to Romania and Hungary without delay while the defence of Warsaw against the Germans should continue unabated.[11] Miles away from the city she loved, Zofia lamented:

O, shame, o sorrow! When the whole country is full of stupefied, hungry people needlessly set in motion, wandering to and fro, with volunteers whom no one is willing to sign up, soldiers abandoned by their commanders and throwing down their weapons by the roadsides. When defeat has been unavenged for countless years, when life is destroyed and ruins and destruction are everywhere. What madness! These sad crowds had been lulled to a deceptive slumber by false reassurances, not warned about anything, deprived of everything, told lies for months on end by the radio and newspapers and now these same heads of state are safe and sound abroad.[12]

Zofia longed to be back in Warsaw, to see if her flat had survived but meantime she helped her hosts care for the many hungry people who called at the manor house.

The landowners had a large herd of dairy cattle and could sell milk to refugees. They had also opened an unofficial bakery. Zofia and Pola volunteered to cut and weigh portions of black bread, so freshly baked that it still steamed. Needy people were given their portions free. Some of these clients told Zofia that they were traveling on to the outskirts of Warsaw, very close to Wołomin where Anna Nałkowska was staying. Zofia's heart leapt at the news, but there was no time to pack her few things and the wagon was overcrowded. With tears in her eyes and 'a thorn in her heart' she watched the wagon lurch away.

From incoming refugees Zofia learnt how dangerous things had become in Poland's eastern territory and she feared for Bogusław who had headed in that direction, but even more for Poland. The same mistakes were being repeated over and over again – vain trust in Poland's strength, empty boasts, proud phrases. It was all so infantile, lamented Zofia, such a lack of responsibility, always hoping that things would work out. 'A person of sober judgement, at the very least someone reasonable is immediately considered to be a bad Pole.'[13]

Zofia thought back to the problem of minorities in Ukraine and in Belarus that she had touched upon in her books, especially in *Unkind Love* and *Walls of the World* and wished she had been more outspoken, but even discreet allusions had been taken badly; she had always felt guilty and in the wrong. When people discussed the future of Poland Zofia could only feel pessimistic, unable to believe that Polish defiant patriotism and its aristocratic sense of honour would ever change.

She didn't share these gloomy thoughts, though, and noted that she was regarded as a model of courage, good health, endurance of character, someone not driven by emotion but by intellect – and always elegant. In fact, Zofia's quiet heroism and sheer endurance would be the hallmark of her war years even though her personal privations and the sufferings of others ate at her heart and soul. Unable to write anything other than her diary, unable to publish, living below the breadline in unheated flats in freezing conditions, Zofia held on, as her diary testifies. A pencil between her fingers and scraps of paper to write on were Zofia's lifeline and means of survival.

Knowing that Warsaw lay in ruins, Zofia nevertheless started on the dangerous journey home and arrived back on 8th October with three candles, a piece of soap, matches, some butter, cheese and bread, walking through countryside so well known to her but changed beyond recognition. People walked along the railway tracks, laden with baggage – either going to the city to sell provisions or returning home with bartered goods. One cyclist had a pack on his back out of which on either side in perfect symmetry stuck the white heads of two live geese.

Buildings were riddled with bullet holes. Zofia and her companion walked past dead horses and bombed out trains. Zofia's legs felt as though they didn't belong to her any more, they were so stiff and heavy and her hands were painful with oedema. Her companion took the milk can Zofia had been carrying and advised her to put her hands in her pockets, which brought her some relief.

And so, finally she reached her own building. There was no glass in the windows, but the house was still standing. Soldiers had sheltered from the bombing – about fifty men, Zofia later learnt, and had left 'a fearful mess', dirty linen, two pairs of spurs stuck into excrement. But her books were untouched and the concierge later brought up some of Zofia's clothes and the few provisions that the soldiers hadn't touched.

So after that twenty-plus mile walk, Zofia and her friend got busy cleaning and tidying. The whole process of getting the flat into some sort of order took the next ten days. Out and about in the war-scarred streets, Zofia met fellow writers and heard news of friends and colleagues. Friends advised her to leave the city and hide out in the country, but Zofia didn't want to be a hanger-on in someone's household, not even in Adamowizna, Zofia V's hospitable home.

Eking out a bare existence, Zofia brought her mother and Hanna home to her flat, a 'house of women' once again. Hanna's Jewish husband Mak had left Warsaw at the recommendation of his tobacco firm *Monopol* and, thanks to his connection with the firm, Hanna and Zofia were able to open a small tobacco shop where they worked from dawn to dusk, selling cigarettes and looking after their increasingly frail mother in ever worsening conditions.

'We are all living in a nightmare, longing to awaken,' wrote Zofia.[14]

The two prize-winning sisters, such important representatives of Polish cultural life, were daily at risk. Their work in the tobacco shop offered them a degree of cover from Gestapo agents, but a chance word could have them shot, or arrested and deported to concentration camp where so many Polish professors and academics perished. Random shoot-outs and raids made the streets of Warsaw highly dangerous – people never knew if they would be rounded up and deported to Germany as slave labourers, or shot on the spot. In addition, the German authorities kept commandeering Warsaw properties. Zofia and her mother were forced to move from one set of rooms to another, each more cramped than the last while Hanna took up residence in her workshop, until it too was bombed. Anna's own confusion and dementia added to the difficulties. She kept wanting to be taken out to cafes and other forms of entertainment. Once, as she alighted with Zofia from a tramcar she thanked the driver politely and informed him proudly that he had just rendered this service to a Nałkowska – thus putting herself and her daughter in danger of immediate arrest.

Cigarettes and the shop took over Zofia's life, so much so that a friend, Tadeusz Breza jokingly dedicated one of his own books, *To the great Mistress of Polish prose and to the modest owner of a small cigarette shop.*[15]

Zofia and Hanna shared the work, while at home Anna longed for diversion to drive away the ever increasing darkness of her disordered thoughts. The temperature plummeted, there was often no heating. They slept dressed in their outer clothing. Zofia bought two little stoves, but often there was no coal or coke.

The sisters had to collect their tobacco supplies from a warehouse, a long journey on foot across icy pavements, or crowded into the second wagon of tramcar with standing room only – the first wagon was 'Only for Germans' who sat in comfort. They made this journey in freezing conditions at five am in order to open the shop at six; if they waited until evening they had to trek across the ill-lit city, fearful lest they arrive home after the obligatory curfew at eight pm.

Yet, Zofia, fifty-five years of age, carrying her 'goods like a porter', walking great distances through the city she loved, felt overcome with delight as she listened to sleigh bells, a sound which brought back her childhood and, breathing the icy air, she remembered holidays in Zakopane and that one visit to Switzerland which had produced *Choucas*.

At home she wrote in bed with her hands numb from cold. Hanna came into the room, wrapped in a fur coat and told Zofia that it was -18 degrees *inside* the flat. They had managed to repair the double panes in their mother's room but the rest of the flat was like a fridge. Zofia went out in quest of coal the next day – and also paid the phone bill that Bogusław had run up last summer when Zofia had been in the spa at Truskawiec – so she was still paying his bills months after their parting.

The two sisters knew they were lucky to have this shop. 'No one is earning anything, everybody wants to sell something, to start a shop, to get into business,' wrote Zofia, and indeed a few weeks later her friend Wanda Melcer appeared at the door selling shoes, which she was carrying from house to house in a suitcase. Zofia bought a pair for her mother.[16]

Christmas Eve 1939 came and went almost unnoticed. Zofia had bought a tree but gave it away to a little boy who had come into the shop and didn't have anything for his family. The Nałkowska sisters worked in the shop

until five pm that day as usual and had many grateful clients. Their customers were all poor, all working men and boys and the sisters sold their cigarettes cheaper than elsewhere. Street urchins bought cigarettes from Zofia
and Hanna – and sold them at a profit on Three Crosses Square.

These street kids soon became a feature of the war-time life of Warsaw.
Thin, hungry and likely to pick their customers' pockets, their courage as
they carried on their forbidden trade and told jokes with cheeky humour
lifted the hearts of people who had been evicted from their plundered
homes and seen their prized possessions dragged out to the street:

'Listen, the travel agents are organising cheap tours to Berlin.'
'Whatever for?'
'So you can spot your own arm chairs.'[17]

One of these street kids, a boy called Wacek boasted to Zofia that he
was a born business man. He had begun his career by stealing cigarettes
from bombed out warehouses. 'Everybody was wading knee deep through
expensive tobacco,' he told Zofia. 'They were all helping themselves, so
why shouldn't I?'

Thanks to young Wacek's business acumen, Zofia actually earned some
money from her books. Wacek loaded her own copies of *Boundary* and
Unkind Love into a case 'as heavy as a rock' and hefted it around his sources.
To his amazement the books sold out, while to Zofia's equal amazement
Wacek refused to take any of the money he had earned, as he was
astounded that this lady in the cigarette shop was so famous and that her
books could actually bring in money – enough for three or four kilos of
butter and far more than the wretched earnings from cigarettes.[18]

Neither sister wanted to cheat anyone, although their honesty was
poorly repaid because the profits were minimal, barely enough to cover
the cost of buying the cigarettes, even after long hours of standing on the
stone floor in their unheated shop without any food or a warm drink, and
then doing the accounts, often until late at night.

Not only did Zofia have to learn the rules of profit and loss, she also
became familiar the brand names of cigarettes, their prices and desirabil-
ity. The little shop, full of poorly dressed men going to work, stamping
their feet to get warm, asking for papers to wrap around bare feet, became
as much a centre of discussion as her literary salon had been, only now

the talk was of war, of the cold, of lack of food and of relatives who had gone out and never returned.

At the same time Zofia was getting postcards and letters from Bogusław with fervent declarations of love. 'Life without you is a nightmare . . . my life is so bound up with yours that my solitary existence is unbearable.'[19]

Yet as she tried to restring the pearl necklace he had broken, to repair a book cover of beautiful Moroccan leather 'rustling like silk' that he had deliberately ripped with a knife and recalled how carefully she had kept all his notes and papers while he had destroyed her letters, these declarations of love meant almost nothing in the cruel, daily realities of overwork, bitter cold, the poorest of poor diets and Mother's needs. There was no meat, no eggs, bread was hard to come by, sugar had long since disappeared from their tea, they lived off porridge and tapioca and were glad of even a little milk.

To collect her cigarettes Zofia had to travel by tram through the 'ruined, Jewish district.' It was not yet an enclosed ghetto and would not be finally walled in until the 16th November 1940, but already in January of that year, Zofia saw 'pictures of frightful destitution, thin caricatures of people in rags, bent under heavy loads, everybody was dragging something along on little sledges or simply pulling their loads over the much- trodden, hard, dirty snow.'[20]

This owner of the little cigarette shop, chatting to workmen at dawn, also helped keep the literary and cultural life of Warsaw alive, even though she could publish nothing. Her writing was confined to her diary, itself a literary masterpiece and still a much borrowed book by older people in Warsaw's libraries who turn back to Zofia's diary to see what their parents and grandparents had lived through. Every reader of Zofia's war time diary marvels at her patience and endurance – as indeed all her friends did.

Tadeusz Breza, who had written the article *The Splendour of Nałkowska*, wrote in a post-war memoir:

If there were a Warsaw cultural prize for the best upholder of intellectual atmosphere during the five years of Occupation I would award it to Nałkowska without any hesitation.[21]

This accolade implies that Zofia took an active part in the secret literary life of Warsaw of which she gives the barest hints and suggestions in her diary; instead, as 1940 ended in severe frost and sub-zero temperatures, Zofia felt her life was a slow suicide, an empty life in which her longing for books and good conversation was as strong as her hunger for food.

Jokes were still being passed from one person to another:

> 'Hey, did you know we can't have a Christmas crib this year?'
> 'Why not?'
> 'Because the Holy Family is in the ghetto, the Three Kings have gone to London and Herod's in Berlin.'[22]

Along with the jokes, carols written in Warsaw and in places of Polish exile, gave a new and deeply-felt expression to the tragedy:

> O, Mother, put off the Nativity until another year. Don't let the Creator witness our torment and fear.
>
> Let your dearest Son be born upon another star, not in our saddest city, torn apart by war.
>
> Because in our city, which you remember from long ago, crosses are growing up, blood red against grimy snow.
>
> Because our children fall beneath shrapnel with never a tear. O, Holy Mary, pray for us, but don't come here.
>
> And if you do give birth in Warsaw among ruin and loss, you'd better throw your New-born straight on to the Cross.[23]

Ruin and loss . . . Yet in the midst of it all Zofia battled on, refusing to give way to exhaustion or her own increasing years; her mother's demands were now overwhelming. Anna had become stubborn and unreasoning, she had lost her grasp on reality. She wanted everyone to notice her, she repeated the same things over and over again, in the cafe or the tramcar or even out in the street, yet she was sweet and charming and Zofia loved her and freely dedicated herself to her in unselfish service.

CHAPTER 16

A rosary of deaths

The only reason I write is my desire to hold on to life, to guard it from loss and annihliation [. . .] I write to give continuation to myself. I'm filled with the horror at the thought that I will pass away without any trace.

The cigarette shop had become Zofia's war-time life. Vivid sketches of her customers in her diary show how war affected the lives of ordinary people in Warsaw:

It's been raining since morning, a damp cold invades the shop and my legs freeze without stockings [. . .]. That handsome man, F. appeared, tired, sad, growing ever thinner from worry and lack of activity. He has combed his black, shining hair so smoothly and is so well dressed in a suit – he only has two. And all in vain, it won't take him anywhere. Like everyone else he doesn't know what tomorrow will bring.

A nice elderly man in rags came in after him. 'Oh my goodness, sir, you're wet through,' I say.

He laughs, 'Ah yes, it's so wet out there.'

'Do sit down,'

'May I really? Thank you, I'll have a little seat because I've still got a long way to go.'

[. . .] 'Do you have some sort of work to go to?'

'Away you go! No, no work at all. I laboured for forty years and now I've got nothing.'

'How do you manage?'

'Ah, well, I hold out my hand to beg,' he confessed embarrassed.[1]

A little later, Zofia wrote:

There's a kind of theatricality in this shop. Every day before we close an elderly flower seller brings her buckets of flowers in from the street. She leaves them on the floor, trusting them completely to our care. There are enormous pink gladioli, huge carnations still tightly closed, golden zinnias, mignonette and beautiful exotic gaillardias [. . .] She tells us that her young daughter is married to a drunkard who beat her so badly that she had to report him to the police.

Among the customers is a charming old lady who comes in every day to buy a packet of the finest rustic nicotine that she shreds at home into the tobacco she can't live without. When we first met her she told us that she would reach her centenary in two months' time, so that means that she is over a hundred now. She's pretty and jolly, smiles with her toothless lips, her blue eyes are large and clear. She has her own flat so although her son doesn't give her anything to eat, because he hasn't got anything himself, he can't drive her out.

Another old beggar lady doesn't have a house, it burnt down, she has no bed or bedding, nothing at all [. . .]. She sleeps in a haystack not far from her burnt out house [. . .]. She's frozen to the bone and sits down on a chair in the shop until she dries out. She asks for some paper, wraps it round her bare feet and then puts on her soaking wet cloth shoes which are full of holes. She never eats anything hot [. . .]. She's scared, she has to walk so far in the rain to that haystack. Ach, she would certainly love to stay, lie down somewhere and drink something warm. Finally she leaves and although she's so grateful that she chanced upon us and told us all about herself, nothing changes in her life. She can't even go to hospital because they won't take her without documents, her papers got burnt and there's no way that she can get new ones.

A hairdresser comes in each morning [. . .] full of jokes and conversational skills. He confesses that before the war he 'played in the theatre' [. . .] closes the door from the street and with a carrying, splendid tenor voice sings away until the window panes shake. As soon as a new customer appears, he falls silent at once, take his four 'clubs' and disappears – and that little extract from a former life disappears like a grotesque hallucination.[2]

One day a rather irritable salesman arrived at the shop with supplies of cigarette papers. He asked the names of the owners of the shop. 'Nałkowska,' Zofia told him and heard him mutter, as he wrote her bill, 'Oh, what a name, what a name!'

'What do you mean, what a name?' Zofia asked.

The agent looked in disdain at this stupid shop assistant. 'I see that you have no idea who Pani Nałkowska is,' he said scornfully.

Zofia couldn't help smiling and the man stared in astonishment. 'How can this be? Is this really you, madam? Oh, but this is amazing! I've read everything you've written. I've always wanted to meet you. I can't believe that you've been reduced to this. Oh, madam, madam, I've seen some dreadful things in this war, but this is absolutely shocking.'

He went away, shaking his head in sorrow.[3]

Winter 1941 set in early. The arctic temperatures were unbearable. People shivered in poorly heated rooms – or rooms without heating at all. Out on the streets the icy wind blew snow into heaps that made pavements impassable, while blizzards of snow stung people's eyes and penetrated the warmest coat – and many people had no winter coats. Within the ghetto Jewish people were required to unstitch every inch of fur from collars and cuffs, from gloves and headgear and relinquish that along with their fur coats to their German masters. On the Polish side of the wall things were not easy either. A customer came in for cigarettes. He had a child's raincoat and a shawl on his arm and explained that he had just taken his children to nursery wrapped in these poor garments and was taking the coat back for his other boy to wear to school. He had carried the younger children in his arms because they had no footwear and how could little ones walk barefoot through the snow?

When conditions in the shop and at home exhausted her to the point of physical and emotional collapse, Zofia sought refuge in the country at Zofia V's house, where at last she could rest, recover lost strength, read and discuss philosophy with Zofia V while the two women washed their stockings. She also contemplated her next novel which would finally be called *The Knots of Life*. The characters occupied her thoughts day and night but she could do little more than make notes. She was profoundly grateful for her friend's unselfish care and marvelled too at Zofia's now seventy year old husband. His disabled body (his growth had been stunted by deformity) seemed so wiry and energetic as he worked in the garden, he then jumped into a horse-drawn trap and clip-clopped off to his pharmacy in Warsaw. This building on the edge of the ghetto had become a secret escape route for people who had been enclosed behind high walls since November 1940 and also a way to bring relief to starving people incarcerated in their own city on official rations of six hundred calories per person per day. It was a capital offence to enter or leave this enclosed area without permission. People who did so were shot on sight. Children who wriggled through gaps in the wall to beg for food for their families were brutally beaten and murdered. These child smugglers are among the unnamed heroes of the Second World War.[4]

Zofia responded to the plight of friends imprisoned in the Warsaw Ghetto. She gave packets of cigarettes to Antoni Reński, a seventeen year old Boy Scout and Resistance hero. Risking his life, Reński smuggled goods into the ghetto and smuggled people out; he was arrested, tortured and endured several concentration camps. He later wrote about some of his experiences in prize-winning books. The cigarettes Zofia gave him were designated for Janusz Korczak, Wacław Nałkowski's greatest friend.[5]

Dr Korczak, an internationally known paediatrician and children's writer and broadcaster could have escaped the ghetto but he chose to stay with the children he cared for in two Children's Homes – and finally went to the death with them in August 1942. Those cigarettes provided valuable currency with which to buy food for the children.

Zofia became aware of the appalling conditions in the ghetto when tramcar number 4 took her through the enclosed area. Armed guards stood at the entrance and the exit and the tram wasn't allowed to stop. No one was allowed to get on or off, but she glimpsed the overcrowded streets, ruined shops and bombed out houses. She refers to this only obliquely in her diary and says nothing about her own work with the underground, but it's clear that she continued to encourage young writers like Reński himself and another seventeen year old Alfred Rogalski 'little Alfred' with whom she discussed Schopenhauer and Spinoza and commented on his manuscripts. 'Little Alfred' perished in the Warsaw Uprising in 1944.

Although she could no longer write, apart from her diary, Zofia fed her soul with books. She read late at night, having done accounts until eleven pm. She read in the shop. She read in queues, on tramcars and in Zofia V's quiet house, she read German literature, specifically Wolfgang Goethe's novel *Wilhelm Meister* as well as the *Confessions of St Augustine* and her old friends, the philosophers, including Bergson, Hegel and Descartes, and many French and Russian classics. 'Reading,' she wrote, 'is not an escape from the frightful life we live today, nor an escape from people. It is rather a way of experiencing these things at the highest level possible, it is discovering oneself in this terrible world.'[6]

Reading was an act of resistance as well as of inner nurture and so were literary gatherings held under the guise of meeting friends. In spite of her increasing deafness and the constant hum in her ears, Zofia was always a marvel of attentiveness and conversational skills. She confided her coping tactics to Zofia V:

> I still manage somehow, the difficulties begin when people speak in low voices or whisper. I only ever ask someone in the family circle to repeat what they've just said. With outsiders I pretend to be a bit distracted, or I remain silent or simply change the subject.[7]

Despite this handicap, friends all remembered Zofia as a great conversationalist and an even greater listener Tadeusz Breza wrote:

> Nałkowska knew how to listen like nobody else, Afterwards there would be a moment of that splendid act of formulation with which without any previous planning she would interrupt the conversation with her usual, 'Stop, stop, wait a moment!' And then she took the thing that had just been said and gave it a brand new form, concise and transparent [. . .]. And how splendidly Pani Zofia narrated her own stories, as well as her literary and philosophical discussions.[8]

Secret literary discussions were held in friends' poorly heated rooms, or in her own overcrowded flat where her mother interrupted the precious moments of conversation with inappropriate comments. Zofia had to bite her tongue and try desperately not to say, 'But, Mother, darling, you've said that already, dearest. The gentleman knows all about that.'

Time was precious because no one was allowed to be out on the streets after eight pm (in the ghetto, curfew was at six pm).

During these difficult days a new friend came into Zofia's hard-pressed life, a dramatist and writer, Jerzy Zawieyski (1902 – 1969). They had met just before the war in 1939 when they had happened to sit in the same row at a theatre production. Recalling that first meeting, Jerzy (who had been born Henryk Feintuch), wrote that he had been amazed that Zofia was so large, tall and, as he put it politely 'generously proportioned.' Unlike most people who praised Zofia's low speaking voice, Jerzy found it rather harsh and noted that she had difficulty in pronouncing certain consonants. In fact, aged fourteen she had spent many hours in front of the mirror trying to correct a defect in pronunciation – according to Jerzy, she still had not overcome it completely.[9]

Jerzy had complimented her on her newly published novel *The Impatient Ones*, she responded with a smile and invited him to her literary gatherings, but their real friendship began when the German authorities forced the Nałkowska ladies to move house. Jerzy lived close by and soon visited them, winning the hearts of Zofia and her mother by saying that he had studied geography from Anna's textbooks. His continuing kindness to Anna in her last years of life touched Zofia. So many friends politely tolerated the old lady but Jerzy sat and engaged with her. Zofia never lost her feelings of gratitude to Jerzy for his support and care during those dark, difficult days and their friendship lasted until Zofia's death in 1954.

All too soon friends succumbed to the cruel realities of Occupied Warsaw. Zofia noted their deaths, recalled their lives and spun their names in her mind, as she said, like beads on a rosary, but one death later that year of 1941 assumed enormous, tragic proportions.

Hanna's Jewish husband Mak had left Warsaw in the first days of the German Occupation. He made his way to France. In August a letter arrived from an unknown source saying that Mak was seriously ill with a life threatening illness. The impact on Hanna was catastrophic. She couldn't write back – there was no address, couldn't send any sort of help and certainly couldn't travel to be with her husband and care for him. Thin, exhausted and almost mortally depressed, Hanna broke down completely. For the next four days the sisters wrote to whomever they could think of, begging for further news, hoping, as Zofia put it, that 'somewhere in this unknown dark Europe' some sort of explanation might be found.[10]

Hanna was so upset that when the next letter arrived she passed it to Zofia without looking at it. 'And how right she was,' Zofia wrote. 'She couldn't have known the truth and gone on living.' Zofia never told her sister the whole terrible truth revealed in that letter.

She took Hanna to the doctor who gave her an injection of tranquilis-
ers and conducted her by horse-drawn transport to her friends in Wołomin.
Zofia begged friends and colleagues from the tobacco company not to tell
Hanna that her husband had died far from home. Hanna reproached
herself bitterly that she had let Mak leave Poland alone.

Hanna was finally told that Mak had died painlessly of a heart attack. In
fact when in May 1941 the inexorable round-ups of all Jewish people, both
French citizens and foreigners, had begun, Mak, guessing the outcome
and not wanting to fall into the hands of the Occupying tormentors, had
jumped from the fifth floor window of the house where he had been staying. Zofia did not dare impart this dreadful news to her distraught sister.
A huge chasm opened between them, Zofia ached for Hanna in her grief,
while the weight of her own knowledge of the truth became obsessive.
Whenever she stood on the window sill to clean the windows, she thought
of Mak standing on the high sill in France, looking at the ground below on
to which he was about to throw himself. She thought about him when she
put blackout papers at the window, thought about him when she heard of
other deaths, wept for him when she walked alone through the streets of
Warsaw and one dreadful night when she and Hanna shared a bed in a
friend's house they talked in whispers all through the night, weeping
together for Hanna's lost happiness, for Mak, dying alone (of a heart
attack) and for the dark truth that only Zofia knew.

Zofia saw her brother-in-law in the face of an unexpected visitor, a
young Jewish boy from the ghetto whom she sheltered and fed. She
dreamt of this death, dreamt that she had told Hanna the truth and awoke
crying out to Mak, 'How could you have done this, how could you?' She
thought again of his horror and dread as he took that terrible leap into the
darkness, thought with dismay that Hanna, believing the story of his
heart attack, would certainly want his body brought home after the war
so that she could plan a memorial sculpture for her husband's grave.

A year later came news of other deaths. From August until September
1942 three hundred and fifty thousand men, women and children in daily
"batches" of from five to seven thousand were deported from the Warsaw
Ghetto and taken in sealed, airless cattle trucks by rail to a specially
constructed killing centre, Treblinka, sixty kilometres east of the city.
Janusz Korczak was just one among many whose names Zofia added to
her 'rosary' of memory. Schulz too . . . Bruno Schulz was murdered in his

home town of Drohobycz on the 19th November 1942, the very day a
contact in the Underground was due to rescue him. It is known that Zofia
had played an active role in the rescue plan, but there's no record of this in
her diary. It may be that this and much other material, particularly relating
to the death throes of the Warsaw Ghetto, were contained in a notebook
that Zofia destroyed one dreadful evening when the Gestapo raided
another flat in the house. Zofia lived her daily life with the constant knowledge that a single denunciation from a customer in the shop or from a
traveller on a tramcar could lead to her death, so now, having in her
possession manuscripts by several young authors, Zofia hastily stuffed
these incriminating papers into the stove. Had she been caught with them,
she would certainly have been arrested, her secret literary activities would
have come to light and the young writers would have been tracked down
and arrested or shot. Shocked by her own deliberate destruction of young
people's work, their hopes and dreams, Zofia then burnt her own notebook, a typical gesture of guilt. There is now a gap in her war-time account
for the period between September 1942 and January 1943. Zofia, whose
life was made meaningful by the act of writing, sorrowed for the loss of
this notebook, almost as if it had been another death, as indeed it was for
her, for whom writing was as indispensable as her own breath.

> The only reason I write is my desire to hold on to life, to guard it from loss
> and annihilation [. . .] I write to give continuation to myself. I'm filled
> with the horror at the thought that I will pass away without any trace.[11]

The destroyed notebook had contained material about 'mother and the
people on the other side of the wall.' Zofia had wanted to create their
memorial in the only way she could, with her words.

On June 6th 1942, that year of so many deaths, Anna Nałkowska had died
surrounded by the care of her beloved and loving daughters who had nursed
her devotedly. Her last years had plunged her ever deeper into dementia in
the pitiless conditions of Occupied Warsaw when her daughters had to stint
on food and Anna couldn't understand why. She had tried to keep darkness
at bay by demanding little outings, by playing the piano – when all else was
lost her poor thin powerless fingers still found their way over the keys.

'I owe everything to your father,' she had said before she died. And
then, 'I want to die now. It's for your sakes. I want to die.'

A new doctor arrived (her usual doctor was unwell) and tortured her with inappropriate care, cupping her, giving her enemas and injections while Zofia watched helplessly and Anna cried out, 'Please stop, I can't bear this treatment any longer.'

She died in great pain although the doctors had assured the sisters that their mother's death would be easy.

If Zofia's diary until then had given a precise and moving picture of the decline and eclipse of a beloved parent, it now became an elegy of love and longing, a requiem expressed in deeply-felt prose.

> We watched as the gravedigger enclosed her grave, as he shut the last opening with a brick – we, the ones closest to her, permitted that last insult which took her away from the world and from our lives for ever. O, thou wonderful, darling, childish one, thousands of times kissed by us, caressed, soothed, completely cared for, known, the only one, the closest one, completely transformed in love for us, always grateful and so trusting . . . trusting.[12]

Hanna, prostrate with grief, was full of reproaches that Zofia had 'driven' her out to her workshop instead of spending precious time with her mother. She left Warsaw to stay with friends, while Zofia spent four days with Zofia V in the quiet summer countryside. Hanna had lost her husband in circumstances that were still unclear to her, she had been unable to mourn for him at his graveside and her mother's death affected her so profoundly that Zofia realised she would never have survived the knowledge of Mak's suicide.

Zofia returned to Warsaw to deal with issues in the cigarette shop and to face the empty house, still full of her mother's presence, full of memories and full of the things her mother had worn and handled.

Zofia was not entirely alone, however. The Nałkowska ladies almost always had a live-in maid. Recently the maids had been university and college graduates who, conscious of the prestige of their diploma, had done only a little light housework and left the heavy work to the two tired sisters. However, a new 'most unusual' (Zofia's words) home help had appeared whose 'stubborn adoration' was going to accompany Zofia to her grave. Thirty-year old Genia was one of twelve children, of whom only five had survived. A village girl with only three years of basic schooling, she had been put to service when she was only ten, had eventually come to Warsaw as a housemaid and had entered Zofia's life sometime in early 1942. She had cared for Anna with great kindness, for which Zofia was eternally grateful; she dressed her body beautifully for visitors to pay their last respects and she was already exhausting Zofia with her almost puppy-like devotion. Later Genia would exasperate her mistress with her stubbornness, tyrannise her and create appalling scenes as Bogusław had done, dominate her completely and at the same time be a constant help and mainstay. Genia was the one who saved for posterity Zofia's manuscripts and letters, her father's briefcase and the piles of handwritten pages and notebooks that made up her diaries, literally snatching them from the flames in 1944.

Friends still called round. Jerzy Zawieyski always brought flowers and Zofia began to wonder if this might develop into a meaningful relationship, although she noted, 'He cares for me as a writer and not as a woman.' Despite her acute and penetrating analysis of other people's feelings, Zofia was perhaps too fond, or too vain, or simply too desirous of devotion to realise that Jerzy could not give her sexual passion because, like Karol Szymanowski, he too 'loved differently.'

August 1942 saw the anniversary of Mak's death and Zofia was glad to entrust Hanna and the shop to 'that strange Genia with her painstaking care and despotic passion' while she escaped the heat and horror of Warsaw for the quiet Mazovian countryside and Zofia V's tender care. However, Genia had become such a feature in Zofia's life that she soon accompanied the sisters to Zofia V's out in the country, where she quickly made herself at home.

August saw the continuing daily deportations of five, six, seven thousand people from the Warsaw Ghetto to their deaths. The sisters returned to Warsaw and visited their mother's grave almost daily – Zofia felt each visit like a homecoming. The cemetery was right beside the Ghetto wall and Zofia noted the impact of these massive deportations which emptied the once overcrowded area. 'That dead town, that place of terror and torment. All the windows and balconies, once so full of overcrowded people – are empty today.'[13]

And then came the break in the diary. When Zofia began again on 15th January 1943 she wondered if she should write it in a different way. But she knew that there was no other way: she had to provide healing for the terrible loss, the great gap left by all those deaths, especially 'those people' (the Jews of Warsaw) who 'were no more.' Their deaths were a kind of torment for her too as she tried to place herself 'within the knot of their immeasurable suffering.' Meanwhile the memory 'beads' on her 'rosary' kept growing. There were so many deaths now that coffins were piled up in the vaults of churches, queueing up for burial.

In April 1943, when Zofia visited her mother's grave she saw 'dark clouds drift above the fresh green of the trees, followed by flames like a long red scarf waving on the wind.' She knew what it meant: on the 19th April fighting had broken out in the Warsaw Ghetto, the first major act of armed resistance in an occupied country, and now the Germans were burning the area to the ground, house by house.

'To hear that over there [. . .] to think about it and live!'[14]

Three days later she reflected that reality is only bearable in small pieces, if we don't see the whole. Although the fires from burning houses from which no one had been evacuated were visible for miles around, news reached the Polish side of the wall only in anecdotal scraps, the echoes of gun fire, the smoke and those endlessly burning fires.

Jewish people in hiding in the Polish part of the city braved the risk of discovery and watched in silence, while, because it was Easter and a holiday, a now notorious carousel went round and round on the Polish side, with crude fairground music. Girls who had come in from the country screamed with annoyance as soot from the burning buildings landed on their Easter frocks.

This fairground and the terrible contrast between the two scenes, the jolly roundabouts and swings which went on while people were being burnt to death became the subject of a poem by Czesław Miłosz[15]. Many Polish people also found it deeply shameful and Zofia was ashamed and shocked too as she tended her mother's grave in the peaceful cemetery beside the burning ghetto area. On her side of the wall the dead had been buried decently beneath the ground, flowers grew on cared-for graves and people whispered a 'Hail Mary' or heaved a sigh to God, while Zofia wrote, in the vaguest possible terms, of 'the fate of those people far away, the fate of these people next to me.'

She was referring to the deaths in the Ghetto and also to the execution of thousands of Polish officers who had been systematically shot and buried in mass graves in the Katyń forest near Smolensk. One of the victims was Jan Gorzechowski's brother. The massacres had been carried out in 1940 on the orders of Stalin who consistently denied all knowledge of the missing Polish officers. When the German Army invaded Russia in June 1941, the mass graves in the forest were discovered and the Nazi Government, well aware of this propaganda coup, broke the devastating news on 13th April 1943.

So now in Warsaw's Powązki cemetery, as Zofia sat beside her mother's grave she thought about these deaths as well as the ones taking place right in front of her. She noticed a caretaker walk between the graves with a watering can, while on the other side of the wall she could see people jump from burning buildings.

In her diary she wrote brief notes, guardedly, to which she added explanations after the war:

> Above the cemetery wall, above the freshest spring foliage of the trees, black clouds rise like columns of smoke. Sometimes you can see flames fluttering in the wind like a red scarf someone is waving. To see this above the dark pansies around the grave and to think about it – and to go on living![16]

A little boy stood on one window sill, parents jumped with children in their arms and Zofia cried out to her diary, 'I can't hold out any longer, I have been changed for ever by them.'[17]

Changed for ever, yes, but Zofia was about to transmute these unspeakable crimes into literature. The caretaker with the watering can appeared in *Medallions*, now considered an indisputable masterpiece.

In this short story the 'cemetery woman' voices her annoyance at the sights and sounds from the other side of the wall. 'It's such a nuisance, you just can't get any sleep because of the shouts and the shooting, the weeping, the explosions and the smell of people being burnt alive inside their homes.' She offers her own commentary on the horrific events which Zofia reports in her story:

> 'They are people after all, so you've got to be sorry for them,' she says [. . .]. 'The worst thing is that there's no way out for them,' she said quietly, as if she was still afraid that someone would hear. 'The ones who put up a fight get killed on the spot. And if they don't fight they get

transported to death just the same. So, what can they do? They burn down their homes and don't let them get out. So mothers wrap up their children in whatever soft things they've got so it won't hurt so much and they throw them out of the window on to the pavement and then they jump out themselves . . .

And even when we don't see it happening, well we hear it like something soft slapping down. Splat, splat! They keep on jumping like that, they would rather jump out than be burnt alive in the fire [. . .]

She picked up her watering can and went off towards the yellow and dark blue pansies on the graves. Overhead a new plane flew over from the direction of the airport and, curving steeply, flew over the walls of the ghetto [. . .][18]

Thus Zofia moulded these horrific facts into an enduring mark of memory.

CHAPTER 17

That smoking wound

> I used to hate hunting because the hares experieced such terror as they were chased by the hunt or caught in a trap. Now I'm one of these hares, just like everyone else.

From the first days of German Occupation terror had stalked the streets of Warsaw as Hitler's henchmen ushered in a regime of unrelenting murder. Then, following the destruction of Warsaw's entire Jewish community, Nazi murderers went on the rampage throughout what was left of the city. German losses in the east intensified and there were fears that the SS and their helpers would wipe out the entire population of Warsaw. Random round-ups in every district of the city intensified. Everyone knew that the victims of this kidnapping were about to be killed, not deported for forced labour as had been originally assumed. It became an act of great courage to leave one's home. As violence on the streets continued, previously overcrowded tramcars ran empty and blood flowed copiously over the pavements.

Despite the terror, young people, particularly Girl Guides and Boy Scouts carried out daring acts of sabotage. The German slogan *Deutschland siegt an allen Fronten* (Germany conquers on all fronts) was quickly changed to *Deutschland liegt an allen Fronten* (Germany lies – has fallen - on all fronts)[1].

These actions had been carried out since the beginning of the war even though the young perpetrators knew that they faced the death penalty. If you were a teenager caught with a paintbrush in your hand defacing a propaganda poster or writing up the defiant slogan *Polska walczy* (Poland is fighting), you could be shot on the spot, or be taken away, beaten to a pulp and hanged. Street executions were an all too common and distressing sight, with bodies hanging from lamp posts or makeshift gibbets all over Poland, yet even this was turned into black humour.

> Hitler and Goebbels were hanged on the same gallows. 'I always told you our war would end in the air,' Hitler said.[2]

People were arbitrarily rounded up, carried away in windowless black vans, then shot at street corners. Their hands were bound, they were blindfolded and their mouths were filled with plaster of Paris. Thus they went to their deaths. Loudspeakers announced their names. On one occasion Zofia counted eighty such names and reflected that now it was happening to 'us' (Poles) as it had happened 'to them' (Jews). And just as the Jews had been unable to escape their fate, so too for the Poles there was now no escape from these huntsmen who stalked their fellow human beings.

> I used to hate hunting because the hares experienced such terror as they were chased by the hunt or caught in a trap. Now I'm one of these hares, just like everyone else.[3]

Women built makeshift shrines with candles and flowers to mark the places where these murders had taken place and knelt and prayed, men removed their hats. Each act of respect and remembrance provoked more vehement shoot-outs, more executions.

Zofia noted how indiscriminate the round-ups were, neither age, nor infirmity nor gender mattered. It could happen at any time to anyone, a frail elderly woman was snatched up and killed, along with two charming young boys, sons of different friends, one age seventeen, the other twenty. Zofia wondered how she would feel when it happened to her.

> I shall still be myself. Right to the last moment I shall remain the 'I' who will accompany me. I shall stay calm, because it's important to keep one's morale to the end. I shall think that my life was lengthy and fulfilled, given to me in its entirety. But they are young, their lives remain unfulfilled. They have mothers, children, wives and their thoughts will be with loved ones left without their care. Perhaps they'll remember the Motherland, or perhaps they won't think about anything

much, being filled with fear. And they will entrust themselves to eternity, which doesn't exist.[4]

Not all the executions were carried out by the German Occupiers, however. The Polish Underground had its own system of justice, law courts and punishments. In October 1943 Zofia was shocked to hear of the death of her dear friend from Grodno days, beautiful Zhenya Exé who had taken Zofia to the fish farm, an important setting in *The Impatient Ones*.

Zofia had given Agnieszka, her splendid character in *Unkind Love*, Zhenya's beauty, high spirits and charm – and now Zhenya was dead, shot by the Underground, accused of being a traitor, or a spy, or perhaps a mistress of one of the German Occupiers. Or perhaps it had all been a mistake, who could know? Perhaps in the end her beauty had proved fatal and she had been trapped into something with a tragic outcome.[5]

Yet, life went on, even though everyone now knew that the Germans wanted to annihilate the Poles. '*Ma nas nie być*' Zofia wrote in concise Polish.[6] We are no longer meant to exist. Yet somehow, living with this terror, you had to accept it, because what else could you do? The Nałkowska sisters and their indispensable maid Genia had been evicted yet again and were now homeless. They set up camp in the ruined loft above Hanna's bombed workshop, without water, heating or sanitation. Refusing to succumb to dirt and dereliction, Zofia cleaned the drawer of her desk in which papers had got damp from water dripping from the roof, washed the china and arranged the cups and saucers carefully on a shelf. Then she dabbed on some French perfume, donned her 'marvellous' fur coat and a little felt hat and went out to brave the terrifying streets in order to take roses to a friend.[7]

Eking out an existence in the leaking, freezing loft of Hanna's one time workshop, Zofia still received friends. Literary discussions continued. One topic gave everyone pause for thought. What would Poland be like after the war? Would writers be able to work freely? The Battle of Kursk in the summer of 1943 had broken the German offensive. It was all too clear that the Soviet Red Army and not the Allied Forces would be the ones who would liberate Poland and now Zofia received secret visitors, people, she wrote cryptically, 'who held different opinions, dangerous and threatening.'[8]

Meantime, at risk of being caught up in a mass arrest, she still coped with the shop. It was too dangerous to travel by tram to the store for fresh orders. She went on foot, listening all the time for the sound of gun fire, wondering which streets were being attacked, on the alert, she wrote, like an animal in a jungle. In the shop she listened to peoples' stories of their personal tragedies. An elderly woman had lost both her sons in Auschwitz and now parented her grandchildren. Several regular customers had 'disappeared.'

One day as she was busy serving customers she heard a loud knocking at the side door. Two German soldiers entered, wearing helmets, armed with machine guns and grenades. Everyone froze, but, wrote Zofia, fears were unfounded – they just wanted to buy cigarettes – though no one knew why, when 'they have better ones and can buy far more.'[9]

Zofia's fifty-ninth birthday on 10th November 1943 went unnoticed except for a comment in her diary.[10] It was freezing in the loft. Food short-ages became ever more desperate. Even the mice in the loft were hungry – Zofia fed them with crumbs and little scraps of food. The daily death toll continued unabated. Zofia added more and more names to her 'rosary'. And again she thought of the Jews in the Ghetto who had lived with death stalking them day after day:

> They got on with their daily lives, got up, got dressed and ate some-thing, knowing all the time what was going on around them. And now it's the same for us. The only way out would be to keep some poison handy at all times. That's quick and easy. But there isn't even any of that.'[11]

On Christmas Eve 1943 Zofia attended a gathering of writing friends. Young male friends, confided their love triangles to her, never guessing that the various participants in these 'knots of life' had done the same. Maria Dąbrowska was there and Zofia chose her table, thinking that this was 'the thing to do', rather than sitting with her young male friends. Maria records the event in her war-time writings. 'Pani Zofia came sailing towards us,' she commented a little icily.[12]

The next day another gathering took place, with rather a lot of alco-hol flowing. Zofia drank *bruderschaft* with Tadeusz Breza, thus marking the moment when they could now call themselves by their first names and use the informal, intimate 'ty', thou. In reality, however, this gathering was to discuss an important matter that saved Zofia and others from destitution. A writer closely involved with the Underground, Zbigniew Mitzner (1910 – 1968), whose unofficial agent was a young and 'unfriendly' Czesław Miłosz, offered contracts to writers for future publication.[13]

The New Year 1944 plunged Zofia into troubled thought and difficult decisions. On the night of 21st December 1943 these men 'who held different opinions' from the present Underground Government took the first steps towards forming a Communist post-war government, the National Home Council, *Krajowa Rada Narodowa*, KRN. This group declared the pre-war government to be illegal along with its war-time successor, the Polish Government in Exile and formed its own People's Army, *Armia Ludowa*, (A.L.) as opposed to the Polish Resistance's active Home Army, *Armia Krajowa* (A.K.).

Their representatives asked Zofia to join them. She had always held left wing views and had taken a critical stance against the pre-war Government as seen in books like *Boundary* and later in *Knots of Life*. Having watched the members of that government take flight in comfortable cars at the start of the war, leaving Poland leaderless, she didn't think much of these men who 'sat at their desks' in London. Nevertheless, she passionately believed in freedom of the word, spoken and written; she never espoused Stalinist doctrines and so she wrestled with her conscience, wondering what decision to take. In her diary she writes that she initially refused, saying that she wasn't competent to serve in that capacity but later, as soon as the war ended, even before the final German capitulation Zofia attended a meeting of the new Government in the ruins of Warsaw. She also served as a representative in Parliament and a minister for the former German area of Opole.

Struggling with these issues, shocked by the scenes she saw around her in the streets, living in the most primitive conditions, Zofia turned to books on biology, physics and psychology and armed with this new reading list spent five or six weeks with Zofia V in Adamowizna, working on her novel and all the time aware of the horrors that were happening in Warsaw.

She had borrowed a book on cognition and logic from a reading room and noticed it bore a stamp from a library that had been inside the Ghetto.

17. Zofia and her husband Gorzechowski's house in Grodno.

18. Zofia and Gorzechowski with their pets, including the greyhound Diana and the deer Basia, Grodno 1924.

19. Jan Gorzechowski in his office. A former war hero who fought for Poland's independence, in 1922 he was appointed Lieutenant-Colonel and Chief of the Military Police in Vilnius and Grodno.

20. PEN Club party in honour of the Russian poet Konstantin Balmont, 1927. Zofia is standing behind Balmont. On his left the writer and translator Tadeusz Boy-Żeleński, and on his right the writer Ferdynand Goetel, the poet Julian Tuwim and the socialist politician Andrzej Strug.

21. Pastel portrait of Zofia made by Stanisław Witkiewicz, 1930. Commonly known as Witkacy, he was a famous painter, novelist, playwright and philosopher. The original portrait is now lost, probably destroyed during World Warr II.

22. Zofia with Karol Szymanowski, the greatest Polish composer of the 20th century, and his sister Stanisława, a renowned singer, Zakopane 1931. Szymanowski was a closet homosexual and a close friend of Zofia's, and she was deeply in love with him.

23. Michał Choromański, Szymanowski's young protégé Zofia had a brief affair with, late 1930s.

24. Bruno Schultz, one of the greatest Polish writers of all time, and close friend of Zofia's.

25. First cover of Schultz's *Sklepy cynamonowe* ("Cinnamon Shops"), 1934. Schultz was a high school teacher at the time while Zofia was already a great literary figure: the first to recognise its greatness, she was instrumental in the publication of the book.

26. Bogusław Kuczyński, Zofia's young and tyrannical lover who lived with her until the outbreak of World War II, late 1930s,

27. Truskavets spa, now in Ukraine, where Zofia met Bruno Schultz for the last time in 1939.

28. Three Crosses Square in Warsaw during the Nazi occupation, 1940.

29. Ruins of the Warsaw Ghetto, which Zofia
famously evokes in her short story collection *Medallions*.

30. First cover of *Medallions*, Zofia's
masterpiece and main text for
Holocaust studies in the U. S., 1946.

31. Tablet commemorating the
"corpse factory" in which soap was
produced from human bodies,
Stutthof concentration camp.

32. Holy Cross Church and Staszic Palace,
with figure of Christ among the ruins, 1946.

33. Bust that marks Zofia's grave, made by her sister Hanna.

34. Zofia's grave in the Powązki Cemetery in Warsaw.

35. Front view of the *Meadow House*, now a much
visited museum hosting cultural events.

That library stamp made Zofia ponder on the intellectual and institutional life that had gone on in the face of death behind those high walls.

> They loved to read, those young girls who worked in warehouses, boys who worked in shops – they were all great readers. And there were shelters for old folk over there, nurseries and institutions of all kinds.[14]

While she was away from Warsaw Zofia reflected day and night on the proposition that the secret agents of the future Communist regime had made to her and found herself tied in a knot of complexity. A woman of words, she was afraid of words that 'are a pretext for hatred, fighting and bloodshed'; afraid too of 'the frightful obvious lies expressed in a naïve, flowery garland of words.' As ever, she could see both sides of any argument and although she had always wanted a left-wing government, she was afraid of what a Communist regime would bring. 'It's always been my thought, but now that it's expressed in someone else's words it is transformed into terror pure and simple.'[15]

The 'acquaintances' who had visited her with their proposal had warned her that the Front was coming ever closer and expressed their fears of the inevitable fighting and air-raids, fears too that, even pitted against the increasingly victorious Red Army, the Germans might still win. However, in July 1944 the Red Army along with the recently formed Communist Polish 1st Army marched to eastern bank of the River Vistula. This army consisted of Poles who had been taken prisoner in the Soviet Union, as well as others (including a number of Jews) who had escaped into the USSR before 1941 when the German invading armies had marched into Russia. Many of these soldiers too were citizens of the Polish Eastern Borderlands which had been occupied first by Stalin in 1939, then by Hitler in 1941 and had been recaptured by Stalin during the western progress of the Red Army in 1943/44. During this time fighters in the Home Army and other branches of Polish Resistance were captured and executed while civilians in Volhynia (Wołyń) had been massacred in a genocide that has been all too little reported. Secret conferences between Churchill, Roosevelt and Stalin in Tehran in 1943 and at Yalta in 1944 had already effectively delivered these territories into Stalin's hands.

Warsaw was turning into a battleground, with barricades and barbed wire in every central street. Zofia still worked in the shop, talking to people who had no idea that she was torn inside with indecision as her customers voiced their patriotic slogans of 'God, Honour and the Fatherland'. These slogans were a given in Poland with its long tradition of fighting 'for your freedom and ours'; always actively engaged in resistance to tyranny with courage and daring that were second to none. Zofia felt committed to sharing the fate of the people of Warsaw although she disagreed with the assassinations and death sentences carried out by Underground paramilitary groups in the name of these same slogans:

> In this tiny, cramped space between the enormous might of two powers which are fatally matched, this narrow strip of the world, a few outdated mistakes and illusions are still locked in struggle. I am caught up in fierce forms of hatred against my will. Between executions, continual evictions, bombs, tanks, trucks, military convoys hurtling across this city, I chance upon all these confidential accusations, abductions, assassinations which are carried out in identical good faith and emotional correctness. Oh, how strange, how sad and how terrible! Yet I still look after the shop [. . .] people in the queue are amazed that they can get every brand of cigarette here, and even more than anywhere else. The accounts tally and the whole thing is running punctually and smoothly.[16]

On the same day that Zofia was balancing her books, a new Communist government was formed the historic city of Lublin, while in Warsaw the Home Army, on orders from the Polish government in exile in London, prepared for an Uprising. Only too well aware of what Soviet government would mean, and seeing German control slacken (alas, as it turned out only temporarily), the Poles wanted to clear the Germans out of Warsaw in order to negotiate with the Soviets as free citizens of an independent, democratic country.

It was never to be.

The Uprising broke out with initial success on 1st August 1944. Zofia, Hanna and Genia had fled to Adamowizna, where Zofia V, usually a rock of calm support, was prostrate with worry for her husband Zet, who was still in the city. The numerous 'guests' in Zofia V's small manor house, all hiding from the Gestapo, included a Jewish lady. Perhaps it was around this time, Zet having returned safely from Warsaw, that a local man, an ethnic German called Wahl, turned up at midnight with four Wehrmacht soldiers and, hammering with their rifles on the door, demanded entrance.

Zofia V pushed her irascible husband to one side and opened the door. Booted feet followed her through the hall as armed men pushed their way through the house.

'I looked at Zofia,' wrote Zofia V in a letter to the author of her exhaustive and definitive biography, Hanna Kirchner. 'She was white, even her lips had gone pale. Leaning against a pillow she stared stubbornly, fearlessly at Wahl.'

The soldiers arrested two young refugees from Warsaw who were to be sent for forced labour to Germany. Zet, swallowing his repugnance, treated Wahl to a liquid lunch next day and when he was well mollified, Wahl ordered their release and then asked, 'Who was that white-faced lady whom I saw in your house yesterday?'

Zet hastily gave a made-up name and Wahl continued, 'What amazing eyes she had! I've never seen such piercingly blue eyes in my life. They looked as if they wanted to kill me. I'm not a coward, but I was terrified. Those eyes said, Memento mori (remember that you will die).'

Six months later Wahl was shot dead in the street by a fighter in the Polish underground.[17]

All too soon other refugees came, bringing horror stories of massacre in the district of Wola, where Ukrainian men in Vlasov's army now ran amok, gang raping and plundering, tearing gold teeth out from their victims' mouths, stealing wedding rings, watches, jewellery. A ten year old girl who had been gang raped was seen with her face swollen from men's bites, while her internal injuries were so severe that blood soaked the stretcher on which she lay.[18]

As Zofia tried to care for refugees, she reflected on the facts of war and concluded that the horrors and bloodshed all boiled down to human agency. She penned words that would become famous: people prepare this fate for other people.[19]

Soon the fires that were burning in Warsaw could be seen from Adamowizna. Already on the 7th August refugees from the burning city arrived, many on foot, bringing more horrific stories of atrocities, of buildings being set on fire, street after street, district after district, of people being dragged out into the yard and shot. Zofia anguished over the young insurgents who 'like children had been dragged into the deadly game of war, dying in their tens of thousands, always heroically and always unwisely.'[20]

She couldn't understand why the insurgents in Warsaw hadn't waited for the Red Army to move in against the Germans, unaware that Stalin had given orders that the Red Army, with its Polish divisions, should not make a single move. Warsaw, 'that smoking wound on the map of the world', was doomed to burn to the ground before the Soviet armies 'liberated' the ruined city.

Zofia began to tick off the names of the districts that had gone up in flames. She thought of her lost life in the city she loved, and, above all, of her friends, of their voices and smiles, their experiences and the friendships that meant so much to her. 'I don't know if they are alive, or if they have died, changed into dirty ash, in the black, stinking mud of burnt corpses.'[21]

Refugees continued to flood out of the burning city. They came wearing only the clothes they stood up in. They were exhausted, hungry, wounded and bereft. Some had escaped from a transit camp in Pruszków about ten kilometres from Warsaw where people were loaded on to trains to be deported to slave labour or concentration camps. Women and girls were sent to Ravensbruck. Sick, wounded and dying people were left out in the open with no help or refuge. It was now three weeks since the Uprising had begun and there was no news of the faithful housemaid, Genia, who had returned to the burning city. There were so many refugees that the manor house was overcrowded. There was almost no food left in the house, nor any money to buy some. Zofia took her share of the heavy housework, washing the floor, carrying buckets of water from the well, lighting the stove and washing piles of dishes.

As the valiant fighters were forced to give ground, people began to escape through the network of sewers, from which many were never to emerge. The wave of terror increased, yet the insurgents kept fighting, forgetting their political divisions, as bombs fell and mines and grenades exploded. 'Warsaw,' wrote Zofia only too truly, 'is to be burnt to the ground.' She was worried about Genia who suffered from asthma and 'was terribly afraid of shootings and bombs' and who had insisted in returning to Warsaw, 'wanting most likely to try to rescue some of our things.'[22]

The manor house was full. People were sleeping on the floor, in the corridor when suddenly Hungarian and Slovak soldiers (fighting on the German side) quartered themselves in the stables and barns. They stole plums, walnuts and apples from the garden, but they were gentle and friendly, however, Zofia knew very well that these friendly Slovaks and their gallant Hungarian officers just had to receive a single order and they too could wreak havoc, rape and kill. So now with a broken spade and a dinner plate, Zofia dug a deep hole in the sandy soil of the garden and dropped into it a heavy suitcase full of her manuscripts and a cardboard box with her diaries. She felt as though she had buried part of herself.[23]

Zofia heard that some friends were safe, but worried about 'dearest' Jerzy Zawieyski who had sent her a card reproaching her that she had left Warsaw without telling any of her friends. By October there was still no action from the Red Army and on 2nd October the defenders of Warsaw were forced to capitulate. German terror did not stop. People were herded over mounds of rubble and shot if they stumbled or lagged behind. The weather had turned cold. An icy wind made life even more wretched. Zofia and Hanna sold what they could, but money was becoming worthless and tempers were frayed, adding to the tension and misery.

Meantime, Warsaw was still being destroyed. It had been part of the Nazi plan right at the start of the war that Warsaw should be totally annihilated. German soldiers continued to lay waste to the city whose resistance had lasted sixty-six days, far longer than anyone had anticipated. The non-participation of the Red Army aided and abetted the enemy, while in Lublin the self-elected Polish Communist Government declared the Uprising illegal and described its leaders as traitors.

Finally on 17h January 1945 the Red Army, along with the Polish 1st Army under General Berling entered the eerily empty ruined city and proclaimed themselves liberators and victors.

Lying ill in bed in Adamowizna, Zofia heard the sounds of machine gun fire. Genia, who had finally arrived safely in November 1944, opened the small window in Zofia's room and reported that the main road was full of traffic and of soldiers. So now there were new uniforms on the roads, and a different language. Zofia, ill with a rising temperature and a bronchial cough typed up the drafts of her novel, *Knots of Life*. She felt an enormous sense of relief, coupled with something akin to disbelief. The arrival of Polish soldiers linked to the Red Army had happened so suddenly that the refugees in Adamowizna had to adjust to this new reality. Living with the expectation that they too could be deported at any minute they had not laid in stores of food, which was so scarce anyway. So now their diet consisted of black bread and potatoes. They had no candles, no matches, no oil; darkness fell at four pm and lasted until seven the next morning. Hanna had an ear infection, Zofia had bronchitis. There was no medicine to be had, but quite unexpectedly visitors arrived, a writer and an editor both known to Zofia before the war. Jarosław Iwaszkiewicz, Karol Szymanowski's cousin and a lifetime admirer of Zofia and her work, had directed them to her. The two men wore the uniform of the Polish 1st Army. For Poles in every part of Poland the sight of Polish uniforms after five long years was a revelation – Zofia called it 'exotic'. There was however one puzzling omission. These new Polish soldiers wore the traditional silver eagle in their berets – but the eagle had no crown, a sign of the political changes that were taking place.

Zofia welcomed the men who told her that schools were being re-opened, architects were being drafted to re-build Warsaw 'that city without any addresses'[24] and publishing houses were starting work once more. With her usual perception, she realised that this new mood was a happy honeymoon period: the new regime would soon tighten the screws. Nevertheless, she was glad that positive things were happening. A fifth edition of *Boundary* was proposed, the first instalments of *Knots of Life* were to appear in a new literary magazine, *Odrodzenie* (Renaissance). The industrial city of Łódź was intended at that stage to be the new workers' capital of the Workers' State and apartments formerly occupied by ethnic Germans had been designated for the use of writers.

'They want to take me there by car, but I am too ill,' Zofia wrote. Nevertheless, she was conducted safely to Łódź along with her friend Pola in a lorry crammed with books rescued from the ruins and with other passengers. The lorry was in a poor state, the roads were no better, the tyres had to be changed three times and the police curfew caught the travellers while they were still on their way. They had to seek refuge in a house beside the road and proceed next day. The young man who had organised the lorry always recalled not the dire conditions of the journey, but the chat on the way as Zofia animatedly analysed the current (very complex) situation and discussed the new possibilities opening up for writers.

So Zofia settled into a sparsely furnished flat in Łódź. A letter to her 'dear' Jerzy Zawieyski gives a brief and vivid description of the fluid, uncertain situation in Poland during these final days of the war:

Here in Łódź there's such a messing and melding of all kinds of stuff, a meeting of people, epochs and places, no foreign city has ever seemed so exotic or cosmopolitan. People from the forests, people from Moscow, from prison camps, from concentration camps, from the ghetto, people about whom we only learn now what their role was in the Underground, what Majdanek really was, or the forest. Only now can I build into my awareness the complex entirety of these years of war. What a spectre! How strange it all is, like the uncoiling of a twisting theatrical scene![25]

It was also dangerous. Trigger happy young partisans representing all shades of political opinion, schooled to obey the most solemn vows, now came out of hiding in the forests or the underground to hear a foreign language and see foreign uniforms on the street – those 'people from Moscow.' For some these 'comrades' were brothers and were welcome; for others they were anathema, a festering sore, salt in the wounds of injured Poland and a symbol of their nation's betrayal.

And now Zofia embarked with total dedication upon a new piece of work as vice-president of the newly formed Commission to Investigate Hitler War Crimes. Life was happening and she was actively engaged in it once more.

CHAPTER 18

Cameos of crime

You alone, no one else, no one in Poland is able to write like this. If you had written in French or English or even in Norwegian you would have been the most famous writer in the world. That incredible precision, that masterful concision – this is all so shattering because it has been done so simply.

Sixty year old Zofia felt her batteries recharged with a new impulse of life and action. Her friends were amazed at her energy and enthusiasm. In spite of her earlier refusal to take part in the new Communist Parliament, she attended its first meeting in the ruins of Warsaw on the 3rd of May, a national holiday which was soon to be replaced by the 1st of May. This first multi-party session seemed to be the voice of left-wing democracy – as opposed to the single party state that lay too immediately on the horizon.

Desperately wanting to believe in the new regime, Zofia stayed with other delegates in Hotel Polonia on the central Aleje Jerozolimskie – Jerusalem Avenue. The hotel had survived destruction although the rooms were unheated, 'icy cold,' wrote Zofia. The view from her window showed her the bombed city centre like a vast amphitheatre, with the remnants of Central Station, splendidly rebuilt before the war, sticking up out of the rubble, a massive skeleton. Just the same, a tram was running along the repaired tracks and people rushed towards it. Others simply flagged down whatever mode of primitive transport might take them to their ruined homes. The city was dotted with scraps of paper pinned to door frames, to torn out window frames, to piles of rubble. These strips of paper contained a whole story of loss and longing: each one bore a name as people sought lost relatives, hoping against hope that someone would come back alive.

A fever of rebuilding had already begun – later the regime would use this enthusiasm for its own ends. Zofia rejoiced that she was part of this outburst of life. When her name was read out in Parliament the auditorium responded with applause.[1]

On 9th May the Second World War ended. The news shook the ruins, 'which are still a city and are still Warsaw' wrote Zofia.[2] Gun shots cracked in celebration, red and white lights flickered across dust and debris and rockets lit the sky.

Zofia had travelled back to Warsaw from her rooms in Łódź to meet her childhood friend Hela Boguszewska (1886 – 1978) and Hela's companion Jerzy Kornacki (1908 – 1981). Hela and Jerzy had set up a writing partnership in 1934 and were partners in life as well, despite the twenty-two year old age gap. They had connected with the new Communist government in Lublin in 1944 but were already disenchanted by the posturing of the instigators. They set up the Commission to Investigate War Crimes, with Zofia co-opted as vice-president. They had already met in Kraków, that undestroyed city, 'embroidered through and through with memory,' Zofia wrote.[3] Before this visit to Warsaw she had gone on a walk through Kraków, visiting old, familiar places, remembering her lost love, Edmund Szalit who had been killed in 1915, recalling the time she had spent in the city with her father when they attended Brzozowski's trial and also looking for the house where her grandmother had lived.

She had also enjoyed good coffee with real cream for the first time in six years and met Jerzy Zawieyski almost every day. 'I am loved,' she concluded, though there were puzzling aspects to this 'kind, dear, timid' man's devotion.

Jerzy Z and Zofia bought ice creams on the Market Square where they were happy to see that the Renaissance buildings of the Sukiennice (cloth market) were, like most of Poland's ancient capital, undestroyed. Among the crowds who thronged the Market Square Zofia noticed wounded soldiers, many on crutches. A crowd gathered around a street musician:

> Sitting on a small cart is a remnant of a person who is playing a mouth organ which is attached to the edge of the cart and fastened at the level of his face with a wire. He has no arms or legs and he's so shrunken that he probably has only part of his trunk. Such a pleasant face, serious and young, his lips so clearly and politely utter the words, 'Thank you ma'am.'

This sight makes everything go dark around me, I feel faint and weak. I turn back towards him, thinking that I could give him a cake or a pear. But I would have had to hold it up to his mouth. You have to put money at the bottom of the cart next to his body. Some family members must have brought him here. He came back home from the war like that to someone.[4]

Zofia, who saw beyond the man's devastated body, wrote his story in a short prose piece called *Błażej or a defenceless man* which became part of a new collection of *Characters* published in 1947.

Along with Hela and Jerzy Kornacki, Zofia interviewed prisoners from Oświęcim (Auschwitz), many still in striped uniforms and all with stories to tell in many different languages. Hela and Jerzy had already surveyed Auschwitz and the adjoining death camp of Birkenau. Zofia begged them to tell her everything in detail. She was particularly interested in the tragic fate of prisoners who had become so emaciated that they had lost all will to live; release had brought them no hope of recovery. Beyond hints and rumours no one outside the concentration camps had known about this – it was all utterly, appallingly new. Zofia pressed her friends for more and more details – she wanted pictures, mental pictures. She wanted to 'see' it all. 'Typical Nałkowska,' Jerzy observed.[5]

The group began investigations in Gdańsk. The commissioners flew in a military aeroplane and she noted meticulously the landscape spread out beneath her; she was seeing Poland from the air for the first time in her sixty years of 'extended biography,' as she liked to joke.

The historic town centre lay in ruins. Their hotel too was partially ruined and the German owners had taken all the equipment when they fled. Zofia slept on an iron bed with a thin pallet and a straw pillow – but the crime scene she witnessed in the Department of Anatomy was shocking beyond any easy description.

A secret guillotine, blessed by a German army chaplain, had stood behind a purple curtain in the Gdańsk prison. The results of its work had been left in the Department of Anatomy for the Commission to see: headless bodies were piled together, having been soaked in some sort of substance, awaiting their turn in the production line, while hairless heads – with oh such human faces - were heaped randomly together, just, wrote Zofia, like potatoes.[6]

But these were not potatoes.

The story entitled *Professor Spanner*, the first of the ground-breaking collection, *Medallions*, described these murdered people with elegiac simplicity in terms reminiscent of a funeral. The carefully chosen language restores their humanity and dignity. It has been suggested that these nameless faces gave Zofia the title *Medallions*. *Medallion*, a locket or cameo, is also the name for portraits of the dead which in Poland are sometimes displayed in an oval frame on their tombstones. Thus the writer's restrained, precise words carve out funeral rites for the unburied.[7]

The victims of this clinical killing had been patients in the local psychiatric hospital, prisoners, inmates of a notorious concentration camp, Stutthof, which was situated in forests along the coast from Gdańsk, as well as, eventually, corpses from other death camps. Among the corpses was the cleanly severed head of a young boy:

> who might perhaps have been eighteen when he died. The slightly slanted dark eyes were not closed, just a little lowered. The full mouth, of the same colour as his face, bore the expression of a patient, sad smile. His brows were even and pronounced. They were raised towards his temples as if in disbelief. He was awaiting in this strangest situation, surpassing his understanding, the final judgment of the world.[8]

Thus the dead are mourned with tender words which transform victims into human beings while the perpetrators remain nameless and the instigator of the criminal procedure is named only in the title of the story.

The Commission viewed a 'scientific' production line of death. Skin was stripped from bodies to produce skeletons for students to study anatomy; other production was carried on as well. Professor Spanner had fled, there had been obvious attempts to burn the building down, but the Professor, an award winning scientist could not hide all the evidence, the neatly stored headless bodies – and a handwritten recipe for making soap.

It has been denied that human fat was used in the making of soap and Zofia Nałkowska was said to have been a victim of Soviet propaganda. However, Jerzy Kornacki's report confirms Nałkowska's story and later research has shown that soap production had indeed been carried out in this particular Department of Anatomy.

The story caused a sensation when it was published in a journal later that year. Nobody else was writing about these recently committed crimes against humanity whose facts were barely being uncovered. And, wrote Jarosław Iwaszkiewicz, nobody else was capable of such clinical precision and simplicity. In a letter to Zofia in December 1945, Jarosław wrote:

> You alone, no one else, no one in Poland is able to write like this. If you had written in French or English or even in Norwegian you would have been the most famous writer in the world. That incredible precision, that masterful concision – this is all so shattering because it has been done so simply.[9]

Zofia's work with the Commission brought her close to Hela and Jerzy who admired her incomparable enthusiasm and energy – and noted with vexed amusement her naïve trust in the new government. She shared with them her dismay that the new pro-regime literary magazine *Renaissance* had attacked 'dear, nice' Jerzy Zawieyski, a practising Roman Catholic. She mentioned one critic in particular whose biting review shocked her because he had 'seemed such a nice man, moderate and kind.'

Jerzy Kornacki wrote a withering response in his private diary. 'What an idiot Zofia is!'[10]

He wrote as a friend, genuinely fond of Zofia who played duets with Hela while Jerzy sang. Soon, alas, others would say similar things and not in a friendly way.

Jerzy Kornacki also wrote positively about Zofia's readiness to chat to people whom she met in the ruins of Warsaw whose stories she relayed to her friends. 'You've got to write about this,' Jerzy told her. And so she did, and crafted these stories into *Medallions*.

One was the story of a Jewish woman, *Dwora Zielona* (green Dwora).

In *Professor Spanner* the scientifically dismembered corpses had been silenced, but in *Dwora Zielona* a woman 'with a black shield over her eye' is given a voice which is all the more eloquent because it is expressed in simple, unsophisticated words.

Zofia met Dwora by chance and, hearing that she had been in a concentration camp, invited her into a cake shop to hear her story but Dwora insisted on taking Zofia into a dark building in Praga, the working class area of Warsaw across the Vistula which the Red Army had entered before it could be completely destroyed. Dwora led Zofia through a dingy hallway up three flights of stairs in total darkness. 'You had to hold on to the rail and feel each broken wooden step carefully with your feet.'

Upstairs the gloomy rooms had been cleaned and here Dwora revealed her story.

'I'm thirty five, only I look much older, no teeth, only one eye.'

Lowering her voice and speaking confidentially, Dwora continued:

'I tell you, ma'am, I wanted to live. I don't know why, because I had no husband, no family, no one at all, yet I wanted to live. I had no eye, I was hungry and cold (*głodna i chłodna*), yet I wanted to live. Why? Well, I'll tell you, ma'am: it was so that I could tell it all just as I've just told you. Let the world know what they did.'[11]

The unexpected encounter meant that Dwora's efforts to live had not been in vain. The elderly writer who had followed her up those dangerous stairs retold her story so that the world might indeed know.

'A charming woman' who worked as a cleaner in the hotel gave Zofia yet another powerful story, *Dno, the pit*.

'I spoke to the hotel manager today and asked if he could give her easier work but it was no use.'[12]

Meanwhile, as President of the Polish French Friendship Society, Zofia hosted writers such as Jean Paul Sartre, flew to Kraków in the military plane for a performance of her play *The Day of his Return*, carried on a friendship that sometimes almost seemed just a little more, with Jerzy Zawieyski, met literary delegates from England and returned to Warsaw, travelling hard class for fifteen hours to a freezing hotel room and the familiar hard pallet and straw pillow. There, as in a ghost story, she reconstructed her past: that mound of rubble had once been a sunlit building where she had lived during her unhappy marriage to Leon Rygier. He had survived the war and was now 'the head teacher of some sort of school or other,' while the housemaid whom Leon had seduced had become his third wife. His brother Henryk, Zofia heard, had died in Auschwitz.

So many memories, all twisted together in the 'knots of life' and here she was now, sixty years old but not yet past her sell-by date, up to her ears in all sorts of duties as well as chiselling the story she had heard from the cleaning lady. *Dno, the pit* is perhaps the greatest story in *Medallions* for the depths of its simplicity and the depths of suffering the wearied, over-worked, heroic woman had undergone.

Other people would have passed the poor cleaner by. Zofia noticed her, heard her story and crafted it into a gem of great price.

The streets outside the hotel were full of the hustle and bustle of life. People made their way across rubble where homes and shops, schools and churches, museums and offices had been. They went on foot, by horse drawn cart, by overcrowded lorry, by bike. Cars hooted, motorbikes raced along, people pushed little carts or even travelled in home-made rick-shaws. Everyone carried bundles, cases, bags of shopping and buckets of produce which they bore on wooden yokes across their shoulders. Zofia noticed a one-legged cyclist, who rode pressing down one pedal only as if it were the most natural thing in the world. She observed a funeral proces-sion in which a coffin painted silver was borne on a horse driven cart so narrow that the coffin could barely fit. Behind the cart walked a young man who had put on his best clothes for the occasion. His face was red with tears. A name plate was attached to the coffin – the dead man was thirty-three and Zofia wrote, 'Along that crowded, lively street only one man accompanied the coffin, but that man wept.'[13]

Zofia rushed from one official meeting to another and returned home on an overcrowded truck, with people being violently jolted every time the driver stopped or started. A cold wind from the Vistula accompanied their open vehicle and in the ruins that had once been the elegant street of Krakowskie Przedmieście, leading to the devastated Old Town, Zofia noticed a group of people who had gathered around the body of a woman. She had fallen off an overcrowded truck. Someone had covered her face with her hat and fur collar and laid her leather brief case on her chest. Zofia noticed her legs clad in grey woollen stockings and shod in neat little boots.

'The truck drivers take risks and go too fast because are nervous. They take passengers illegally for a back-hander – but they are a real blessing for people who have to traverse Warsaw.'

Soon afterwards the lorry broke down and Zofia went on foot. Classical music was relayed through a loud-speaker, music such as she had not heard for so many years. She stood still to listen beside a flower shop that had risen out of the ruins. Chrysanthemums, begonias and roses played their own music with colour and scent and Zofia felt shaken, yet happy, moved to joy and love and tears.[14]

During their researches into those unspeakable war crimes the Commission visited the death camp Chełmno, a mere fifty kilometres from Zofia's post-war place of residence in Łódź. The Commission included Wacław Barcikowski (1887 – 1981), a lawyer who in the 1930s had defended left-wing activists and Communists (including the future premier of Poland, Władysław Gomułka). Small wonder then that in People's Poland Barcikowski rose to a top position as judge in the High Court. Compromised by his activities during the Stalinist period, he later resigned. Wacław had got to know Zofia quite intimately towards the end of the war when he had been one of the many refugees hiding in Adamowizna. He wrote about the visit to Chełmno in a memoir which focussed on Zofia's interest and reactions.[15]

The Commission had no clear idea why the historic centre on the banks of the River Ner had been designated as a destination for their investigations. Despite the fact that Chełmno is only about fifty kilometres from Łódź no-one had heard of the death camp situated on the edge of the town where over 350,000 people had been murdered. Local people were none too keen to answer questions, they shuffled uneasily, not at all sure that it was safe to speak – they had been deported by the Occupying forces, had only just returned to their homes and still couldn't believe that the invincible German armies had been defeated.

But they had heard of Zofia Nałkowska and, reassured by her presence, started to relay facts which shocked the Commission to the core. They pointed out the village church which had been packed full of victims who were then transported by narrow-gauge railway to the grounds of a palace, hidden behind a high fence. The Nazis had later blown up the palace and the outbuildings, but two survivors came forward to tell their stories. One of them. Michał or Mordecai Podchlebnik (1907 – 1985) later bore witness at the trial of Adolf Eichmann in Jerusalem in 1961 and also took part in Claude Lanzmann's documentary film Shoah (1985).

Inside the fence the Commission felt their feet crunch through a white dust encrusted with crushed bone which covered the whole terrain as far as the eye could see. Michał told them that they were walking over ash from the crematorium and over crushed bones that the murderers hadn't managed to dispose of before their escape.

Barcikowski writes that the Commission were too shocked to proceed. Zofia covered her face and whispered, 'This is monstrous! People shouldn't do things like this.' She asked Michał to scoop a little of this ash into a small container so that she could show it as evidence later.[16]

Michał explained that the people brought to the palace with its imposing gateway had been told that they must have a shower and then they would be taken on their onward journey. The Commission were shown photographs taken by the murderers of groups of young people who had been given soap and towels and now posed for the camera before they undressed and got into waiting trucks which would transport them to death.

These trucks, which could hold anything from a hundred to two hundred people, were gassing machines.

Michał had to bury gassed bodies who had been stripped of gold fillings and wedding rings, and had been degradingly searched for hidden valuables. One terrible day he had seen the gassed bodies of his wife and children.

> The boy was seven and the little girl was four. Then I lay down on my wife's body and told them to shoot me.
>
> They didn't want to shoot me. The German said, 'This man is strong, he's still fit for a bit of work.' And he beat me with a club until I got up.'[17]

Podchlebnik's story is the ninth in *Medallions*.

In November that year Zofia turned sixty-one. She found it unbelievable that at this advanced age she was still so engaged in a whirlwind of activity that she had hardly time to write.

In that month too a young man very diffidently approached her with a manuscript, excusing himself that this was not a piece of literature, but would Pani Zofia be kind enough . . .?

The young man was Marek Edelman (1922 – 2009), the youngest leader of the Jewish Fighting Force and the manuscript on which Zofia heaped generous praise was called *The Ghetto is Fighting*, his account of the Uprising in April-May 1943 whose fires Zofia had witnessed as she tended her mother's grave. She wrote an introduction to the account:

> The manuscript of this little book was brought to me by a young author, not previously known to me. I read it at one sitting, not even looking up for a moment. 'I am not a writer,' he said. 'This hasn't got

any literary merit.' Just the same, his 'unliterary' account achieves something that not all masterpieces succeed in doing. In words that are serious, purposeful, restrained, free from platitude, it gives the minutes of collective martyrdom and perpetuates the mechanism of its course. It is also an authentic document of collective spiritual power rescued from the biggest disaster that the history of nations has ever known.[18]

New Year 1946 saw Zofia and Hanna, 'two elderly women, both mourning lost loved ones,' in their apartment in Łódź listening to a concert on the radio while their two Siamese cats amused themselves and Genia, 'funny and alarming', busied herself in the background. A cyclamen on the table had been given to Zofia as a mark of gratitude from an unknown woman who had lost her husband in Auschwitz and 'to whom I offered some sort of useful service.'[19]

Two weeks later she was up in the air once more, travelling with a group of writers, including Jarosław Iwaskiewicz and Tadeusz Breza – who although he was a friend had just written a penetrating but unkind critique of Jerzy Zawieyski's latest drama.[20] They flew to Copenhagen where they had a stop over and thence to Hamburg – this was because they were not allowed to fly over East German territory which was under Soviet occupation.

Fog detained them in Hamburg for three rather wretched days. They saw nothing of the bombed city and were glad to wing they way to Paris – the pilot responded to Zofia's questions about the logistics of flight and showed her inside the cabin.

In Paris, where Zofia spent four delightful months, the Polish writers gave readings and met people. Zofia, who had always loved Paris, found it strangely consoling that the city had survived, unlike Warsaw. In fact, returning to those ruins, even though rebuilding work was going apace, was rather depressing, while back home in her apartment in Łódź Zofia witnessed a 'crime scene' that was strangely symbolic.

Lovers of animals from earliest childhood, Hanna and Zofia were delighted to have two Siamese cats in their new home in a city neither sister had known well and which still seemed a bit foreign. The female cat produced five little pure white kittens, so tiny they looked, the sisters agreed, like rats or guinea pigs:

By day, they played and showed off, at night they curled up together, affectionate and fluffy, a beautiful mass of catty life. But love for his wife and children wasn't enough for this affectionate, fat, soft, loving tom cat. Now the hubbub begins, he yowls all night for love but the tabby cat ignores him. She's not interested. Laying aside her doubts and moral considerations Hanna phones a certain number. The girl is only too glad to agree and brings another Siamese tabby who is also pining for love. Now the concern is that that jealousy should not lead to conflict and every effort is made to keeping the animals apart.

But it all goes wrong. The trusting little visiting cat sneaks through a tiny gap and in full view of Hanna and the indifferent cat family, in the blink of an eye this alien cat eats up her lover's kitten – in spite of Hanna's efforts to save it. She squeezed the cat's throat as hard as she could and forced its jaws apart. She had saved so many mice, sparrows, lizards from the jaws of different cats in *Meadow House*, but covered in blood and badly scratched, she couldn't save the kitten.

When I arrived on the scene the floor had been cleaned, the stains on Hanna's dress had been washed and the tiny corpse had been cleared away. Neither parent had noticed anything, they didn't pay any attention to the crime. Genia, however, beat up the murderous tabby, as a way of satisfying her offended moral feelings.[21]

The cat's 'cannibalism' made a small domestic humoresque, but animals always carried meaning for Zofia. The sixth story in *Medallions* is called *Wiza*, a term which derives from *Wiese*, the German word for a meadow. We must forget all about a beautiful meadow studded with wild flowers where children might make daisy chains, or shy violets could lead a German poet to write about love. In the hellish reversal of all things good, the *wiza* in German concentration camps was a vast area where prisoners had to stand all day without food or drink while their block was being cleaned.

They drove the women out on to the *wiza* every day for a whole week. They crowded together to try to warm themselves [. . .] One day it was still cold but the sun appeared in the afternoon. Then they all moved together towards the side (of the yard) where the trees didn't hide the sun from view. They moved in that direction like animals do, not like people, or like some sort of mass.

That day the Greek women sang their national hymn, but not in Greek,
They sang a Jewish hymn in Hebrew. They sang very beautifully, standing
in the sunshine, loudly and strongly as if they were healthy. But it wasn't
physical strength, if you please, ma'am, because they were the very ones
who were the weakest. It was the power of longing and yearning.[22]

The young woman who narrated this story also recounted that once,
when she had been peeling potatoes along with another prisoner, they
had chanced upon three baby mice, hairless and pink, curled inside a
hollow that had been nibbled out of one of the potatoes. Her companion
had wanted to give the mice to the cat, but the young woman refused to
do so.

'You see, I had a sudden thought – how is the cat going to eat these
mice?' And she added reluctantly. 'I was just like the Gestapo because I
was curious to see what it would look like.'[23]

Rather than give way to this degraded curiosity, she had pushed the
potato deep into the hay, hoping that the mother would find the babies
again and rescue them.

Zofia's finely chiselled cameos were published to great acclaim in various literary journals but by the time the collection known as *Medallions*
appeared in book form in 1947, public mood had changed and critics tore
the little book apart.

Nałkowska, some critics claimed, had not given the correct political
message. Her sub-title had been the simple (and now famous) slogan
ludzie ludziom zgotowali ten los. The literal translation of this succinct apho-
rism is 'people to people have prepared this fate.' Critics, riding the rising
tide of socialist realism, condemned this sub-title, arguing that it should
read 'fascism prepared this fate . . .'

These critics had entirely missed the point. They failed to see that, for
Zofia, the whole shocking reality of these war crimes was that *people* had
performed these unspeakably depraved actions on their fellow human
beings. Animals might be expected to behave brutally. It is in their nature.
But people? The concept 'crimes against humanity' would be used for the
first time in the Nuremberg Trials[24] and this is exactly the idea that is the
basis of *Medallions.*

Other readers, brought up in the romantic tradition of Polish martyrdom, expected to find heroic deeds, people flinging themselves into the
fires of hell against all the odds. These readers did not realise that Zofia
had shown the depths of hell without any flag waving or rhetoric. They
failed to appreciate the heroism of the quiet endurance of the characters
in *Medallions* or their bravery in bearing witness at great personal cost.

Some critics complained that the book had only scratched the surface
of Nazi war crimes, while others protested that the scenes Nałkowska had
presented were so drastic and horrific that the book would only ever find
a small specialist readership. *Medallions* was an 'immoral' book and 'our
young people shouldn't be poisoned by the nightmare of the Occupation.'[25]

Perhaps the most off-beam reflection however came from Zofia's rival
Maria Dąbrowska. At a small literary gathering Zofia read out one of her
stories from *Medallions*. 'Very weak,' scoffed Maria (who had read a light
hearted piece about how difficult it was to be famous). 'Presented with icy
elegance from an inner emptiness – it was boring and offensive.'[26]

Time would tell how wrong she was. The story she objected to was
Beside the Railway Track, the central story. It has become the most accessi-
ble and most popular for young people who study *Medallions*.

In this story, a young Jewish woman who has been daring enough to
jump from the speeding train carrying her to a death camp, falls beside the
railway track and breaks her leg. Villagers gather, wondering what to do,
one of them is a brash "smart aleck" type 'who saw it all and couldn't
understand it,' the anonymous narrator wrote.

> Her hands were covered in blood. Her death sentence was in her
> knee, fixed as if she had been nailed to the ground. She lay quietly for a
> long time and covered those eyes that were too dark with her closed
> eyelids.
>
> When she finally opened them, she saw new faces around her. That
> young man was still standing there. She then asked him to buy her
> some vodka and cigarettes and he duly obliged. [. . .] There was a
> continuous stream of new people. She was lying among people but
> could not count on their help. She lay like a wounded animal which
> hunters had forgotten to finish off. She was drunk and dozed. This
> power which separated her from them all with a ring of terror was
> insurmountable.

Time passed. An elderly peasant woman who had been standing there and had gone off, managed to get back. She was out of breath. She drew closer and pulled out a tin mug of milk and some bread which she had been hiding under her shawl. Bending down, she hastily placed them into the wounded woman's hands and left straight away, only pausing further off to see if she was drinking the milk. As soon as she spotted two policemen coming from town, she disappeared, covering her face with her shawl.

The others had left as well. Only the small-town smart aleck who had brought her vodka and cigarettes still kept her company. But she didn't want anything more from him.

[. . .] When she opened her eyes at dusk no one was with her except the two policemen and that young man who now no longer went away at all. She asked them to shoot her but without any conviction that they would do it. She placed both her hands on her eyes so as not to see anything.

The police still hesitated not knowing what to do. One tried to persuade the other but he said, 'You do it.'

She heard the young man's voice. 'Just give it to me.'

They still held back and argued. From under her lowered eyelids she saw the policeman taking the revolver out of its holster and handing it to the stranger.

The people standing further off in a small group saw him bend over her. They heard the shot and turned away in disgust.

'They could at least have called somebody, but not like this . . . like a dog.'

[. . .] 'But why he shot her is not clear,' said the narrator. 'I can't understand it. You would have thought that he was the very one who felt sorry for her.'[27]

Those last words sum up the phenomenon now known to history as the Holocaust.

CHAPTER 19

Restored to Life

What torments me? Formulas and slogans that don't achieve anything. Complete neglect of the psychology of those masses who are boiling from top to bottom, repelled by this propaganda. The kielce pogrom, divisions of regular armed forces in the forests, certainly convinced of the rightness of cause and having no way back [. . .] Mutual belief in the rightness of the cause closes people's eyes to the rest of the world.

The dictates of the new Communist regime were soon felt by writers. Former friends became bitter critics and the politically motivated detractors didn't spare Zofia either. Back from four months in Paris and hosting foreign delegations in Warsaw, Zofia found pressures from the new activists difficult to deal with.

What methods they use, what ideas, what tone! I fence myself off from unbearable thoughts of all this, and strengthen myself in my own feelings of rightness with splendid reading, brought here [to her apartment in Łódź] with such difficulty [. . .]. It's all happening against the background of waves of warfare flooding Europe. Does this mean war all over again? Armed fighting has already broken out on our terrain [. . .]

Whether talk is just empty phrases or of significant things – it all takes place against the rumble of those shots along the highway or in the forests, amongst murders, arrests, attacks and all the accessories of political warfare, so one reads splendid books, one is active without pause, putting on a good face in a game that gets worse all the time, having as consolation only this, that death is near and it's not worth choosing what sort of death it will be.[1]

Perhaps her sympathies really lay with an elderly man who came to the door of her apartment selling milk.

Her domestic help Genia (devoted yet increasingly dominant), who normally dealt with such matters, was out and so Zofia opened the door herself. The elderly man's appearance aroused her compassion. He was hardly able to walk, let alone climb stairs. He complained about his legs and when Zofia asked what was wrong with them he explained that he had been in a concentration camp. He added that on his return home his wife refused to let him into her flat. She needed a man who was hale and hearty. He had to live in the cellar and cook his own meals. She used to take the milk round the doors, but she now worked in a textile factory and so he had to do the milk round instead.

He had to rise before dawn, trek out to the country to collect the milk churns which he then carried round the doors, up and down stairs, measuring each person's supply of milk from his big churn.

Responding to Zofia's warm sympathy, he then asked, 'If you please, ma'am, why does this workers' state wear the workers out?'

'What do you mean?' Zofia asked and he told her that in the textile factory where his wife worked, the workers now had to operate four machines, not two as previously. The threads – which were of poor quality – tore easily and as fast as his wife's 'little hands' could work the shuttle and repair one hole, another machine went wrong and she had another hole to mend. Then she and other workers got into trouble, but it wasn't their fault, it was the speed they were supposed to work at while the din and constant noise were overwhelming.

Zofia didn't record her comment – did she agree with him? She did however note that his concern was for the working conditions endured by his wife – even though she had shut him out of the house.

Many of Zofia's critics condemned her for her supposed love of high society, for attending receptions in the palaces of the new regime just as she had done before the war. But Zofia was also a woman who could talk to simple people and allowed them to express their sorrows.

Yet she naively went along with some of the tightening dictates of the new regime. The signing of peace and the suicide of Hitler in 1945 by no means meant the end of conflict. On June 30th 1946 Poles were asked to vote in a referendum, Three times YES (*Trzy razy TAK*), which affirmed the supposed legality of the new government, accepted agricultural reform and agreed to Poland's borders in a shift westwards that meant the loss of the Eastern Borderlands from which people were now 'resettled' in former German territories, causing immense suffering and psychological trauma for thousands of Germans, Ukrainians, including the Lemko people, and the displaced Poles.

Zofia voted in the referendum and commented on the orderly crowds at the booths, but in fact the voting did not go off so peacefully all over Poland and the results which tightened the grip of the one party state were clearly falsified.[2]

Now firmly under the control of Moscow, Poland had lost its independence while ethnic cleansing in formerly Polish territories like Volhynia have left deep scars in the consciousness of Poles. Further brutalities were also carried out against Ukrainians who were deported from south-west Poland and racial hatred was fuelled by attacks on Jews, not least a notorious pogrom in the Polish city of Kielce in which Jewish returnees from concentration camps or from the Soviet Union were terrorised and murdered.

Zofia was clearly affected by this unrest, well aware of the constant sound of shooting, street executions and killings, 'all the accessories of political warfare,' she wrote. Her diary entries are sad and tired. Although people had always been her meat and drink, she tried to avoid them. She was tired, she wrote, of empty phrases and formulae that ignored the needs of the mass of people.

She had been shocked by the murders in Kielce and seemed to believe the official propaganda (now firmly refuted) that the massacre had been carried out on orders of right wing partisans. Armed and well trained military units were indeed still operating. Zofia noted that these men, who had sworn to fight to the death for their cause had no way of going back on their solemn oaths and knew very well that to lay down their arms was tantamount to hearing their own death sentence. The new regime was already imprisoning, torturing and executing men and women who had devoted their lives and their health to the cause of an independent, non-Communist Poland.

Zofia felt that the only way to neutralise the opposition was to open a way of return, but she also knew this was hopeless.

What torments me? Formulas and slogans that don't achieve anything. Complete neglect of the psychology of those masses who are boiling from top to bottom, repelled by this propaganda. The Kielce pogrom, divisions of regular armed forces in the forests, certainly convinced of the rightness of cause and having no way back [. . .] Mutual belief in the rightness of the cause closes people's eyes to the rest of the world.[3]

This entry is ambiguous. She doesn't state whose empty phrases are making her so anxious, nor whose eyes are closed to the rest of the world, although the 'armed forces in the forests' refer to the units of the underground Home Army who had vowed to fight for free Poland all through the Second World War and, bitterly opposed to the new occupying forces, feeling isolated and betrayed could not deny their most sacred vows.

Zofia also had to endure conflict at home. Hanna couldn't stand the domestic help Genia who was slavishly, even violently devoted to Zofia, yet demanding and autocratic. Like the former live-in lover, Bogusław, Genia, too, this uneducated young woman, in service from the age of ten, wanted to shape Zofia into the image of the great lady, and when Zofia remonstrated she became hysterical, even threatening to jump out of the window.

So Zofia booked into a spa situated in south-west Poland in the Sudeten mountains near the Czech border. In spite of her very real ill-health she put up with great discomfort during the long, tiring journey.

She started off with other passengers in a 'wreck of a car', but the next stage was even worse. She was taken in some sort of cart which left the road to jolt over fields, a heart-stopping ride – and she was supposed to be going to the spa because of serious heart issues! Two very young Russian soldiers joined the odd little convoy – an even younger German was with them. Aware that she might have been stumbling into something unpleasant, even dangerous, Zofia engaged the soldiers in conversation – one of them proudly informed her that Maxim Gorky (1868 – 1936) was a marvellous writer.

After this strange trio had left two more young men flagged the cart down. They looked like Polish partisans, suntanned and fair, with high military boots, but they spoke in a mixture of Yiddish and Polish. One of the young men was clearly upset and afraid. 'I won't make it, won't make it,' he repeated. His friend tried to reassure him, but his thin young face was flushed, his eyes were swollen. 'Fifteen of our people have gone already . . . I knew in my heart something was wrong – and when I got there it was all over.'

Touched by all the emotions the young men were expressing, Zofia longed to question them and hear more of their drama, but they ignored her – little knowing that she would capture in ink the brief story that she had heard, writing sadly, 'So now they're having to run away from us as well.'

Unfortunately for the passengers who wanted so urgently to get to their destination, the driver had his own agenda and turned into a little town to find his daughter who was working in a factory there, but although he drove his unwilling passengers all over the town, asking at house after house, the daughter couldn't be found.

When Zofia finally arrived at the spa she found that there was no room for her, so she booked into a hotel. There was no hot water for the travel-stained, elderly woman who was exhausted and hungry after her journey. The bus terminus was right beneath her window, there were constant clouds of dust and endless honking of horns. But beyond the window she saw hills and forests and this view comforted her.[4]

Everywhere there were signs of former German occupation, from names of the various houses within the sanatorium, the young German chambermaid and finally, something that gave Zofia pause for thought.

A German doctor who was obviously very well known in the spa had come as a patient. He picked up a newspaper from the table and sat reading it, but as a medical man, he was given preference to jump the queue. Zofia took his place and had a look at the paper he had been examining. It contained a list of the doctor's former patients who had come from all over Germany and beyond to seek a cure from this eminent man. The list ended in 1941 – and Zofia copied down all these names, as a record of their untold stories; many of the towns and cities that they had come from no longer belonged to Germany.

Zofia spent a month in the spa town. As ever, she kept up appearances, making up her face carefully before her appointment with the doctor, but since she had been referred because of heart problems and the doctor was a gynaecologist she didn't feel that her medical issues had actually been resolved when she returned to Łódź. All too soon she was off on her travels again – and would continue making tiring, though stimulating journeys for the rest of the year. She travelled with other writers, all officially representing the new regime. They spent a month in what was soon to become the Czech People's Republic, visiting Prague, Bratislava, Brno, the Tatra mountains (where deep snow in late October reminded Zofia of her stay in Switzerland and of *Choucas*, the book she had written there) and back to Prague once more. She was also reminded that she was half Czech and that the language she heard around her was her mother's birth language, spoken by her grandmother right to the end of her long life.

She arrived back in Łódź for her sixty-second birthday, and then left for Yugoslavia where in Belgrade she was shocked to meet quite unexpectedly her former lover, Miroslav Krleza, who had aged beyond recognition. He, of course, told her that she looked as young as ever – but he sought no further meeting with her. She recalled the happy time they had spent in Warsaw and in Paris, his encouragement as she struggled to write *Boundary* and also thought with regret of his multi-lingual letters to her that had been destroyed in the fires of Warsaw. Nevertheless, she searched through local bookshops and eventually bought one of Krleza's books to replace the one that had been lost.

Zofia's Yugoslav trip, which included Zagreb and Lubliana, lasted almost ten days, a real meeting of Slav nations with all the Slavonic languages, including Russian being spoken as delegates gathered and shared their work. Zofia voiced from her heart sentiments that seem more than a little contrived, out-dated and only too politically correct: that this unity of People's Democracies was the one thing that would save the world from the horrors of fascism and a future world war.[5]

Back home in Poland. Zofia took time to wander around the ruins of Warsaw where she noticed smart handbags 'as big and beautiful as any in Paris' being sold in makeshift shops, along with silk blouses and in another shop, 'lots of sausage'.

She also attended a ball in the Palace of Wilanów, given in honour of ex-President Roosevelt's son, Elliott, and his film star wife, while in her personal life she received adoring letters and visits from Jerzy Zawieyski and rather more ambivalent ones from her former lover Bogusław, who, having lived in Romania, Italy and London, had acquired and lost a wife and was now planning to come back to Poland.

Her work with the Polish-French Friendship Society drew new young writers into her circle and although she tried to receive visitors only in the evenings, her days were filled with people. She heard their war time stories and those of her families and noted that precisely these experiences define the people of post-war Poland, making laughter difficult and sharpening dissension, not least in the field of literature.

Her work also involved her in travel between Łódź and Warsaw, mostly in very difficult conditions, to stay in Warsaw in unheated rooms lacking all amenities. She had thought that her work with Parliament would be over now that she had finished investigating war crimes, but she was pressured to stay on. She pleaded ill health, begged to be allowed to work as a writer although she felt that she was becoming passé and her once eminent surname now had little relevance, but her pleas were ignored and Zofia found herself forced to voice platitudes she didn't believe in.

A visit from Jerzy Zawieyski moved her and puzzled her – he was so different from the way he had seemed to be during the happy days they had spent in Kraków right at the end of the war. Or, she wondered naively, was it her fault that this affair that had seemed so promising hadn't taken off, that she was just too old and tired and that Genia always got in the way of any relationship.

Jerzy told her he was moving back to his old flat in Warsaw – which had been partially rebuilt and that, amazingly, many of his books and some of his furniture had survived. Zofia permitted herself momentary sigh for all that she had lost from her Warsaw home and remained grateful to Genia for books and papers she had rescued before they went up in flames. She met up with old friends, one of whom noted that Zofia's hearing was getting steadily more difficult, although they had still managed to sustain a brilliant conversation. Photographs at that time do not show Zofia at her best, she looks strained and tired, smiling too brightly and clearly struggling to hear, yet not wanting to let it show.

Out and about in Warsaw, Łódź and Kraków, Zofia always made time for disabled beggars. She grieved over their fate, and gave money (Jerzy Zawieyski called her a saint), but Zofia felt that this was only to insult them further, almost acquiescing in the war crimes that had destroyed their homes, their families and friends and robbed them of limbs and sight.

Old women made her think of her mother whose grave had remained unvisited for the past three years – and then severe pneumonia left Zofia in such a weakened state that she felt she was dying. She thought again of her mother in her last illness, and felt that it was time for her to die too, that she should fight no longer and simply cut short her 'extended biography' with gratitude that she had lived so long.

Her doctor decided otherwise. From the University of Łódź he brought a new treatment, still not formally patented and not readily available: penicillin.[6]

Zofia recovered and still in a greatly weakened state began to receive visitors and flowers – a huge amount of people, she wrote, a score of them from morning till night, all bringing flowers and good wishes. Jerzy brought his close friend Staś and this visit plunged Zofia into confusion.

'Jerzy . . . what am I to think? Should I believe? No, that's going too far. This is a man who has an infinite desire to be liked. As he is.'[7]

She was still unable to believe that although Jerzy adored her for being Nałkowska the writer, his affections were focussed elsewhere – on his friend Staś.

A month later a four page letter from Bogusław, who had heard of her illness, and referred to her affectionately as '*ty*, thou' rather than '*pani*, madam' filled her with mixed emotion.

Visitors continued to pour in and Zofia gradually regained her strength. Friends drove her to drink the health-giving mineral waters in the spa called Krynica, twenty-eight miles from Nowy Sącz, surrounded by peaceful views of wooded mountainsides. Here Hanna wrote to her, 'I am weeding our last garden'[8] – their mother's grave, and Zofia was filled with sadness that Hanna was there alone. Another card from Zofia Villaume brought news of a very old friend from their teenage years, Maria Komornicka whose brilliance had won her the love of Cezary Jellenta and possibly of Wacław Nałkowski himself. Maria had reverted to her female persona and was living in great poverty in a home for the elderly. Zofia V had visited her, praising her poems 'filled with a dark mysticism, clairvoyance, uncanny, written from the verge of madness.' Zofia N wrote in her diary, perhaps a little less than sincerely, 'I should like to visit her too, if I could.'[9]

But she never did.

Zofia spent July and August in Krynica, drinking the waters, going for walks, listening to concerts and piano recitals, chatting to other writer friends among the spa guests, reading and writing letters. Jerzy Zawieyski wrote from the Baltic coast, telling her about a saintly priest, Father Zieja (1897 – 1991) to whom Jerzy had owed his conversion into the Roman Catholic Church in 1942.

Jerzy begged her to send him some of her writing – even if, he implored, semi-jokingly, it was just a piece about squirrels (referring to a previous letter). He adored her writing, he told her. 'Your word, which is unique, always opening new discoveries, steeped with wisdom and charm. Your enormous talent - this is my great good which I honour and from which I learn.'[10]

Zofia would perhaps have preferred a different sort of adoration and felt desperately lonely in spite of his letters and visits from friends.

Yet, in spite of this high praise and in spite of reading good reviews of her pre-war novel, *The Impatient Ones* ('a masterpiece, the quintessence of wisdom and clarity, no one else writes such transparent prose which burns with the clearest crystal')[11] Zofia felt unable to write creatively until one day a dog came to her table in the restaurant, 'a lonely dog with a charming little face.' Zofia quickly understood what had brought the dog to her and fed him some titbits from her plate. So now they were friends and very soon the dog's master was drawn into the little circle. It turned out that he was a pre-war acquaintance, and was now editing a popular magazine, *Prekrój* (Cross-Section). He begged Zofia to write some of her famous character sketches for the magazine and lent her his typewriter.[12]

So now with the help of another friend, Teresa, a professional musician and a member of the Polish-French Friendship Society who assisted with the typing, Zofia started work once more.

The dog Fafik had unwittingly restored Zofia to life as a published writer. Thanks to this canine intervention some of her best literary pieces emerged into print. The first one was devoted to the mouth organ player whom she had met in Kraków, the man who had come home from the war with no arms or legs.

More *Characters* followed and were published in *Przekrój*, a journal that exists to this day in Poland. Zofia Nałkowska was in orbit once more.

Most definitely in orbit – as regards her unexpected visit to Moscow on 4th November, just six days before her sixty-third birthday when 'it happened' as Zofia travelled with other writers (all men, as usual) in mixed sleepers on the Berlin – Moscow Express.

They crossed the new Polish-Belarussian border into countryside which until recently had been part of Poland, so well-known to Zofia during her unhappy second marriage.

The conversation in the well-appointed coaches was witty and filled with laughter as the Polish delegates engaged with Russian and Belarussian dignitaries, all serving the Party line. By contrast the view beyond the window was of a desolate land: little wooden houses without any trees, fields devoid of any sign of cultivation, shabbily clothed women with knotted bundles, others with headscarves pulled low over their brows, all of them moving in an orderly fashion towards the goods wagons which were their means of transport.

Even the coaches further into Russia looked no better than Polish third class, whereas 'our coach . . . is European.' And Zofia wondered as she sat alone in her compartment, thinking it all through, 'Where is justice?'

Then, unexpectedly, into the compartment, intruded a stranger. He apologised at once and backed towards the door but didn't leave. He told Zofia in Russian that she was like an Empress.

'H'm,' Zofia thought. 'An interesting compliment in the land of the Soviets.'

She guessed the intruder had had too much to drink but he seemed harmless enough.

So, laughing prettily, Zofia explained that he hadn't just mistaken the compartment, he was in the wrong about her, because she was no longer young and, although he had praised her abundant hair, she was in fact going grey.

'Madame, I know you're not a twenty-year old, but you are so beautiful, you're majestic, you're so wise.'

Amazed, Zofia understood that he was sincere and his next words surprised her even more.

'Chase me away,' he begged.

Zofia rose. 'Go, then,' she said as firmly as she could.

And suddenly she felt a scattering of gentleness fall on her face and her hair, like the delicate touch of petals from a flower.

Filled with a deep sense of shame, Zofia ordered him to leave. He obeyed but returned at once, sighing, 'If only I had met you ten years ago.'

It's getting serious now, Zofia thought, and corrected him sternly, 'Not ten, but twenty.'

'No, no, I didn't mean that . . . excuse me . . .' And again the most delicate kisses that Zofia had ever experienced. She replied with only one, justifying it to herself that he was so modest and humble, so charming and sweet,

'Will you forgive me?' he begged.

'Yes indeed, forgiveness is the only thing I can offer you . . .'

And with that, he left and Zofia told herself 'He's probably a bad poet.'

For the rest of the journey he was always in her company and next evening as she sat in the compartment with a colleague she didn't care for as a person or as a writer, the 'bad poet' came in, pushed past her colleague, knelt before he and gave her a book of his poems, dedicated to her.

She read them all night and discovered that he wasn't such a bad poet at all. Later she read that he was thirty-seven, the son of a blacksmith, a much awarded poet and that in this land of socialist realism Romanticism was far from dead and still had a part to play.

'Well, well, what a surprise! I was sorry that I had been so off-putting,' Zofia concluded wryly.

The next seventeen days were filled with official delegations, with visits to theatres and museums, to the Mausoleum where Lenin's embalmed body lay, and with banquets and recitals of prose and poetry. The Polish delegation met many distinguished Soviet writers, including, Samuil Marshak, the translator of Robert Burns (1887 – 1964) who told her, 'Realism isn't a literary movement, it is happiness.' Zofia doesn't record her reply.

Even though she went to the hairdresser and had her hair done specially, Zofia had no occasion to meet her poet-lover again, except at a final banquet when they made eyes at one another, in true teenage fashion across a crowded room.

Zofia noticed how poorly-dressed Muscovites crowded into art galleries and theatres. She noted that there were far more women everywhere than men. She chatted to the floor ladies, who did twenty-four hour shifts on each hotel landing and was particularly impressed by the way old women ('who in Poland would have been begging outside churches or shut away in old folks' homes, waiting for death') were actively employed in cloakrooms, collecting winter coats, or in theatres, selling tickets and programmes as well as guarding works of art in the galleries, making sure no one entered each room without having given their outdoor coats and boots to the cloakroom lady.[13]

She wrote quite fulsomely (and it would appear to modern eyes foolishly) about the happy fate of these elderly women in an article which was published on her return to Poland.[14] Yet when we consider the old women Zofia met on the streets in Poland, to whom she gave what money she could afford, perhaps her remarks are less naive than they might appear.

One such old woman had touched her deeply at the beginning of November before her Moscow visit when she had gone after a gap of three years to visit her mother's grave.

It was the Feast of All Souls when people in Poland traditionally honour the dead by clearing fallen leaves away from the graves, laying down wreaths and flowers and lighting candles.

Amongst the ruins of Warsaw, beside a tram stop Zofia saw on old woman sitting on the bare ground. She searched her pocket for small change and bent down to offer it to the old lady, but opened her wallet instead.

The old woman's blue eyes looked up at her and Zofia saw their beauty. They got into conversation. We can imagine tall Zofia who was by now greatly impeded in her hearing, bending very low to catch the old lady's tale of woe. Her right hand and left foot had been badly injured by an exploding grenade during the Uprising. Both her sons had been killed. She had no one left to care for her. Doctors refused to treat her, telling her she was 'on the way out'; she dreamt of a place in an old folks' home where at least she could be looked after.

Zofia was moved to tears. This could have been her own mother! And those eyes were so beautiful! Zofia longed to take her home and care for her.[15]

Instead she caught a tram and rode in the open wagon through an icy wind to the cemetery. All around her people were adorning the graves of their loved ones with flowers and candles. Zofia bought a wreath and spent a long time at her mother's graveside in tears and in deep thought.

Then, having heard that Zofia V had come to Warsaw for the Day of the Dead, Zofia went to visit her, crossing the ruins in darkness, missing her way and finally getting a taxi.

The two friends had their first meeting for three years. Zofia V was full of praise for Zofia's achievements while Zofia N wanted to bring her dear friend back to Łódź to let her revive her intellectual life, so long dormant, to get her away from her reclusive life style deep in the country and let her be restored to life as Zofia herself had been, thanks to the advances of medicine and a charming, greedy dog.

CHAPTER 20

Knots of Life

They've withdrawn journals with my articles, or with articles about me. the only criterion is this realism, such an undefined loose sort of term. All this roars in my head with a tangle of problems that I simply can't solve. How can I write in way that will meet their demands, in a way that, although I'm on the wrong side I can still save for today's reality things that are really worthwhile creatively, which means the truth that is arrived through reason?

Zofia's last novel *The Knots of Life* had taken ten years to write.[1] It begins with a brilliant description of a ball on the eve of the Second World War to which Nazi leadership had been invited. *The Romance of Teresa Hennert* had opened the new era of Independent Poland with a searing critique of the politicians and generals of the new Second Republic, men who had been ready to die for Polish freedom but had no idea how to govern. Now, just before the demise of that Republic, *The Knots of Life* made a closure to the themes that had run through Zofia's entire opus.

The book had cost more emotional pain than any of her previous work. Zofia created a larger than life hero, full of charisma and charm, warm and generous to his friends, faithful to his Leader and his ideals, faithless to his wife. In other words, a replica of her second husband, Jan. While she was writing an earlier draft, Zofia learnt of Jan's death in London, alone in hospital following a severe illness.[2] He had left a considerable sum of money that she was entitled to claim, but she refused to do so. However, his death meant that she now had a free hand in creating his fictional look-alike, knowing that he would never now read it and be angered at seeing himself in his wife's work.

Such are the complicated knots of life that just three weeks before learning of Jan's death, Zofia heard that her first husband, Leon Rygier had also just died,[3] so now, no longer a deserted wife, Zofia was truly a widow, entangled in a weird relationship with her domestic help Genia, 'this being who is weak physically but powerful morally who fills the finale of my fate, her dedication and worship define my life'.[4]

Genia, uneducated, intelligent, adored her mistress yet terrorized her and cut her off from her friends.

> Dare I say it's easier for me when she's not there? Her stubborn, passionate care, her iron will, frightful stormy decisions – all this shatters any kind of concentration, robs me of the ability to want anything. Whatever I ask her for, even the most normal thing, arouses her resistance, anger, arguments. And yet this is the only person left who is close to me, the very closest person, completely bound up with my fate, bound with all sorts of feelings.[5]

She was also caught up in the complications of the adoration of the playwright and author, quiet Jerzy Zawieyski and the passionate, demanding letters of her former lover Bogusław who returned to Poland in 1948.

Jerzy knew about Bogusław but the latter didn't know about Jerzy, while Genia made no secret of her preference for Bogusław, handsome, tall and distinguished looking. She felt he was a much better partner for her illustrious mistress that the slightly built, unhandsome Jerzy. We can almost imagine Zofia tearing her still abundant hair when she wrote, 'I'm using Jerzy to free Bogusław from feeling obliged to love me out of pity!'[6]

The sixty fourth year of Zofia's 'extended biography' was therefore knotty indeed.

The title *Knots of Life* is based on the inscription that Zofia had discovered in her teenage years on a tombstone in an abandoned Jewish cemetery. Now, a lifetime later she chose the phrase as a summation of her life's work, although the book, which had been eagerly anticipated, had never enjoyed a great readership. Contemporary readers who have rediscovered Zofia's work praise *The Impatient Ones*, but are dismissive of *The Knots of Life*, claiming that it is not innovative enough. However, no one can deny the stunning writing that leads the reader into the heart of aristocratic, privileged Poland and then blows it all apart in the onslaught of war.

In her own day her friends admired the novel; a few even understood that rather than harking back to the past, Zofia's genius lay in her ability to write for the future. Unfortunately, though, publication had come at the wrong time: the proponents of socialist realism attacked the novel cruelly. Zofia was particularly wounded by the review of a younger writer whom she counted a friend.

'The book is false," he claimed. 'Why did such a mistress of psychological analysis as Nałkowska make such a cardinal mistake in her attempt at a realistic, social-psychological novel?'

And the critic concluded, using one of those empty phrases that Zofia found so irritating, that it was all down to what he called 'psychologism.'[7]

She understood that he probably had to write in this way, but 'how could he?' She felt hurt by his 'sour tone of voice' and was devastated that his review denied any worth to the book that she had adjusted to suit the new requirements. Suffering the strictures of the new regime, she wrote bitterly: 'They change you into a rag and wave you around.'

She refused to travel to the newly Polonised city of Szczecin (formerly German Stettin) for a Socialist writer's conference. 'Only to learn that my *Knots* are false and worthless.'[8]

Jerzy Zawieyski, who had also fallen foul of the new requirements, stoutly defended Zofia at the conference, but writers who had been ardent admirers cooled towards her. Zofia felt that she had been pushed to the margins of life and had no further contribution to make to Polish literature. She felt doubly saddened because she believed in the basic truth of socialism and felt that the regime was wrong in the methods that it used.

Three years later she wrote sadly:

They've withdrawn journals with my articles, or with articles about me. The only criterion is this realism, such an undefined loose sort of term. All this roars in my head with a tangle of problems that I simply can't solve. How can I write in way that will meet their demands, in a way that, although I'm on the wrong side (*she means the pre-war, non-Communist era*) I can still save for today's reality things that are really worthwhile creatively, which means the truth that is arrived through reason?'[9]

In the midst of these concerns Zofia met Bogusław in Warsaw; they had lunch together for the first time in nine years. Bogusław begged her to come and live with him in a town north-east of Warsaw. 'Let's just go away together,' he urged her.

Zofia refused, 'My past experience doesn't encourage me to travel with you, sir. You might lose me on the way.'[10]

Instead, she relived her pre-war walk around Warsaw, and, walking in tears around the ruined city, this 'wound in the world' she made a personal pilgrimage, 'a procession of despair' that was also an elegy to all her former life, to all that she had loved and lost.

Wounded in her writing life, enduring ill-health and deafness with that constant hum in her head, Zofia decided that all that was left to her (besides taking poison) was to translate other people's masterpieces, since she could write none of her own. A photograph shows a group of writers beneath a banner with the slogan: *Writers – engineers of the human soul, Stalin.* Maria Dąbrowska is in the centre. Her cropped hair gleams in the light. She's hatless and looks relaxed, while Zofia, formally hatted, sits at the very edge. She looks strained and unhappy – it's clear that she's struggling to catch what is going on around her.

And indeed she was now receiving death threats. The first had been sent in a letter, early in 1948, then a call came from two young men who wanted Pani Zofia to help them travel to Greece. This sounded convincing enough as Zofia was deeply involved with people and their needs. The year had begun with her helping a young couple to go to Sweden. The thirty-three year old husband was seriously ill and they had heard that in Sweden doctors could perform an operation to help him.

Zofia only had to look at the young man to know that all the effort and expense were useless, but who was she to destroy his hopes?[11] So this phone call from the two young men didn't dismay her – but they insisted that they had to meet Zofia personally in her own home.

Genia screamed, 'No, no, you mustn't let them come here.'

They decided the best solution was to keep a chain on the door, then another threat came over the phone. 'This is the undertaker calling. Your coffin is ready.'

Genia was beside herself and even Zofia couldn't prevent a cry of alarm. Genia rushed out to get help from friends in the same building. An hour passed – and before Genia returned the young men appeared at the door.

'We want to apologise for that call, it was all a joke,' they said.

Zofia accepted their apology but Genia rushed in to say that the intrud-
ers should produce identification papers. Zofia glanced out of the window
and saw two men with machine guns in the yard. So the young men were
to be arrested! She immediately phoned the police and told them that it
was all a mistake, the two young men were boys of eighteen, they were
perfectly polite human beings who regretted the upset they had caused.[12]

She also caught up with the mother of her friend, Zhenya Exé who had
been executed by the Polish Underground in 1943. Now she heard from
the bereaved mother that the death sentence had been a mistake. Zhenya's
contacts with the Gestapo had been misunderstood by the Underground
and Zhenya had been shot in her own home with her teenage son looking
on. The murderer shot Zhenya's husband too and escaped through one of
the windows.[13]

So now this bereaved Russian mother became a regular visitor to Zofia's
house; Jerzy Zawieyski wrote admiringly that Zofia's concern for people
in need was so infectious that he never now passed a beggar by without
giving something.

Jerzy had initiated the letter writing friendship in 1943; it lasted until
Zofia's death in 1954. His are full of adoration, ambiguous declarations of love, complaints and also rebuke: why doesn't she write more
often, why doesn't she make more time for him, why doesn't she write
another masterpiece? He rushes to her defence whenever he reads a
negative review. This epistolary love affair is a garland of words, a
soothing of wounds.[14] He opens up the world of Roman Catholic faith
to her, she gently suggests that his writing might be improved if he
could distance himself from his need to reflect Catholic dogma.
Another name occurs from time to time, Staś. Zofia calls him 'your
kind friend', not guessing the real relationship between the two
ardently Catholic men.

Unable to respond physically to Zofia's need for a sexual partner, Jerzy
nevertheless felt genuine compassion for her:

> I don't think anyone has really loved you. I've always thought that in
> truth you have never experienced great tenderness and true goodness
> [. . .] My heart breaks when I see you surrounded by people at all the
> receptions you hold in your house. All your literary friendships are so
> inconstant and superficial [. . .] This is the story of your life, all these

insincere people are quite indifferent, they only see in you your beauty and fame [. . .] I'm in no way like any of the men who surround you, but no one else besides me understands your inner life.[15]

From Jerzy's letters we learn much about Zofia's busy, complex agenda as she represented various committees, wrote letters in French and Polish, helped petitioners who approached her as a Member of Parliament and supported younger writers (including Jerzy) by trying to find translators for their works. She was no longer nominated for literary prizes or for foreign travel. Instead she retreated to health resorts and spas for several weeks at a time. A lover of people, Zofia was also a lover of silence and was always devoted to nature. Out in the country, she enjoyed feeding sparrows, felt sorry for a tethered goat and recorded the movements of a rare black squirrel.

Aided by Bogusław and Genia (who now rode a motorbike and was equipped with helmet and goggles) Zofia moved from Łódź to Warsaw, but the flat had no hot water, sporadic electricity and had to be approached over a huge mound of rubble.

Finally in December 1950, she was given rooms in the House of Writers in the heart of Warsaw, the city where she truly belonged.

She moved in with her faithful, masterful Genia, with her Alsatian dog Shocking and with a Siamese cat who was expecting her first litter of kittens. The house was freezing, so Zofia put her cat in a warm basket. Genia helped the inexperienced mother cat give birth while Shocking watched puzzled from afar. The first kitten was born dead but four more followed and Shocking allowed the small white fluffy bodies to curl up beside him.[16]

The agendas of the new regime grew ever more restrictive. Zofia was used as a figurehead for the regime who needed heroes, cultural icons and martyrs. When she was obliged to give speeches she mostly quoted her father. Wacław Nałkowski suited the image of a Marxist thinker who had sacrificed himself for the cause. Bogusław was actively trying to create a Nałkowski Museum and so Zofia visited her beloved *Meadow House*. The forests were no more, the pine trees had been cut down and only stunted bushes remained where once she had ridden through woodland with Jan Gorzechowski.

The house bore the scars of war. The front doors were broken, the glass panes had gone. Zofia learnt that a ghetto had been created in the nearby town Wołomin and *Meadow House* had been taken into that enclosed area from which people had been deported by train to Treblinka from August to October 1942.[17]

It must have been hard for Zofia as she imagined the frightened, desperate families who had been crowded into the small, low-ceilinged rooms of *Meadow House*. She herself felt like a ghost, come back from a vanished world as she went up to her own room and thought about the books she had written here, the lovers and husbands she had received. Only Bogusław was left, a lover no longer although still actively engaged in her life.

'Everything had meaning only once it had been refracted through *Meadow House*,' she wrote in a dairy that was becoming increasingly a note-taking exercise.[18]

Friends feared that she was beginning to become a little forgetful, but it could well have been her difficulties with her hearing which she still tried, not usually successfully, to hide. Genia, formerly barely literate, now became Zofia's secretary, a task that would later lead her to work as custodian in a literary archive until her death in 1980.

Zofia's cultural activity took her to the seat of power, associating with much hated political leaders: Jakub Berman (1901 – 1984), head of the notorious Secret Police, and the hard-line Stalinist President Bolesław Bierut (1892 – 1956). Such contacts alienated some Polish readers who couldn't believe that the author of *Medallions* could make such associations. Zofia doesn't record her impressions of these men in her diary, she simply mentions meeting them as part of her duties on the Constitutional Committee; her main work was with much humbler projects, collecting funds to help workers in need, associating with young people (a photograph shows her hatless with a group of schoolgirls who all wear the scarf of the Communist Youth Movement).

In her flat in Warsaw, looking over the empty space where the Royal Castle had once stood, Zofia received delegations of women workers who wanted her to dedicate their copies of her books. She heard their pleas for a crèche for young working mothers and worked actively on their behalf. She was invited to speak at workers' gatherings and in 1951 she began to work with her editor on her *Selected Works*, a task that involved her prodigious memory as she made choices that would suit the regime.[19]

She also helped her sister Hanna to move back to Warsaw. Hanna too was pressured by the dictates of socialist realism. Having become more resigned at last to the death of her husband Mak, Hanna had re-married and Zofia (along with Bogusław) helped the couple find accommodation in the capital.

She kept up with her friends, Hela and Jerzy Kornacki, Jerzy Zawieyski and her dear Zofia V who ached for Zofia, seeing her loneliness beneath the façade of activity and adulation. 'Others come and go and you are left with nobody except that impossible megalomaniac Genia,' she wrote in a letter which she never sent.[20]

This letter from Zofia's oldest and closest friend describes in minute detail the writer's Warsaw rooms overlooking the great Zygmunt Column, still toppled to the ground and the huge gap where the Royal Castle had been – not to be rebuilt until the 1970s. We see Zofia N's exquisite taste in furnishing, crystal and porcelain on the sideboard, a fruit bowl, a gift from the Czech Minister of Culture, four fading roses, a present from faithful Jerzy Zawieyski – and then Genia, bustling in, disturbing the two friends.

'Time for tea.'

Passing her office Zofia N indicated a cupboard. 'My diaries are in there, my whole life. Don't let just any old person get hold of them.'

Genia butted in. 'Zofia's going to Vienna. She's going to speak at a women's conference.'

'But Genia,' Zofia V protested. 'Pani Zofia is exhausted.'

'She's got to keep on working,' Genia said, and Zofia V wrote in that undelivered letter, 'So it's come to this, this is the way Genia bosses you.'[21]

Zofia was also actively involved in the needs of her constituents in Opole. She responded as best she could to their needs, made the long journey to this former German town in south-west Poland, where she appeared as a distinguished literary figure and read some of Wacław Nałkowski's work. However, this award-winning writer, decorated with many awards, head of Polish PEN Club, member of the Polish Academy of Literature, president of the Polish-French Friendship Society, vice-president of the Committee of the Defenders of Peace and the League of the Fight against Racism, MP and a Member of the Commission of Culture, sensed deep down that both her father and herself were now merely historical figures in the new People's Poland.

Her seventieth birthday came and went. On 12th December 1954 Zofia attended a discussion in Parliament about decisions for Opole. She returned home about 8 pm. The next morning Genia found her slumped across the bed, fully dressed. She was still breathing and in hospital seemed to regain consciousness but only enough to mutter indistinct phrases. The doctors diagnosed a cerebral haemorrhage. More strokes followed and Zofia died on the 17th December 1954 at six o'clock in the evening.

'Death strikes us at any moment in our life,' she had written,[22] and death struck her when she was still fully active and engaged.

She was given a State funeral. Genia dressed her body. Maria Dąbrowska whose earlier friendship had turned to bitterness, admitted that Zofia Nałkowska looked beautiful in her coffin. Friends gathered round to pay their respects. Zofia was buried in the Powązki Cemetery in Warsaw. Hanna Nałkowska created the bust that marks her sister's grave, but her real memorial, beside her books, is her beloved *Meadow House*, now a much visited museum where the unseen ghost of Zofia Nałkowska surely presides over the concerts and literary events which are held here. She would be more than a little sad at the billboards and advertisements of capitalism that line the busy highway outside her favourite house, but she would be pleased at the way the little house is presented, at her photographs and displays of her books translated in many languages.

Let us leave her there, sitting beneath her portrait. Her abundant chestnut brown hair is gathered in a knot at her neck. She rather artfully overstretches her neck, anxious to hide any wrinkles, but perhaps she simply wants to take a closer look at a group of young people who have gathered for a letter-writing session to help them improve their grammar and style.

And that is the thing this master craftswoman of 'transparent prose which burns with the clearest crystal' would appreciate most of all.

Portrait of the writer as an old woman
(Zofia Nałkowska, Warsaw, 1884-1954)

Her genius acclaimed when she was just fifteen,
now, enduring war-time hell,
she rises each hungry dawn to sell
tobacco, carting cartons up an icy hill.
Cigarettes provide a frail smokescreen
to keep forbidden authors, forbidden works alive.

Her diary lists a litany of names:
lovers, friends, musicians, poets - lost -
black holes within the galaxy of fame.
Her notes compose their requiem,
expose the pain of war, protest its waste:
"I write. From smoke and silence and too many tears."

As Warsaw is smashed to smouldering smithereens
she edits dressmaker-like, her latest manuscript,
Cuts pencilled pages, reshapes ribbons of words,
lips pursed with pins.

Horn-rimmed spectacles enlarge eyes young men
still praise. Shoes white with ash, she is a delegate
to grotesque chambers, the first to disclose the fate
fabricated by human minds for human kind;
from that crucible of crime creates
exquisite cameos, her masterpiece.

Women note her modish *maquillage*,
repeat rumours of a lover – "Imagine, at her age!"
Feted in London, Paris, Moscow, Prague,
in as many languages she holds centre stage,
"Young sir, my powder compact, please, it's on the chair,
and yes, if you would, my silver fur . . ."

She lets no standards slip; her style her defence
against ageing, deafness, her feared future tense;
her private journal shows
what anguish accompanies her public pose.

A woman with a scalpel pen, large and generous,
her gift was to make others feel great and glamorous,
while with ruthless precision she prises life apart
and probes the subtle workings of the human heart.

Notes

Chapter 1 Youth absorbed in the third person

1   Jerzy Zawieyski in *Memories Wspomnienia o Zofii Nałkowskiej*, ed
    Barcikowski p 308 Czytelnik, 1965
2   Maria Kuncewiczowa *Memories* p. 173
3   Tadesuz Breza *Memories* p. 97
4   M Dąbrowska, *Dzienniki powojenne 1945 - 1949*, quoted in ZN
    Dziennik, diary, p. 398 Book 6 volume 1
5   Iwaszkiewicz, Nałkowska archives, quoted Hanna Kirchner p 574
    Nałkowska or a life in writing Nałkowska albo życie pisane Fortuna i
    Fatum, Warszawa 2011
6   ZN *Count Emil* p. 176
7   ZN *My father* p. 30
8   Ibid p. 22
9   Ibid p. 30
10 Diary 21.12.1899 pp. 52, 53
11 Ibid p. 52
12 Ibid pp. 23-24
13 Ibid pp. 53, 54
14 Ibid p. 226
15 Ibid p. 214
16 Ibid p. 251
17 Ibid pp. 195 - 192
18 Ibid p. 257
19 Quoted by Jan Kott in *Memories* p. 165

Chapter 2 Icy fields – the challenge of a woman writer

1   ZN *Icy Fields* p. 13, this edition published Warsaw 1907

2   *Diary* p. 271

3   Ibid p. 288

4   *Icy fields* p. 13

5   *Diary* p. 281

6   Ibid p. 292

7   Ibid p. 305

8   Ibid p. 308

9   Ibid p. 348

10   Ibid p. 311

11   Ibid p. 320

12   Ibid p. 326

13   See Hanna Kirchner *Nałkowska, or a life in writing,* various references

14   *Diary* p. 328

15   Ibid p. 329

16   *Icy Fields* pp. 59 – 60

17   *Diary* p. 334

18   Ibid p. 345

19   Ibid p. 341

20   Ibid p. 346

21   Ibid p. 348

22   Stefania Podhorska, *Memories of ZN* p. 266

Chapter 3 Life in its entirety

1   ZN quoted in *Views near and far* Warsaw 1957 p. 280

2   Ibid p. 237

3   ZN *My father* p. 40

4   *Diary 1899 – 1905* p. 76

5   *Views* p 13

6   Ibid p. 337

7   Ibid pp. 48 – 49

8   Quoted Hanna Kirchner *Nałkowska . . .* p. 79

9   ZN *Prince* Warsaw 1907 pp. 160 – 161

10   Zofia Villaume quoted these words to Hanna Kirchner who recorded them in a footnote to ZN *Diary 1945 – 54* vol 6 p. 457

11   ZN *Views* p. 280

12   See Hanna Kirchner *N . . .* p. 98, ZN *Diary 1909 – 17* p. 65

13   Maria Kucewiczowa *N as I remember her, Memories* p. 168

14   ZN *Koteczka* Lwów 1909

15   Andrzej Franaszek, *Miłosz, a biography* (Bellknap Harvard 2017) p. 100
16   *Diary 1909 – 1917* p. 36
17   Hanna Kirchner *N . . .* p. 101

Chapter 4 Laying out life in patterns
1   Karolina Beylin in *Memories* p. 39
2   Mieczysław Bibrowski in *Memories* p. 47
3   ZN *Diary 1909 – 1917* p. 258
4   Ibid p. 258
5   Ibid p. 261
6   Ibid p. 262
7   Ibid p.159
8   Angelika Kuźniak, *Stryjeńska Diabli nadali*, Wołowiec 2015
9   Adam Mickiewicz *Do Matki Polki*, to a Polish Mother, author's translation, *Loss and Language*, Chapman Publications 1994
10   ZN *Diary 1909 – 1917* p. 162
11   *Diary 1930 – 1939* p. 221
12   ZN *Narcyza* Kraków 1910 p. 129
13   Ibid p. 130
14   HK footnotes to *Diary 1909 – 1917* p 180-181
15   *Memories* pp. 39/40
16   *Diary* p. 357.

Chapter 5 Encircled by fire
1   *Diary 1909 – 1917* p. 439
2   Ibid pp. 280 – 281
3   Ibid p. 341
4   Ibid p. 343
5   Ibid p. 347
6   Cezary Jellenta, *Deep Twilight* re-issued PIW 1985 p. 68
7   Ibid p. 89
8   Ibid p. 89
9   *Diary* p. 388
10   Ibid p. 389
11   *Gloves* p. 209
12   *Diary* p. 389
13   Ibid p. 390
14   Ibid p. 410

15   Ibid p. 412

16   *Icy Fields* p. 26

17   *Snakes and Roses* p. 200

18   Breza, *Memories* p. 103

19   *Snakes* p. 236

20   *New Culture* 1952 p. 47

21   Ibid

22   *Diary 1916* pp 420 – 421

23   Ibid p. 432

24   Doblin, *Journey to Poland* p. 29, this edition Paragon House US 1991

25   Ibid p. 41

26   *Diary* p. 435

27   Ibid p. 437

28   Ibid p. 439

29   Ibid p. 451

30   Ibid p. 453

31   Ibid p. 455

32   Ibid p. 464

33   Ibid p. 473

34   ZN *Views near and far* p. 14

Chapter 6 Independent employment

1   ZN *Diary 1918 – 1929* p. 39

2   ZN *Count Emil* p. 30, pp. 166-167

3   Ibid pp. 112 – 113

4   Ibid pp. 176 – 178

5   Trans Jenny Robertson *Loss and Language* p. 28 Chapman 1994

6   Quoted in Adam Zamoyski, *Warsaw 1920* p. 53

7   *Diary* p. 37

8   Ibid p. 39

9   Wanda Melcer *Memories* p. 232

10   Ibid p. 224

11   Ibid p. 227

12   Ibid p. 233

13   Jerzy Zawiejski *Memories* p.335

14   *Diary* p. 79

Chapter 7 Living on the edge

1 ZN *Diary 1918 – 29* p. 103
2 ZN *Views from Near and Far* p. 303
3 Thomas Venclova, *Vilnius: a personal history* p. 7
4 Ibid p. 51.
5 Alfred Doblin, *Journey to Poland* 1924 p. 99
6 Juliusz Słowacki *Beniowski* song VI pp. 326 – 327 (this edition PIW ed. Jerzy Pelc)
7 ZN *Views* p. 314
8 Ibid p. 137
9 Translated into English by Megan Thomas and Ewa Małachowska – Pasesk, Nothern Illinois University Press, 2014
10 *The Romance of Teresa Hennert*. Lecture, Symposium on Nałkowska 2016
11 Irzykowski, quoted Kirchner p. 206
12 *Diary* p. 103
13 *Diary* p. 112
14 Nadzieja Drucka *Memories* p. 126 see also *Three quarters* LTW Publishing 2011
15 Ibid
16 Nadzieja Drucka, *Three quarters* pp. 9 – 69
17 Ibid p. 125
18 Ibid pp. 128 – 129
19 ZN *Diary 1945 – 1954* end note p 457
20 ZN *Stories* pp. 64 -65
21 Ibid p. 65
22 *Diary* p 181
23 Ibid
24 Ibid p. 125
25 Ibid
26 Ibid p.129
27 Ibid p. 130
28 Ibid p. 138
29 Ibid
30 Ibid 119
31 Ibid p. 192 (footnote, ed. Hanna Kirchner, slightly adapted).
32 Ibid p. 153

Chapter 8 Unkind love – and a curtain impossible to name

1   ZN *Unkind Love* (Niedobra miłość) is the title of ZN's next outstanding novel, while the curtain refers to her hearing loss.

2   Her views on age will be shown in a cruel (yet ultimately compassionate) caricature in her greatest novel, *Boundary*, while the shameful loss is her increasing deafness and constant humming in her head caused by tinnitus.

3   North Illinois University Press 2014, Found in Translation award 2015

4   ZN *Choucas* pp. 26. ZN is one of very few authors to deal with this theme, another will be Stefan Żeromski in his novel, *Przedwiośnie* (Foretaste of Spring) 1925.

5   *Choucas* p. 35 and p. 146

6   Ibid p. 35

7   Ibid p. 119

8   Ibid p. 68

9   Ibid p. 130

10   Ibid p. 148

11   *Diary 1918 – 1930* p. 176

12   Ibid p. 184

13   Ibid p. 175

14   Nadzieja Drucka *Three quarters*, p 102

15   ZN *Meadow House, Dom nad łąkami*, quoted in *Selected Works* p. 382

16   ZN *Views near and far* p 315

17   *Diary 1930 – 35* footnote p. 76

18   Ibid p. 182

19   Ibid p. 190

20   Ibid p.187

21   Ibid p. 190

22   Ibid p. 192

23   Ibid p. 193

24   Ibid p. 255

25   Ibid quoted footnote p. 307

26   Ibid footnote p. 323

27   Ibid p. 233

28   Ibid p. 344

29   Ibid p. 330

30   Ibid p. 358

31   Ibid p. 310

32   ZN *Unkind Love* pp 87 – 89

33   Ibid p. 89

34   Ibid p. 253

35   Ibid pp. 50 – 55

36   Quoted Hanna Kirchner pp. 885 – 887

37   ZN *House of Women*, in *Selected Works* p. 673

38   *Diary* p. 416

39   Ibid p. 417 footnote

40   Ibid p. 419

41   Ibid footnote p. 418

Chapter 9 House of Women

1   ZN *Diary* pp. 282 – 285

2   *Diary 1918 – 1929* p. 297

3   *Diary 1930 – 1939* vol 1 pp. 77 – 78

4   *Diary* p. 76

5   Ibid p. 94

6   Ibid p. 81, 88 – 90

7   Ibid p 118 – 119

8   Ibid p. 121

9   Ibid p. 137

10   Ibid p. 161

11   Ibid pp 177 – 178

12   Ibid pp 176 – 177

13   Ibid pp 178 – 179

14   Maria Dąbrowska, *My wonderful life, diaries in a single volume*, Warsaw 2002 p. 368, 371

15   ZN *Diary* p. 183

16   Ibid p. 207

17   Ibid pp. 224-5

18   Słonimski *Chronicles* 1927 – 1939 PIW 1956 p. 234

19   ZN *Diary* p 282 – 283

20   Ibid pp 282 – 285

21   Ibid pp, 291-2

22   ZN *Walls of the World* pp. 156 – 157

23   ZN *Walls of the World, Marcjia's Family* p. 91

24   *Diary* p. 297

25   Ibid pp. 304 – 305

26   Ibid

27   Wanda Melcer *Memories* pp. 247 – 249

28   *Diary* p. 311

29   Ibid

Chapter 10 My highest level

1   *Diary 1914 – 32* p. 342

2   *Diary 1930 – 39* vol 1 p. 327

3   Ibid p. 330

4   Ibid p 336

5   Ibid p. 337

6   Ibid pp. 339 – 341, see also Timothy Snyder, *Sketches from a Secret War, A Polish Artist's Mission to Liberate Soviet Ukraine,* Yale University Press 2005

7   *Diary 1914 – 32* quoted Snyder p. 25

8   Ibid p. 342

9   Gregorz Rąkowski, *Wołyń,* 2005, also Dr. M Orłowicz, *Przewodnik,* Łuck 1929

10   *Diary* p. 350

11   Ibid p. 354

12   Ibid p. 355

13   Ibid p. 360

14   Ibid p 365

15   *Diary 1930 – 39* vol 2 footnote p 14

16   *Diary 1930 – 39* vol 1 p. 378

17   Ibid p. 378

18   Jerzy Ficowski, *Regions of the Great Heresy,* 1967, trs Theodora Robertson, Norton and Company 2003 pp. 63 – 64

19   Ibid pp. 105 – 106

20   *Diary* p. 380

21   Ibid p. 388

22   Ibid p. 387

23   Maria Kuncewiczowa, *Memories,* pp. 169 – 170

24   *Diary 1930 – 39* vol 2 p. 14

25   *Diary 1930 – 39* vol 1 p. 398

Chapter 11 Literature rejuvenates

1   *ZN Views near and far* pp. 322 – 325

2   *Diary 1930 – 39* vol 1 footnote p. 444.

3   Ibid p. 443

4   Ibid p. 447
5   Ibid p. 450
6   Ibid p. 467
7   Ibid p. 467
8   Ibid pp. 454 – 476
9   *Diary* 130 – 39 vol 2 p. 10
10   Ibid p. 10
11   Ibid p.10
12   Ibid pp. 15 – 24
13   ZN *Views near and far* p. 319, pp. 326 – 327
14   Ibid pp. 322 – 325

Chapter 12 Boundary and beyond

1   *Diary 1930 – 1939* vol 2 p. 79
2   Ibid p. 33
3   *Służąca do wyszystkiego* (*Maid of all work*) Joanna Kuciel-Frydryszak, Warsaw 2018
4   *Boundary* (this edition Warsaw 1994) p. 25
5   Ibid p. 26
6   Schulz ZN *against the background of her new novel*, p. 269
7   *Boundary* p. 253
8   *Memories* p. 229
9   *Diary* p. 36
10   Ibid p. 48
11   Ibid p. 61
12   Ibid p. 71
13   Ibid p. 75
14   Ibid p. 79

Chapter 13 Storm clouds near and far

1   Wittlin, *Literary News* p. 6
2   Ibid
3   *Diary 1930 – 39* vol 2 p. 85
4   Ibid p. 85
5   Ibid pp 108 – 109
6   Barcikowski *Memories* pp. 9 – 13
7   *Diary* p. 115
8   Ibid pp. 136 – 138
9   Ibid p. 135

10   Ibid pp. 150 – 153

11   Ibid p. 164

12   Ibid p. 178, 181

13   *Literary News* as above

14   *Diary* p. 169

15   Ibid pp 187 – 193

16   Ibid pp 196 – 197

17   Ibid pp 209 – 212

18   Ibid pp 217 – 224

19   Ibid p 229

20   Ibid p. 240

21   Ibid p. 297

22   Ibid p. 307

Chapter 14 Taken to the gates of hell

1   Bruno Schulz in *Skamander nr 108 – 110* 1939, reprinted in B. *Schulz Prose* pp 493 – 509 Kraków 1964

2   *Diary 1930 – 39* vol 2 p. 323

3   Ibid p. 335

4   Ibid p. 337

5   Ibid p. 395

6   Bruno Schulz in *Skamander* nr 108 – 110 1939, reprinted in B. Schulz *Prose* pp 493 – 509 Kraków 1964

7   M Janion Wydawnictwo Sic!, Warszawa 2000

8   *Diary 1930 – 39* pp. 397 – 399

9   Ibid p. 404

10   Ibid p. 406, see also footnote pp. 407-408

11   Ibid p. 416

12   Ibid pp. 410 – 419.

13   Ibid p. 425

Chapter 15 Bombardment

1   Breza, *Memories* pp. 97 – 98

2   W. Bartoszewski *1859 Days of Warsaw* p. 25 Kraków 1959, 1984

3   ZN *Wartime Diaries* pp. 25 ff

4   Bartoszewski pp. 30 ff

5   Buczkowski, *Warsaw Jokes* 1939 – 1944, p. 19 (compiled from secretly circulated brochure printed in February 1941, whose author was

later shot. This edition printed in Warsaw in 1947 drew on other material from Underground newspapers and journals)

6   *Wartime Diaries* pp. 30 – 35
7   *Knots of Life* p. 302 Warsaw 1984.
8   *Wartime Diaries* p. 46
9   Ibid pp. 48 – 49
10 Ibid p. 50.
11 Bartoszewski *1859 Days of Warsaw*, Krakow p. 44
12 Ibid p. 49
13 *Wartime Diaries* p. 54
14 Ibid p. 58
15 Ibid p. 100
16 Ibid p.111
17 Ibid p. 104
18 *Warsaw jokes* p. 20
19 *Wartime Diaries* p. 117
20 Ibid p.116
21 Ibid p.110
22 Breza, *Memories* pp 97-98.
23 *Warsaw Jokes* p. 21
24 Stanisław Baliński, *Kolęda Warszawska* 1939, printed in Ginalska Polish Christmas, London 1961

Chapter 16 A rosary of deaths

1   *Diary* pp. 267 – 269
2   *Wartime Diaries* p. 134
3   Ibid pp 134, 137 – 8
4   Ibid p. 133
5   See among others Jenny Robertson *Don't go to Uncle's Wedding*, Azure 2000
6   *ZN or a life in writing* H. Kirchner p. 519 – 520.
7   *Diary* p 228 – 229.
8   Ibid p 141.
9   Breza *Memories* pp. 97 – 98
10 Zawiejski *Memories* pp. 312 – 313
11 *Diary* pp. 188 ff
12 Ibid pp. 267 – 269
13 Ibid p. 239
14 Ibid p. 261

15   Ibid p. 279

16   Miłosz *Campo di Fiori*, Warsaw Easter 1943, in various collections, here *Warsaw in Poetry* p. 203, 1996

17   *Diary* p. 279

18   Ibid p. 279

19   ZN *Medaliony*, Warsaw 1963 pp. 27 – 34

Chapter 17 That smoking wound

1   ZN *Wartime Diaries* pp. 303 – 305

2   Aleksander Kamiński *Kamienie na Szaniec* (Stones on the Battlements) pp. 101 ff Warsaw 1999, see also Bartoszewski

3   *Warsaw Jokes* p. 44

4   ZN *War time Diaries* pp 303 – 305

5   Ibid p. 316

6   Ibid p. 299

7   Ibid p 303

8   Ibid p. 301

9   Ibid p. 307

10   Ibid p 306

11   Ibid p. 308

12   Ibid p. 311

13   Ibid footnote p. 470.

14   Ibid p, 319 and footnote p. 470

15   Ibid p. 402

16   Ibid pp. 351 – 352

17   Ibid pp 354-5

18   *Diary 1945 – 54* vol. 3 p. 484

19   *Diary* p. 367

20   Ibid p 367

21   Ibid p. 367

22   Ibid p 363 – 367

23   Ibid p 374

24   Ibid pp 376 – 378

25   Ibid p. 385

26   ZN and JZ *Letters 1945 – 1954* ed Hanna Kirchner p. 50 Warsaw 2000

Chapter 18 Cameos of crime

1   ZN *Diary 1945 – 54* vol 1 p. 126

2   Ibid pp. 47 – 48
3   Ibid p. 53
4   Ibid p. 77
5   Ibid p. 78
6   *Diary* book 6 vol 1 footnote p. 55
7   *Profesor Spanner, Medaliony* (Medallions) p. 8 (author's translation; the English version, translated by Diana Kuprel, is published by North Western University Press)
8   Hanna Kirchner *ZN, life in writing* p. 592
9   *Profesor Spanner* p. 8
10   *Diary* p. 126
11   Ibid footnote p. 57
12   *Medallions* p. 46
13   *Diary* p.101
14   Ibid p. 107
15   Ibid p. 108
16   *Memories* pp. 5 – 38
17   Ibid p. 23
18   *Medallions, This man is strong* p. 61
19   Marek Edelman, *The Ghetto is Fighting* in *Warsaw Ghetto* Warsaw 1988 p. 19
20   *Diary* p. 133
21   JZ letter *Diary* p. 133
22   Ibid pp. 234 – 235
23   *Medallions* pp. 53 – 54
24   Ibid p. 51
25   See Philippe Sands *East West Street* pp. xxi, 111 Weidenfeld and Nicholson, 2016
26   Hanna Kirchner, *ZN or a life in writing* pp 588-590
27   Ibid 590
28   *Medallions* pp. 38 – 41

Chapter 19 Restored to Life

1   ZN *Diary 1945 – 54* vol 1 p. 264
2   Ibid p. 249
3   Ibid p. 255
4   Ibid p. 264
5   Ibid pp. 268 – 271
6   Ibid pp. 295 – 353

7   Ibid pp. 420 – 421
8   Ibid p. 430
9   Ibid p. 451
10   Ibid p. 452
11   Ibid p. 453
12   Ibid p. 439
13   Ibid p. 457
14   Ibid pp 502 – 506
15   ZN in *Views near and far* pp. 440 – 442, Warsaw 1957
16   *Diary* pp. 500 – 502

Chapter 20 Knots of Life
1   ZN *Diary* 1945 – 54 vol. 1 p. 443
2   Ibid p. 561
3   Ibid p. 557
4   Ibid p. 557
5   Ibid p. 582
6   *Diary 1945 – 54* vol 2 p. 602
7   *Diary 1945 – 54* vol 1 p. 575
8   Ibid vol 2 p. 25
9   Ibid p. 25
10   Ibid p. 443
11   Ibid pp 543 – 545
12   Vol 1 pp. 536 – 537
13   Ibid pp 546 – 549
14   Ibid pp 538 – 539
15   *Niesie mnie rzeka smutku* – A river of sadness carries me – letters ZN
     and JZ 1943 – 1954 ed. Malina Kluźnik introduction Hanna Kirchner,
     Warsaw 2000
16   Ibid pp. 189 – 190
17   *Diary* vol 2 p. 471
18   Lives connected with Wołomin p. 108 (Wołomin Town Council 2009)
19   Ibid pp. 255 – 257
20   *Diary* vol 2 p. 443
21   *Diary* vol 3 p. 458
22   Ibid pp. 454 – 456
23   ZN *Granica* (Boundary), KAMA, Warsaw 1994, p. 25

Bibliography

Books in English by Zofia Nałkowska

trs Ursula Phillips *Boundary* (NIUPress,2016)

trs Ursula Phillips *Choucas* (NIUPress, 2014), winner of Found in Translation Award

trs Diana Kuprel *Medallions* (Northwestern University Press, Illinois, 2000)

trs Ursula Phillips, *The Impatient Ones* (completed but not yet published)

trs Megan Thomas and Ewa Małachowska-Pasek *The Romance of Teresa Hennert* (NIUPress, 2014)

Books in Polish by Zofia Nałkowska

Kobiety Women (including *Lodowe pole* Icy Fields), novel Warsaw 1906, Kraków 1912

Książe Prince, novel Warsaw 1907, 1929

Koteczka, czyli białe tulipany, Little kitten or white tulips, short stories Lwów 1909

Narcyza (Narcisssa), novel Kraków 1910, 1967

Noc podniebna (Heavenly Night), novella Warsaw 1911

Lustra (Mirror), novella Kraków 1913

Węże i róże (Snakes and Roses) novel Kraków 1915

Moje zwierzęta (My Animals), short stories Warsaw 1915

Tajemnice krwi (Secrets of Blood) short stories Warsaw 1917

Hrabia Emil (Count Emil) novel, Warsaw 1920, 1922

Charaktery (Portraits) sketches, Warsaw 1922, Lwów 1938

Na torwowiskach (on the peat bogs) short stories, Warsaw 1922

Romans Teresy Hennert (Romance of Teresa Hennert) novel, Warsaw 1924, 1965

Dom nad łąkami (House on the Meadows) short stories, Warsaw 1925, 1953

Małżeństwo (Marriage) novella, Warsaw 1925

Choucas, an international novel, Warsaw 1927, 1968

Księga o przyjaciołach (Book about Friends) short stories, co-authored with M. Wielopolska , Wasaw, Kraków 1927

Niedobra miłość, a provincial romance (Unkind Love), Warsaw 1928, 1952

Dom Kobiet (House of Women) a play in three acts, Warsaw 1930, Lwów 1937

Dzień jego powrotu (The Day of his Return) drama, Warsaw 1931

Ściany świata (Walls of the World) short stories, Warsaw 1931

Między zwierzętami (Among my Pets) short stories, Lwów 1934

Granica (Boundary) novel Warsaw 1934,

Renata Słuczańska (3 act play) Warsaw 1935

Niecierpliwi novel, Lwów 1939, Warsaw 1964

Medaliony, Medallions short stories, Warsaw 1946 – 1947

Charaktery dawne i ostatnie (Former and Final Portraits) Warsaw 1948, 1968

Węzły Życia novel, Warsaw 1948, 1950, 1954, 1968

Mój ojciec (My Father) Warsaw 1953, 1955

Pisma wybrane (Selected Works) Warsaw 1954, Warsaw 1956

Widzenie bliskie i dalekie (Views Near and Far) articles etc Warsaw 1957

Dzienniki 1899 – 1954, (diaries), including *War-time Diaries*, (vol 4 is in 2 part, vol 6 in 3 parts) all edited and introduced with notes by Hanna Kirchner, published from 1970 - 2001

Niesie mnie rzęka smutku (Letters between ZN and Jerzy Zawieyski 1943 – 1954) introduction Hanna Kirchner, edited by M. Kluźniak Warsaw 2000

Books in Polish about Zofia Nałkowska

Authors various *Wspomnienia o Zofii Nałkowskiej*, (Memories of ZN) Warsaw 1965

Iwona Kienzler *Nałkowska I jej mężczyźni* (Nałkowska and her men), Warsaw 2015

Hanna Kirchner, *Nałkowska albo życie pisane* (Nałkowska or a life in writing) Warsaw 2011, the definitive biography of ZN with analysis of all her works by Dr Kirchner who edited and annotated all ZN's diaries.

Sources connected with Nałkowska

Maria Dąbrowska *Życie moje cudowne* (Warsaw 2002)

Nadzieja Drucka *Trzy czwarte* (Łomiańki 2011)

Alfred Doblin, *Journey to Poland 1924*, (New York 1991)

Jerzy Ficowski trans and edited Theodosia Robertson *Regions of the Great Heresy* (NY, London 2003)

Cezary Jellenta, *Wielki Zmierzch* (Warsaw 1985)

Angelika Kuźniak, *Stryjeńska* (Wołowiec 2015)

Ed Marzena Kubacz, Agata Sobczak, *Życiorycy z Wołominen związane* (Wołomin 2009)

Muzeum im Zofii i Wacława Nałkowskich, *Dlaczego warto dziś czytać Zofię Nałkowską* conference papers 1994

Muzeum im Zofii i Wacława Nałkowskich in Wołomin *Górki jak legenda* (Wołomin 2012)

Józef Wittlin *Sól ziemi* (novel 1935, Kraków 2014)

Stefan Żeromski, *Przedwiosnie* (novel Warsaw 1924)

General Sources

W. Bartoszewski, *1859 Dni Warszawy* (Znak 2nd edition 1984)

Norman Davies, *Rising '44* (Macmillan 2003)

Marek Edelman et al ed Tomasz Szarota, *Getto walczy* in *Warszawskie getto* (Warsaw 1988)

Aleksander Kamiński, *Kamienie na szaniec* (Warsaw 1999)

Jan Karski, *Story of a Secret State* (Hodder Mifflin 1944)

Joanna Krajewska *Spór o literatr kobiecą w Dwudziestoleciu między wojennym* (Poznań 2004)

Claude Lanzmann, *Shoah*

Ursula Phillips ed *Polish Literature in Transformation* (Lit Verlag 1989)

Philippe Sands, *East West Street* (Weidenfeld and Nicholson 2016)

Grzegorz Rąkowski, *Wołyń* (Pruszków 2005)

Alexandra Richie, *Warsaw 1944* (Collins 2013, 2014)

Jenny Robertson, *Don't go to Uncle's Wedding* (Azure 2000)

Antoni Słonimski *Kroniki Tygodniowe 1927 – 1939* (Warsaw 1956)

Timothy Snyder, *Sketches from a Secret War* (Yale 2005)

Peter Stachura, *Poland 1918 – 1945* (Routledge 2004)

Tomas Venclova, *Vilnius, a personal history* (Vilnius 2011)

Adam Zamoyski, *Warsaw 1920* (Harper Collins 2008)

Acknowledgements

This book could never have been written without the diaries of Zofia Nałkowska, thoroughly annotated by Professor Hanna Kirchner. Every other book about Nałkowska depends upon the work done by Professor Kirchner. The day I discovered her biography, *Nałkowska or a life in writing*, in a marvellous bookshop in Sopot was a red letter day indeed, even though the book weighed one and a half kilos and filled my suitcase. Thank you, Professor Kirchner for gracious permission to use material from your major biography and for your lifelong work on Zofia Nałkowska.

I'm grateful to the friendliness, welcome and support from Dr Marzena Kubacz, curator of the Zofia and Wacław Nałkowscy Museum in Wołomin near Warsaw. Dr Marzena opened the house to me, gave me books to read and encouraged me in this project.

Pani Joanna Wróblewska- Kujawska, a great niece of Zofia, kindly gave permission to use material in her possession and dealt with my e-mails with great courtesy while her son Pan Jan Kujawski passed on the permission with gentle humour which lifted my spirits. Very many thanks to you for your kindness and readiness to help.

I'm also grateful to my dear friend of many years Dorota Mieczkowska who always offers the generous hospitality of her home whenever I come to Warsaw.

Thank you so much, Wojciech Maslarz for embracing this project and giving me so much support face to face and via Messenger.

Dr Ursula Phillips has not only translated three of Nałkowska's books, she also invited me to share in an international symposium on Nałkowska to which she wore an amazing T-shirt with ZN's portrait photographed across it, a joyous symbol of the woman we had gathered to celebrate.

Thank you, Ursula for your patience in answering my queries and for sharing your knowledge.

Dr. Elwira Grossman of Glasgow University encouraged me from the very first draft. I'm grateful to you, Elwira and to Professor Karin Friedrich in Aberdeen for your warm support, while Krystyna Szumelukowa in Edinburgh was always encouraging and pointed me in the direction of possible funding.

Which leads me to thank Marek Straczyński in *Dom Kombatantów* in Edinburgh for taking this writing project up with the committee of the Polish Ex-Combatants Association Trust Fund. Thank you most sincerely for the generous grant which helped make publication of this book possible. My thanks too to the Polonia Aid Foundation Trust whose kind funding also supported this publication. Magda Raczyńska of the Polish Cultural Institute in London gave an instant kind response. I really can't express my gratitude sufficiently to all three foundations which do so much to support Polish cultural life in the UK.

A huge thank you to the team at Scotland Street Press, to Nancy Birch, Anne Sophie Fraser whose artistic skills produced the beautiful cover and Valentina Auletta for her meticulous work on the text and the endnotes.

My biggest thanks go to Jean who believed in this book from the very beginning and has done so much to support it from draft to publication. Jean is already well known for the top quality of the books she produces. I feel privileged to be on the list of Scotland Street Press whose vision embraces far horizons.

Finally, thank you, Stuart, my at-home consultant in all matters Polish. You have shared a lifetime of involvement in Poland and your knowledge sustained me through the research and writing of this book.

Timeline for Zofia Nalkowska

10.11. 1884 Birth of Zofia Nałkowska, the second child of Wacław and Anna, the first daughter had died

1888 Birth of her sister Hanna

1895 The family settled in the house outside Warsaw referred to in the text as Meadow House and immortalised by Zofia in her book *The House above the Meadows.*

18.9.1899. In her diary entry the young Zofia writes that 'my intelligence developed early.' Publishes her first poems.

1901 Zofia completed her education at a a privately run school in Warsaw

1902 writes in her diary that she 'perceives everything in a literary way.'

1903 Publishes her first short novel, *Fields of Ice*

11.02.1894 marries Leon Rygier in the evangelical church on Królewska Street, Warsaw

1904 publishes first novel, *Women*, dedicated to her mother

1905 Zofia now lives in Kielce with her husband and publishes stories in the local paper, the Kielce *Echo*

1906 Zofia publishes a paper on women's rights

1907 Her marriage is already failing. She speaks at the Congress of Polish Women, demanding equal sexual rights for women. She becomes emotionally involved with dying revolutionary Ludwik Liciński, returns to Meadow House, publishes a revolutionary novel *The Prince* and works on short stories, including *Little Kitten or white tulips*

1909 publishes her third novel, *Contemporaries*. Along with her father attends the trial of Stanisław Brzozowski and conducts a meaningful but platonic love affair with Edmund Szalit

Travels to Italy as a paid companion of a rich woman where she undergoes self-education in art and culture, while feeling ill-at-ease in the world of high finance.

1911 Death of Wacław Nałkowski. Anna and her two daughters live in great poverty in Meadow House. Zofia works on her father's texts, publishes her novella *Heavenly Night* and a major novel *Narcyza*, in which she uses material from Liciński's life and death.

1913 publishes *Mirror*, a novella

1914, first threat of war. Zofia publishes *Snakes and Roses*. The three women return to Warsaw for safety. Zofia has more love affairs, mostly platonic. The war marks a turning point: she immerses herself in other people's lives and reflects this in her writing.

1915 publishes *My animals*, short stories about her pets. The Russian front retreats from Meadow House, the women return to check on their possessions. Zofia starts on a series of short stories, *The Secrets of Blood* which examine the underlying manifestations of war and violence in society as a whole and in human lives.

1916 Jan 'Jur' Gorzechowski makes his first appearance in her life

1918 end of First World War, Poland consolidates its national life and regains lost territory

1919 an attempt is made on Jan Gorzechowski's life. The Polish-Soviet war begins

1920 Zofia publishes *Count Emil*, a contemporary romance. Bolshevik troops surround Warsaw

Zofia starts work in the Office of Foreign Propaganda, her first paid employment.

1922 Zofia publishes *Characters*, psychological sketches and *Beside the peat bogs*, a series of sketches and forerunner of her successful *House on the Meadows*

25.06.1922 marries Jan Gorzechowski

1923 Moves to ex-army barracks near Vilnius and then to Grodno with Jan

1924 Publishes *The Romance of Teresa Hennert* to great acclaim

1925 Zofia starts visiting prisoners in Grodno

1925 Goes with Jan to a sanatorium in Leysin, Switzerland. Zofia gathers material for her 'international novel' *Choucas*. Notes her tinnitus and hearing difficulties

1925 Zofia publishes the popular *House above the Meadows* and a novella called *Marriage*. She returns to Grodno, records facts about the prisoners and words on *Choucas*.

1926 along with Jan is a guest of Józef Piłsudski

1927 Zofia leaves her unhappy marriage and returns to Meadow House, attends International Congress of Author's Rights and becomes the Vice-President of PEN Club. Organises protests for political prisoners and becomes acquainted with Maria Dąbrowska. Publishes *Choucas* and co-authors *A book about my friends* (her pets). Attends a Presidential ball in the Royal Castle

Amidst increasing political and ethnic tensions, Jan is appointed commandant of the fortress prison of Brzeszcz (Brest)

1928 Zofia visits Nice with her mother. Publishes *Unkind Love*, immediately classed as a masterpiece

1929 Jan now lives in Warsaw. Zofia returns to him and is removed by her mother to live with her at 4 Marszałkowska Street where her literary salon becomes the hub of Warsaw's cultural life, a "mini-Paris"

1929 in recognition of her literary work, Zofia is awarded the Freedom of Łódź

1930 Her drama *House of Women* is a huge success. Zofia tours with her play. Visits Lublin, her father's home territory and Zakopane where she witnesses the tragic death of Julian Ejsmond, is betrayed openly by Jan and secretly falls in with Karol Szymanowski, a love only revealed with the publication of her diaries years after both their deaths

1930 European tours. Visits Zagreb and Prague

1931 Reflects in the nature of evil. Publishes her second drama, *The Day of his Return* and short stories *Walls of the World*, a prototype for both *Boundary and Medallions*

1931 Worsening financial and political situation, Zofia and other women writers tour Yugoslavia and Greece

1932 Zofia and her mother face extreme poverty. She continues her tours, visiting Volhynia and Estonia. Begins an affair with a Croatian playwright Krleza and starts work on *Boundary*

1934 A highly repressive prison camp is opened in Bereza-Kartusa as a means of crushing dissent. Writers involved in protest. Zofia is the only woman in the Polish Academy of Literature (PAL). She encourages budding writers, Gombrowicz, Schulz, starts an affair with Bogusław Kuczyński, twenty-two years her junior.

1934 As a representative of PEN Club Zofia enjoys her first ever sea voyage to Edinburgh via London. Returns to Poland and Bogusław.

1935 Stays in Nowy Sącz and writes a travel piece highlighting the people she meets, including Jewish women, describes the dress and customs of Hassidic Jews. Publishes her great masterpiece, *Boundary*. Acclaim and prizes are heaped upon her

1936 A "trial" of one of the main characters of *Boundary* is staged in Warsaw – another success. Bogusław is becoming more demanding and violent. Zofia's increasing deafness, her devoted care of her mother as she plunges into dementia sap her creativity, she turns to translation and starts on *Madame Bovary*

1937 Death of Szymanowski. Zofia travels to Copenhagen and Paris for the 15th International PEN Club Congress, returns via Berlin

Mother has to sell Meadow House. Zofia visits Gdynia, returns to her domestic difficulties – and plans new novel

Film premier of *Boundary*. Zofia's lifelong friend Zofia V offers her refuge in her house in Adamowizna, outside Warsaw.

1939 publishes *The Impatient Ones*, a dark, difficult novel, unafraid to tackle psychosis, domestic violence, murder, suicide - yet offering larger than life characters and memorable scenes. It is only now being discovered as a truly great novel.

Zofia begins a new novel, *The Knots of Life*. In June visits a spa near Drohobycz and enjoys the company of Bruno Schulz – their last meeting.

1st September 1939 Germans invade Poland. Warsaw under bombardment. Zofia and Bogusław join the stream of refugees fleeing eastwards. 8th October Zofia returns to Warsaw to a house without windows. Mother and the two sisters now live together. Hanna's husband has fled to France, the two sisters run a small shop selling cigarettes, and are forced to move with their sick mother from one set of rooms to another.

1941 Hanna's husband commits suicide in France. A new friend enters Zofia's life, a dramatist Jerzy Zawiejski and a new housemaid, the redoubtable Genia who will adore and tyrannise Zofia to the end of her days.

1942 Death of Anna Nałkowska. The sisters tend her grave, from which Zofia witnesses the deportation of thousands from the Warsaw Ghetto.

19th April 1943 Ghetto Uprising, Zofia witnesses the fires, the people jumping from burning buildings and begins a story which will feature in *Medallions*

1st August 1944 Warsaw Uprising. Zofia now lives with her friend and many refugees in Adamowizna. All through the war, Zofia has kept on reading and writing her diary.

January 1945 The Red Army march into ruined Warsaw. A new "reality" begins. Zofia is given a flat in Łódź, an industrial city intended become the new capital, but Varsovians return to their ruined city with Zofia among them, recording in her diary the sights she witnesses.

6th April Zofia joins the Commission for examining Nazi War Crimes in Poland. Despite her ill health and the terrible conditions of travel as well as the enormity of the crimes she witnesses, Zofia is truly inspired. She crafts these crimes into *Medallions*, her shortest and greatest book whose success brings her a new readership and new admirers.

1947 publishes *Medallions*. Travels to Prague and Moscow, is elected Member of Parliament for Opole, works on a book about her father.

1st September 1948 Jan Gorzechowski dies in London. Zofia publishes *Knots of Life*, models her main male character on her husband. Also publishes her last set of *Characters*. She feels increasingly uncomfortable with the new regime, is used a figurehead. Her work doesn't meet the demands of socialist realism and her bools fall out of favour.

1949 Zofia is President of League against Racism

1950 moves to a new flat in The House of Literature in the centre of Warsaw. Visits Meadow House and learns about its fate during the war. Prepares her *Selected Works*, published in 1954. She prepares a volume of her articles and essays, *Visions near and far*, published after her death

8th December 1954 Zofia attends a meeting about her constituents in Opole, returns home and is discovered next day, fully dressed and unconscious.

17th December 1954 Zofia dies in hospital having never fully regained consciousness.

Timeline for Polish History

1905 Revolution in Tsarist Russia leads to a slight freeing-up of strict censorship

1914 First World War begins, hopes for Polish Independence, though Polish soldiers fight each other in the opposing armies

1917 Treaty of Brest-Litovsk, Soviet Russia withdraws from the war

1918 Poland is restored to map of Europe, negotiations to define western borders

1919 Polish-Soviet War begins in an effort to regain eastern borders

1920 Treaty of Warsaw between Józef Piłsudski and the Ukrainian leader Petlura

1920 August "Miracle of the Vistula": Polish forces save the capital and drive Soviet troops eastwards

1920 October Creation of Republic of Central Lithuania

1921 Treaty of Riga establishes Polish eastern borders in the Second Republic

1926 May coup Piłsudski overthrows the government but declines the presidency which goes to Ignacy Mościcki

1932 Soviet-Polish non-aggression Pact

1934 Polish-German non-aggression Pact

1935 May 12th death of Marshal Piłsudski

1939 Molotov-Ribbentrop secret treaty – agree to carve up Poland between USSR and Nazi Germany

1939 Polish-British Common Defence Pact

1939 August 31st staged "incident" in Gliwice (Gleiwitz) is used as pretext for invasion of Poland

1939 September 1st Nazi invasion of Poland, 'Blitzkrieg'

1939 September 17th Soviet invasion of Poland from the east

1939 September 18th Fall of Warsaw

1940 February 10th deportation of Polish citizens from eastern territories to Soviet gulags begins

1940 Katyń massacre of Polish officers

1941 June 21st Hitler invades Russia, extermination of Jewish communities in the east goes hand in hand with German advance

1941 30th July Sikorski/Mayski agreement. Poles released from Gulags/slave labour, General Anders forms Polish Army

1941 16th November Warsaw Ghetto is completely enclosed.

1942 Hitler's "Final Solution" is implemented, extermination camps go into action

1942 July – September: over 350,000 people from the Warsaw Ghetto are deported to Treblinka

1943 April 19th – May 15th: the Warsaw Ghetto Uprising, the whole area is razed to the ground

1943 July 4th General Władysław Sikorski perishes in an aeroplane crash

1944 July 22nd Soviet-backed Polish Committee of National Liberation is established in Lublin

1944 August 1st – October 2nd Warsaw Uprising; 5th – 12th August massacres in Wola district

1945 January 17th Soviet backed Polish troops and Red Army enter destroyed Warsaw

1945 February 4th – 11th Yalta conference, no Polish representation

1945 May 8th End of World War in Europe

1945 June 8th Trial of the Sixteen, notable leaders of the Polish Underground are arrested, tried and executed

1945 August 2nd Potsdam Conference. Polish and German borders are shifted westwards. Poland loses its eastern territories established in 1921 and becomes a Soviet satellite Stalin promises "free elections"

1946 June 30th The People's Referendum "Three times Yes" – Poles agree to border changes

1946 July 4th Kielce pogrom

1947 Operation Vistula, forcible deportations of ethnic Ukrainians and Lemkovs to USSR

1947 Auschwitz war crimes trial

1949 Polish Writers Congress. Socialist-realism becomes only permitted style, no independent publishing allowed

1952 Adoption of Constitution of the Poland People's Republic, one party-rule

1953 Death of Joseph Stalin.

Index

Adamowizna; 141; 148; 158; 180; 182; 183; 185; 195

Akhmatova, Anna; 23

Alexander III, Emperor of All the Russias; 4

Armia Krajowa (Home Army); 180; 181; 182; 205

Armia Ludowa (People's Army); 180

Auschwitz; 179; 190; 193; 197

Barcelona; 119

Barcikowski, Wacław; 195

Beck, Józef; 129

Belarus; 59; 77; 157

Belgrade; 207

ben Solomon Zalman, Elijah (Vilna Gaon); 58

Benešić, Julije; 106

Bergson, Henri; 167

Berlin; 141; 160; 162; 210

Berling, Zygmunt; 185

Berman, Jakub; 220

Beylin, Karolina; 36

Bick, Maximilian (brother-in-law); 62; 114; 119; 130; 133; 137; 151; 158; 168; 169; 171; 172; 221

Bierut, Bolesław; 220

Birkenau death camp; 190

Birmingham; 98

Birnbaum, Zdzisław; 31

Boguszewska, Hela; 77; 115; 189; 190; 192; 221

Bowes-Lyon, Elizabeth; 117

Bratislava; 206

Breza, Tadeusz; 141; 159; 161; 167; 179; 197

Brno; 206

Brzechwa, Jan; 140

Brzozowski, Stanisław; 26; 27; 28; 88; 189

Burns, Robert; 212

Cambridge University; 14

Chaplin, Charlie; 102

Chełmno death camp; 195

Choromański, Michał; 91; 101; 102; 107

Choynowska, Stanisława; 66

Ciano, Galeazzo; 146

Clyde river; 117

Commission of Culture; 221

Commission to Investigate War Crimes; 4; 187; 189; 190; 191; 192; 195; 196

Committee of the Defenders of Peace; 221

Communist; 26; 61; 69; 103; 110; 131; 144; 145; 156; 180; 181; 182; 185; 188; 189; 202; 204; 220

Conrad, Joseph; 115; 117

Copenhagen; 140; 197

Croatia; 93; 107; 108

Dąbrowska, Maria; 3; 79; 84; 85; 87; 92; 104; 123; 131; 136; 137; 179; 200; 217; 222

    Nights and Days; 79

Dawid, Jan; 54

Department of Anatomy; 190; 191

Descartes, René; 167

Diana (greyhound); 58; 65; 74; 77; 78; 84; 94; 111

Dmowski, Roman; 21; 53
Doblin, Alfred; 46
Dostoyevsky, Fyodor; 80; 81; 144
   Crime and Punishment; 80
   Humiliated and Insulted; 80
   Poor People; 80
Drohobycz (now Drohobych); 109; 110;
   112; 114; 115; 147; 170
Drucka, Nadzieja; 63; 64; 75
Dugas, Ludovic; 95
Dwora Zielona; 192; 193

Edelman, Marek; 196
   The Ghetto is Fighting; 196
Edinburgh; 4; 115; 117; 119
Eichmann, Adolf; 195
Ejsmond, Julian; 89
Exé, Zhenya; 138; 139; 178; 218

First World War; 38; 39; 60; 63; 88; 91; 105;
   125; 131; 141; 146
   Armistice; 50
Flaubert, Gustave
   Madame Bovary; 32; 136
France; 73; 80; 146; 147; 150; 168; 169

Gdańsk; 128; 190; 191
Gdynia; 115; 140
Gestapo; 66; 151; 158; 170; 182; 199; 218
Goethe, Wolfgang; 126; 166
   Confessions of St Augustine; 167
   Wilhelm Meister; 167
Gojawczyńska, Pola; 151; 154; 156; 186
Gombrowicz, Witold; 108; 111; 133
Gomułka, Władysław; 195
Gorky, Maxim; 205
Goryszewska, Genowefa (Genia); 171; 172;
   178; 182; 184; 185; 197; 198; 203; 205;
   208; 215; 217; 218; 219; 220; 221; 222
Gorzechowski, Jan (second husband); 137;
   144; 219
   fight for Polish independence; 46
   previous marriage; 46
   controlling and despotic behaviour; 47;
   48; 62; 63; 64; 70; 75; 84
   hunting activity; 51
   death; 214

Great Britain; 150
Greece; 98; 217
Grodno; 59; 60; 61; 62; 63; 65; 66; 67; 69;
   70; 71; 73; 74; 75; 76; 77; 78; 80; 82;
   96; 117; 138; 154; 178
Grodno Society for Care of Prisoners; 66
Gross, Magdalena; 109

Hamburg; 1; 197
Hegel, Georg Wilhelm Friedrich; 167
Hitler, Adolf; 25; 116; 156; 176; 177; 181;
   187; 203
Holocaust; 101; 201
Hungary; 4; 156

Italy; 18; 207
Iwaszkiewicz, Jarosław; 186; 192; 197

Janion, Maria; 145
   To Europe, yes, but together with our dead;
   145
Jellenta, Cezary; 14; 40; 209
Jewish, Jews; 14; 31; 42; 43; 44; 45; 46; 53;
   58; 60; 62; 82; 101; 105; 114; 121; 122;
   129; 140; 143; 145; 153; 158; 161; 165;
   168; 169; 173; 176; 177; 179; 181; 182;
   192; 196; 199; 200; 204; 215
Joyce, James; 140
Józewska, Julia; 104
Józewski, Henryk; 103; 104; 105

Kaplan, Regina; 110
Kielce; 23; 26; 78; 204; 205
Kirchner, Hanna; 3; 98; 183
Kochanowski, Jan; 126
Komornicka, Maria; 13; 14; 15; 209
Korczak, Janusz; 55; 166; 169
Kornacki, Jerzy; 189; 190; 191; 192; 221
Krajowa Rada Narodowa (National Home
   Council); 180
Kraków; 4; 5; 18; 27; 45; 59; 79; 88; 91; 101;
   117; 120; 138; 155; 189; 193; 208; 210
Krleža, Miroslav; 106; 207
Krynica; 137; 209
Kuczyński, Bogusław; 113; 144; 115; 116;
   117; 118; 119; 120; 123; 125; 129; 130;
   131; 132; 133; 134; 135; 136; 137; 139;

140; 141; 143; 144; 147; 148; 149; 150;
    151; 152; 153; 157; 159; 161; 172; 205;
    207; 209; 215;
    unsuccessful writing career; 117; 118;
        120; 133; 134; 143; 148
    tyrannical behaviour; 118; 120; 136; 137;
        143; 148
    launches literary magazine Studio; 123;
        133
    separation from Zofia; 153
    re-enters Zofia's life; 216; 219; 220; 221
Kuncewiczowa, Maria; 111
    Foreign Woman; 111

Lanzmann, Claude; 195
League of the Fight against Racism; 221
Leysin; 72
Liciński, Ludwik; 22; 25; 26
Łódź; 186; 187; 189; 195; 197; 202; 206;
    207; 208; 213; 219
London; 4; 111; 113; 116; 117; 162; 180;
    182; 207; 214
Lubliana; 207
Lublin; 33; 88; 140; 182; 185; 189
Łuck, now Lutsk; 103; 104; 105
Łuków; 154
Lwów (now L'viv); 14; 87; 147; 155

Majdanek; 187
Makedon'ski, Gabriel; 138
Malinowski, Bronisław; 90
Marshak, Samuil; 212
Marxist; 26; 35; 219
O'Brien de Lacy; 63
Meadow House; 18; 19; 28; 30; 31; 32; 35;
    36; 39; 40; 41; 48; 62; 76; 83; 87; 88;
    94; 96; 106; 107; 108; 111; 114; 115;
    116; 120; 127; 141; 198; 219; 220;
    222
Melcer, Wanda; 54; 55; 66; 99; 127; 144;
    159
Mickiewicz, Adam; 18; 32; 52
Miłosz, Czesław; 26; 58; 147; 173; 180
Mitzner, Zbigniew; 180
Monopol (tobacco firm); 158
Mościcki, Ignacy; 150
Moscow; 187; 204; 210; 213

Munich; 32
Mussolini, Benito; 116; 146

Nałkowska, Anna (mother); 5; 6; 15; 23;
    35; 36; 80; 94; 110; 118; 119; 130; 133;
    135; 136; 137; 148; 156; 158; 159; 162;
    168; 170; 171; 172
    geography textbooks; 36; 42; 94; 130;
        133; 168
    dementia; 119; 136; 158
    death; 170
Nałkowska, Celina; 5
Nałkowska, Hanna (sister); 3; 5; 6; 20; 31;
    35; 36; 55; 62; 94; 119; 130; 133; 135;
    137; 139; 141; 151; 158; 159; 160; 168;
    169; 171; 172; 178; 182; 185; 186; 197;
    198; 205; 209; 221; 222
    beauty; 31
    sculptress work; 31; 35; 47; 222
    marriage to Maximilian Bick; 62
    death of husband; 169
    remarries; 221
Nałkowska, Zofia (1884-1954)
    physical description; 3; 37; 100
    tinnitus; 3; 47; 74
    teenage years; 6; 7; 8; 9; 11
    diary writing; 9; 13; 17; 27; 56; 77; 84;
        86; 98; 117; 119; 124; 136; 153; 157;
        161; 174; 204; 221
    early poetry; 11
    translation work; 11
    marriage to Leon Rygier; 12; 17; 20; 21;
        23
    love for animals; 20; 37; 58; 65; 197; 210
    fight for sexual equality; 22; 24
    feminism; 24; 33
    friendship with Zofia Villaume; 25; 26;
        37
    unconsummated affair with Edmund
        Szalit; 27; 28
    views on war; 41; 183; 199
    first meeting with Jan Gorzechovski; 45
    ill-health; 47; 135; 137; 140; 141; 148;
        186; 205; 208
    marriage to Gorzechowski; 56; 57; 62;
        64
    moves to Grodno; 59

voluntary work in prison; 66; 67; 69
leaves Grodno and Gorzechowski; 76
travels to France with her mother; 80
friendship with Karol Szymanowski; 90;
    92; 98; 103
affair with Michał Choromański; 101;
    102
friendship with Bruno Schulz; 110; 115
relationship with Bogusław Kuczyński;
    112; 114; 118; 131; 132; 150
helps Bogusław launching his literary
    magazine; 123
is awarded the State Literary Prize for
    Literature; 130
separation from Bogusław Kuczyński;
    153
manages a tobacco shop with Hanna;
    158; 159; 160; 163; 164; 166; 179; 182
war-time life; 163; 165; 170; 178
premature deafness; 167; 220
death of her mother Anna; 170
meets Bogusław again after nine years;
    216
dies of a cerebral haemorrhage; 222
Nałkowska, Zofia (themes)
abortion; 28; 127
age; 125; 142
crime; 35; 44; 61; 97; 122; 146; 174; 192;
    196; 198; 199; 200
domestic violence; 64; 144; 214
ethnic minorities; 61; 81; 124
failure of the Second Republic; 69; 128;
    146; 214
family life; 86; 124; 127; 144; 146
hunting; 48; 51
infanticide; 43; 44
love; 28; 43; 61; 73; 82; 144; 146
murder; 44; 64; 81; 97; 138; 146
nationalism; 72; 73
psychosis; 47; 126
suffering and pain; 44; 73
suicide; 44; 146
war; 40; 41; 44; 45; 73; 81; 145; 195; 196;
    199
Nałkowska, Zofia (works)
Boundary; 24; 69; 76; 80; 97; 100; 104;
    106; 108; 110; 118; 123; 124; 125; 127;

128; 130; 131; 134; 136; 138; 142; 143;
    144; 146; 160; 180; 186; 207
Choucas; 71; 72; 73; 78; 81; 125; 159;
    207
Count Emil; 48; 50; 51
Heavenly Night; 28; 36; 89
House of Women; 83; 86; 87; 88; 89; 93;
    105
Icy Fields; 11; 16; 22; 42
Knots of Life; 43; 100; 146; 151; 152; 165;
    180; 185; 186; 214; 215
Medallions; 1; 4; 35; 44; 81; 97; 101; 123;
    174; 191; 192; 193; 196; 198; 199; 200;
    220
Mirrors; 36
Narcysa; 25; 29; 32; 33; 34
Prince; 21; 22; 23
Secrets of Blood; 41; 45
Snakes and Roses; 42; 43
Teresa's Nights (radio play); 120; 123
The Day of His Return; 66; 97; 98; 101;
    103; 107; 193
The Impatient Ones; 86; 134; 135; 138;
    141; 142; 144; 145; 146; 147; 168; 178;
    210; 215
The Romance of Teresa Hennert; 60; 61;
    62; 64; 75; 81; 100; 124; 138; 214
Unkind Love; 60; 61; 80; 81; 82; 83; 124;
    129; 132; 157; 160; 178
Views near and far; 98
Walls of the World; 47; 61; 66; 68; 96; 97;
    157
Nałkowski, Wacław (father); 8; 9; 14; 15;
    166; 219
early life and education; 5; 33; 140
geography work; 5; 20
socialist ideas; 9; 14; 50
death; 35; 127
friendship with Janusz Korczak; 55
Nice; 80; 95
Nietzsche, Friedrich; 6, 11
North Western University Press; 123
Nowy Sącz; 119; 120; 122; 137; 209
Nuremberg Trials; 199

Odrodzenie literary magazine; 186
Office of Foreign Propaganda; 54; 99

Opole; 180; 221; 222
Orzeszkowa, Eliza; 60

Paderewski, Ignacy; 53
Paris; 15; 18; 52; 80; 107; 108; 111; 112; 116;
    135; 140; 177; 197; 202; 207
Pawiak prison; 35
PEN Club; 88; 89; 90; 101; 108; 115; 117;
    221
Phillips, Ursula; 69; 72
Piłsudski, Józef; 21; 46; 47; 53; 58; 59; 69;
    74; 77; 78; 93; 100; 103; 104; 119; 120
Podchlebnik, Michał or Mordecai; 195; 196
Poland's independence; 47; 48
Polish Academy of Literature; 3; 110; 120;
    128; 221
Polish Literary Academy; 134
Polish Tobacco Monopoly; 62
Polish Writers' Union; 99
Polish-French Friendship Society; 193; 207;
    210; 221
Polish-Soviet War; 53; 88
    Battle of Warsaw; 54
Poniatowski, Stanisław; 60
Powązki Cemetery; 174; 222
Prague; 93; 147; 206; 207
Proust, Marcel; 80; 125
    In Search of Lost Time; 80
Pruszków; 184
Przekrój literary journal; 210
Pushkin Press; 131

Ravensbruck; 184
Red Army; 155; 178; 181; 184; 185; 192
Reński, Antoni; 166
Reymont, Władysław; 21
    Chłopi, Peasants; 21
Roman Catholic Church; 209
Romania; 113; 146; 156; 207
Roosevelt, Elliott; 207
Roosevelt, Theodore; 181
Rygier, Henryk; 193
Rygier, Leon (first husband); 12; 16; 17; 18;
    21; 22; 23; 25; 27; 30; 55; 78; 88; 125;
    193
    first meeting with Zofia; 12
    previous affairs; 16
    infidelity; 23; 24; 27
    separation from Zofia; 30
    death; 215
Rygier, Tadeusz; 18

Sartre, Jean Paul; 193
Schopenhauer, Arthur; 166
Schulz, Bruno; 109; 110; 112; 114; 115; 120;
    123; 124; 126; 132; 133; 144; 145; 147;
    148; 169
    The Street of the Crocodiles; 109; 110; 120
Scotland; 60; 116
Second Republic of Poland; 61
Second World War; 3; 45; 66; 86; 103; 141;
    142; 144; 145; 166; 205; 214
    Battle of Kursk; 178
    end; 189
    horrors of the concentration camps;
        190; 191; 193; 195; 196; 201
Siberia; 25; 41
Słonimski, Antoni; 93; 115; 140
Słowacki, Juliusz; 59; 79
Spinoza, Baruch; 166
St Petersburg; 21; 63
Stalin, Joseph; 105; 145; 156; 174; 181; 184;
    217
Starzyński, Stefan (Mayor of Warsaw); 150
Stryjeńska, Zofia; 32
Stutthof concentration camp; 191
Switzerland; 71; 72; 73; 74; 138; 159; 207
Szalit, Edmund Joachim; 27; 28; 45; 88; 189
Szczawińska-Dawidowa, Jadwiga; 54; 55
Szczecin; 216
Szyfman, Arnold; 87; 90
Szymanowski, Karol; 89; 90; 91; 92; 98;
    101; 103; 107; 128; 134; 135; 138; 172;
    186

Tarnów; 101
Tatra mountains; 88; 206
Tehran; 181
Treblinka death camp; 55; 169; 220
Truskawiec; 147; 159

Ukraine; 91; 103; 109; 129; 147; 157
Union of Soviet Socialist Republics; 58; 60

Vienna; 72; 93; 100; 102; 221
Villaume, Zofia; 14; 15; 18; 21; 24; 25; 26;
    27; 37; 48; 64; 77; 100; 107; 141; 148;
    158; 165; 166; 167; 171; 172; 180; 182;
    183; 209; 213; 221
Vilnius; 56; 57; 58; 59; 62
Vistula River; 14; 41; 114; 181; 192; 194
Volhynia; 103; 104; 105; 181; 204

Wacek; 160
Wahl; 183
Warsaw; ; 3; 4; 5; 6; 14; 15; 18; 19; 20; 21;
    25; 28; 31; 32; 35; 38; 40; 41; 42; 45;
    47; 50; 53; 54; 55; 56; 60; 61; 62; 66;
    69; 70; 77; 78; 79; 80; 82; 83; 87; 90;
    92; 100; 101; 102; 103; 106; 108; 109;
    111; 112; 113; 114; 117; 120; 123; 129;
    130; 134; 135; 137; 138; 141; 142; 143;
    147; 148; 149; 150; 151; 152; 153; 154;
    155; 156; 157; 158; 160; 161; 162; 163;
    166; 168; 169; 170; 171; 172; 173; 174;
    176; 180; 181; 182; 183; 184; 185; 186;
    188; 189; 192; 193; 194; 197; 202; 207;
    208; 213; 216; 217; 219; 220; 221; 222
    Market Square; 18; 101; 189
bombardments; 41; 150; 151; 152; 153;
    155; 157; 159; 161

Uprising; 103; 166; 182; 184; 185; 196;
    213
Marsałkowska Street; 134
Three Crosses Square; 135; 160
Ghetto; 166; 169; 170; 172; 173; 179; 180
Aleje Jerozolimskie (Jerusalem Avenue);
    188
destruction; 188
Witkiewicz, Stanisław (Witkacy); 22; 90;
    133
Wittlin, Józef; 136
Sół ziemi (The Salt of the Earth); 130
Wołomin; 19; 156; 169; 220
Wróblewski, Tadeusz; 135

Yalta; 181

Zagórska, Aniela; 115; 117
Zagreb; 93; 101; 102; 207
Zahrt, Gustaw; 141
Zakopane; 88; 89; 90; 91; 101; 112; 133; 159
Zawieyski, Jerzy; 167; 172; 185; 186; 189;
    192; 193; 197; 207; 208; 209; 215; 216;
    218; 221
Żeromski, Stefan; 108; 128
    Przedwiośnie (On the Eve of Spring); 128
Zieja, Father; 209